N 2

When Kristy and her friends set up the Babysitters Club, they little think it will be so successful. The idea is simple – parents make a single phone call and reach a team of babysitting experts, ready and willing to look after their children for them. The parents are happy, the kids are happy, everybody's happy! And if things don't always go according to plan, at least there's a lot of fun to be had on the way!

The Babysitters Club

COLLECTION 2

Book 4
MARY ANNE
SAVES THE DAY

Book 5
DAWN AND THE
IMPOSSIBLE THREE

Book 6
KRISTY'S BIG DAY

Ann M. Martin

Hippo

Scholastic Children's Books,
Commonwealth House, 1 – 19 New Oxford Street,
London, WC1A 1NU, UK
A division of Scholastic Ltd
London ~ New York ~ Toronto ~ Sydney ~ Auckland

Mary Anne Saves the Day
Dawn and the Impossible Three
Kristy's Big Day
First published in the US by Scholastic Inc., 1987
First published in the UK by Scholastic Ltd, 1990
First published in this edition by Scholastic Ltd, 1998

ISBN 0 590 19878 5

Typeset by Rowland Phototypesetting Ltd,
Bury St Edmunds, Suffolk
Printed by Cox & Wyman Ltd, Reading, Berks.

3 4 5 6 7 8 9 10

CONTENTS

The Babysitters Club

MARY ANNE SAVES THE DAY

1st CHAPTER

"Kristy! Hey, Kristy!" I called.

It was Monday afternoon, almost five-thirty, and time for a meeting of the Babysitters Club. I had just stepped onto my front porch. At the house next door, I could see Kristy Thomas stepping onto her front porch.

Kristy is the chairman of the Babysitters Club. She's also my best friend in the whole world. We've grown up together. And since my mother died when I was really little, leaving just Dad and me, Kristy's been like my sister, and Mrs Thomas is like my mother. (Kristy's parents got divorced a few years ago and her dad walked out, but my father has *not* been like a father to Kristy. He's not warm and open like Mrs Thomas.)

"Hi, Mary Anne," Kristy answered.

We ran across our front lawns, crunching through the remains of a January snow, and met between our houses. Then we crossed the street to Claudia Kishi's house. Claudia is the vice-chairman of the club. We hold our meetings at her house because she has a telephone in her bedroom.

The Babysitters Club is really more of a business than a club. This is how it works: On Monday, Wednesday, and Friday afternoons, the club meets from five-thirty until six o'clock. Our clients call us on Claudia's line to tell us when they'll need baby-sitters. Then one of us takes the job. It's simple—but brilliant. (It was Kristy's idea.) The great thing is that with four of us taking the calls, anyone who needs a sitter is bound to find one.

Of course, our club isn't perfect. For instance, the members—Kristy, Claudia, me (I'm the secretary), and Stacey McGill, who's our treasurer—are only twelve years old. The latest we can stay out is ten o'clock. In fact, only Stacey is allowed out that late, although recently sometimes Claudia has been allowed to sit until ten, too. Kristy and I have to be home by nine-thirty on the weekends, and nine o'clock on week nights. That nearly cost us our club. Recently, another bunch of girls copied us and set up a business called the Baby-sitters Agency. They were older than us and could stay out until all hours. A lot of our clients started using them instead, but the agency folded because the kids who worked for it weren't great baby-sitters, so now we're back to normal, glad that the new year is starting off smoothly.

Kristy rang the Kishis' bell, and Mimi answered the door. Mimi is Claudia's grandmother. She lives with the Kishis and watches out for Claudia and her sister Janine, since both Mr and Mrs Kishi work.

"Hello, girls," said Mimi in her pleasant voice. The Kishis are Japanese. Claudia and Janine were born in the United States. Both of their parents came to America when they were little. Mimi was in her thirties, I think, when she left Japan, so she still speaks with an accent. I like her accent. It's soft and nice to listen to.

"Hi, Mimi," we replied.

"How is the scarf coming, Mary Anne?" she asked. (Mimi taught me how to knit. She's helping me make a scarf for my father.)

"It's fine," I said. "I'm almost done, but I'll need you to help me with the fringe."

"Of course. Any time, Mary Anne."

I kissed Mimi quickly on the cheek. Then Kristy and I got prepared to run up the stairs and into Claudia's room. We have to do it fast. If Janine is home, we like to try to get by her bedroom without having to talk to her.

Janine is a genius. Honest. She's only fifteen and already she's going to lectures at Stoneybrook University. She corrects absolutely everything you say to her. Kristy and I avoid her as much as possible.

That day, we were lucky. Janine wasn't even home. When we ran by her room, it was dark.

"Hi!" we greeted Claudia.

"Hi," she replied, her voice muffled. Claudia had her head in her pyjama bag as she rummaged around at the bottom of it. In a moment she straightened up, proudly holding out three Mars bars.

Claudia is a junk-food addict. She buys sweets and cakes and chocolate and other things and hides the stuff all over her room. She eats it at any time (and eats her meals, too) and never seems to gain an ounce, or to get so much as the hint of a pimple.

She handed us each a bar, but I turned mine down. Dad gets upset if I don't eat a proper dinner (or breakfast or lunch), and I don't have a very big appetite. Claudia tossed the chocolate back in her pyjama bag. She wasn't going to offer it to Stacey when she arrived, since Stacey has diabetes and can't eat most sweets.

"Any calls yet?" I asked. It was just barely 5.30, but sometimes our clients called early.

"One," replied Claudia. "Kristy's mum. She needs someone for David Michael on Thursday."

Kristy nodded. "Our regular two-day-a-week sitter finally quit. Mum'll be calling more often for a while."

Kristy has two brothers in high school, Sam and Charlie, and a little brother, David Michael, who's six. Sam, Charlie, and Kristy are each responsible for David Michael one afternoon a week. Mrs Thomas had had a baby-sitter lined up for him for the other two days, but I knew the sitter had been cancelling a lot.

"Hey, everybody!" called a voice. Stacey entered Claudia's room, looking gorgeous, as usual.

If you ask Stacey, she'll tell you she's plain, but that's crazy. Stacey is glamorous. She moved to Stoneybrook, Connecticut, from New York City last summer. She's very sophisticated, and is even allowed to have her hair permed, so that she has this fabulous-looking shaggy blonde mane, and she wears fabulous clothes—big, baggy shirts and tight-fitting trousers—and amazing jewellery, like parrots and palm trees. She even has a pair of earrings that consists of a dog for one ear and a bone for the other ear.

I'd give anything to be Stacey. Not to have diabetes, of course, but to have lived in New York City and to be able to dress up like a model every day. My father lets me dress like a model too—a model of a six-year-old. I have to wear my hair in plaits (that's a *rule*), and he has to approve my outfit every day, which is sort of silly since he buys all my clothes. And what he buys are corduroy skirts and plain sweaters and blouses and trainers.

Just once, I'd like to go to school wearing skintight turquoise trousers, Stacey's "island" shirt with the flamingos and toucans all over it, and maybe bright red, high-top sneakers. I'd like to create a sensation. (Well, half of me would. The other half would be too shy to want to attract any attention.)

Stacey often creates a sensation.

So does Claudia. Although she's not quite as sophisticated as Stacey (you can't top having lived in New York), she's pretty glamorous herself. Her black hair is long and silky, and she does something different with it almost every day. Sometimes she wears it in lots of skinny braids, sometimes she twists it on top of her head. At the moment, she was wearing it loose, but had pulled the sides back with big yellow clips shaped like flowers.

Luckily, Kristy dresses more like me than like Claudia and Stacey. It's nice to have someone to feel babyish with. Mrs Thomas doesn't put any dressing restrictions on Kristy; it's just that Kristy doesn't care much about her appearance. Her brown hair is usually sort of messy, and she wears clothes only because it's against the law to go to school naked.

"What's going on?" asked Stacey.

"One call so far," replied Kristy. "My mum needs someone for David Michael on Thursday afternoon."

I opened our record book. The Babysitters Club keeps two books: the record book and a notebook. The record book is just what it sounds like—a book in which we keep our club records. Not only does it have our baby-sitting appointments, it has the addresses and phone numbers of our clients, and records of things like what rates our clients pay, how much each of us earns at each job and which of us has paid our club subs. Stacey keeps track of anything to do with money and numbers.

The Babysitters Club Notebook is more like a diary. Kristy asked us to write up what happens at every job we go to. This is important because then the rest of us learn about our clients' problems, habits, and special needs. For instance, after Claudia baby-sat for Eleanor and Nina Marshall the first time, she wrote up the job and mentioned that Nina is allergic to strawberries. Since we all have to read the notebook entries, it wasn't long before the whole club knew never to give Nina a strawberry.

As you can see, our club is well-run and well-organized. We have Kristy to thank for that, even if she *is* bossy sometimes (well, a lot of the time).

I turned to the appointment section of the record book. "Let's see," I said. "Thursday

. . . Claudia, you're the only one free. Do you want to sit for David Michael?"

"Sure," she answered.

I entered the job information in the book, and Claudia called Mrs Thomas back at her office to tell her who the sitter would be.

As soon as she hung up, the phone rang.

Claudia answered it since her hand was still on the receiver. "Hello, the Babysitters Club . . . Yes? . . . Oh, hi. Okay. 'Bye."

I had already turned the pages of the record book to Saturday.

"That was Watson, Kristy. He needs someone for about two hours on Saturday, from two till four."

Watson is Kristy's mother's fiancé. They plan to get married in the autumn. Watson's divorced, just like Mrs Thomas, and has two little kids: Karen who's five, and Andrew who's three. They stay with him every other weekend. When Watson becomes Kristy's stepfather, Karen and Andrew will become her stepsister and stepbrother.

Even though Kristy loves Karen and Andrew and would want the job on Saturday, our club rule is to offer each job to everybody. "Well," I said, "it looks like nobody is baby-sitting on Saturday so far."

"No," said Stacey, "but I have a doctor's appointment."

"And Mimi's taking me shopping then," said Claudia.

"Well, that leaves you and me," I told Kristy. "You can have the job. I know you want to see Karen and Andrew."

"Thanks!" replied Kristy happily.

I was being nice, but I was also being chicken. There's this weird old woman, Mrs Porter, who lives next door to Watson. Karen says she's a witch and that her name is really Morbidda Destiny. She's very frightened of her. So am I. I didn't mind passing up the job.

Claudia called Watson back.

The phone rang two more times, and we set up two more jobs.

The next time it rang, Kristy answered it. "Hello, the Babysitters Club . . . Hi, Mrs Newton!"

Mrs Newton is one of our favourite clients. She has an adorable little boy named Jamie . . . and a new baby! Lucy wasn't even two months old. Mrs Newton didn't let us sit for Lucy very often, so a call from her was pretty exciting.

Claudia and Stacey and I listened eagerly to Kristy's end of the conversation, wondering if Mrs Newton needed a sitter just for Jamie or for Lucy, too. Each of us was hoping for a chance to take care of the new baby.

"Yes," Kristy was saying. "Yes . . . Oh, Jamie *and* Lucy." (Claudia and Stacey and I squealed with delight.) "Friday . . . six till eight . . . Of course. I'll be there. Great. See you." She hung up.

Kristy would be there?! What happened to offering jobs around? Claud and Stacey and I stared at each other. I don't know what my face looked like, but I could see a mixture of horror and anger on the others' faces.

Kristy, however, was beaming. She was so thrilled at the possibility of taking care of Lucy, that at first she didn't even realize what she'd done.

"The Newtons are giving a cocktail party on Friday and they need someone to watch the kids while they're busy with the guests," she explained. "I'm so excited! Six till eight . . . I'll probably get to give Lucy a bottle—" Kristy broke off, finally realizing that nobody else looked nearly as happy as she did. "Oh," she said. "Sorry."

"*Kristy!*" exclaimed Claudia. "You're supposed to offer the job around. You know that. It's *your* rule. I'd like to sit for Lucy, too."

"So would I," added Stacey.

"Me, too." I checked our record book. "And we're all free then."

"Boy," said Claudia sullenly. She produced a large piece of chewing gum from under the quilt of her bed, unwrapped it, popped it in her mouth, and chewed away. "Some people around here sure are job-hogs."

"I *said* I was sorry," exclaimed Kristy. "Besides, look who's talking."

Uh-oh, I thought. This doesn't sound good.

"What do you mean, look who's talking?" said Claudia.

"Well," Stacey began, and I could tell that she was trying to be polite, "you *have* done that a lot yourself. Remember that job with Charlotte Johanssen? And the one with the Marshalls?"

"And the one with the Pikes?" I added cautiously. It was true. Claudia had forgotten to offer a lot of jobs.

"Hey, what are you guys? Elephants? Don't you ever forget anything?"

"Well, it *has* been a problem," said Kristy.

"I don't believe this!" cried Claudia. "*You*"—she pointed accusingly at Kristy—"break one of our rules, and everyone jumps on *me*! I didn't do anything. I'm innocent."

"*This* time," muttered Stacey.

"Hey," said Claudia. "If you're so desperate to have new friends here in Stoneybrook, don't argue with the ones you've got."

"Is that a threat?" exclaimed Stacey. "Because if it is, I don't need you guys. Don't forget where I'm from."

"We *know*, we *know*—New York. It's all you talk about."

"I was going to say," Stacey went on haughtily, "before I was interrupted, that I'm tough. And I'm a fighter, and I don't need anybody. Not stuck-up job-hogs"—she looked at Claudia—"or bossy know-it-alls"—Kristy—"or shy little babies." Me.

"I am not a shy little baby!" I said, but as soon as I said it, my chin began to tremble and my eyes filled with tears.

"Oh, shut up," Kristy said crossly. Sometimes she has very little patience with me.

But I'd had it. I jumped to my feet. "No, *you* shut up," I shouted at Kristy. "And you, too," I said to Stacey. "I don't care how tough you are or how special you think you are because of your dumb diabetes, you have no right—"

"Don't call Stacey's diabetes dumb!" Claudia cut in.

"And don't bother to stick up for me," Stacey shouted back at Claudia. "Don't do me any favours."

"No problem," Claudia replied icily.

"Hey," said Kristy suddenly. "Who were you calling a bossy know-it-all before?"

"Who do you think?" replied Stacey.

"*Me!*" Kristy glanced at me.

"Don't tell me to shut up and then expect me to help you," I told Kristy.

Kristy looked as if someone had just informed her that scientists had discovered that the moon was in fact made of green cheese.

"Maybe I am shy," I said loudly, edging towards the door. "And maybe I am quiet, but you guys can*not* step all over me. You want to know what I think? I think you, Stacey, are a conceited snob; and you, Claudia, are a stuck-up job-hog; and you, Kristin Amanda Thomas, are the biggest, bossiest know-it-all in the world, and I don't care if I never see you again!"

I let myself out of Claudia's room, slamming the door behind me so hard that the walls shook. Then I ran down the stairs. Behind me, I could hear Claudia, Stacey, and Kristy yelling at each other. As I reached the Kishis' front hall, Claudia's door slammed again. Two more pairs of legs thundered down the stairs.

I ran home, half hoping that either Kristy or Stacey would call after me. But neither one did.

2nd CHAPTER

The last thing I wanted to do after our big fight was eat dinner with Dad, but he expects us to have a proper meal in the evening. Sometimes he fixes it, sometimes I do, but we always sit down in the kitchen and eat dinner at 6.30.

Luckily, Dad was still at work when I got home from Claudia's that night. I was crying, and in no mood to speak to anybody. I slammed angrily around the kitchen. I took a pan of leftover stew out of the refrigerator, slammed the fridge shut, stuck the pan in the oven, and slammed the oven shut. Then I got out plates and glasses, knives and forks, and slammed two cabinets and a drawer. I banged the things down on the table one at a time. Eight bangs.

Then I went upstairs to wash my face. By the time Dad got home I looked a lot better and felt a little better.

"Mary Anne?" he called.

"Coming," I answered. I headed down the stairs, my hair neatly combed, my blouse tucked carefully into my skirt, my kneesocks pulled up and straightened. Dad says it's important to look nice at mealtimes.

"Hi," I said.

"Hello, Mary Anne." He leaned over so I could kiss his cheek. "Is dinner started?"

"Yes." (Dad hates when people say yeah. He also hates *shut up, hey, moron, jerk,* and a long list of other words that creep into my vocabulary whenever I'm not around him.) "I'm heating up the stew."

"That's fine," said Dad. "Let's just toss a salad. That will make a nice dinner."

Dad and I got out lettuce, tomatoes, a cucumber, and some carrots. We chopped and tossed silently. In no time, a crisp salad was sitting in a glass bowl in the centre of the kitchen table. My father took the stew out of the oven and served up two portions.

We sat down and bowed our heads while Dad said grace. At the end, just before the "Amen," he asked God to watch over Abigail. (Abigail is my mother.) He does that before every meal, as far as I know, and sometimes I think he overdoes things. After all, my mother has been dead for almost eleven years. I bless her at night before I go to sleep, and it seems to me that that ought to be enough.

"Well, how was your day, Mary Anne?"

"Fine," I replied.

"How did you do on your spelling test?"

I took a bite of salad, even though I wasn't a bit hungry. "Fine. I got ninety-nine. It was—"

"Mary Anne, *please* don't speak with your mouth full."

I swallowed. "I got ninety-nine," I repeated. "It was the highest grade in the class."

"That's wonderful. I'm very proud of you. Your studying paid off."

I nodded.

"Did you have a meeting of your club this afternoon?" he asked.

"Yeah . . . *yes*."

Kristy, Claudia, and Stacey are all surprised that Dad allows me to be in the club and to do so much baby-sitting. What they don't know is that the only reason he likes our business is that he thinks it teaches me responsibility and how to plan ahead, save money, and that sort of thing.

"What went on? Anything special?" Dad attempted a smile.

I shook my head. There was no way I was going to tell him about the fight we'd had.

"Well," said Dad, trying hard to make conversation, "my case went . . . went very well today. Quite smoothly, really. I feel certain that we're going to win."

I shifted uncomfortably in my seat. I didn't know what case he was talking about, but I had a feeling I *should* have known. He'd probably told me about it. "That's great, Dad."

"Yes. Thank you."

We ate in silence for several minutes.

"This case is interesting because it demonstrates the extreme importance of honesty in business dealings," he said finally. "Always remember that, Mary Anne. Be scrupulously honest and fair. It will serve you in good stead."

"All right, Dad."

We ate in silence again, and it dawned on me that Dad and I sat across from each other at that table twice a day each weekday and three times a day on the weekends. If a meal averaged half an hour, that meant we spent over four hundred hours a year eating together, trying to make conversation—and we barely knew what to say to each other. He might as well have been a stranger I just happened to share food with sixteen times a week.

I pushed my stew around my plate.

"You're not eating, Mary Anne," my father said. "Are you feeling all right?"

"Yes, fine."

"Are you sure? You weren't filling up on snacks at the Kishis', were you?"

"No, Dad, I sw—I promise. I'm just not very hungry."

"Well, try to eat your vegetables, at least. Then you may start your homework."

Dad made starting my homework sound like some kind of reward.

I forced down as much as I could manage. Then my father turned the radio on and listened to classical music while we cleaned up the kitchen. At last I escaped to my bedroom.

I sat down at my desk and opened my maths book. A clean sheet of paper lay before me, along with two sharpened pencils and a pink rubber. But I couldn't concentrate. Before I had made so much as a mark on the paper, I got up and flopped down on my bed.

I remembered calling my friends: a conceited snob; a stuck-up job-hog; and the biggest, bossiest know-it-all in the world. I sincerely wished I hadn't said those things.

Then I remembered being called a baby and being told to shut up. I sincerely wished Stacey and Kristy hadn't said *those* things.

I wished I could talk to somebody. Maybe I could phone Claudia. The only thing *she'd* said that afternoon was for me not to call Stacey's diabetes dumb, which really wasn't mean. But I am not allowed to use the phone after dinner unless I'm discussing homework.

I could ask my father for special permission to use the phone for non-homework business, but he'd want to know what that business was.

I sighed.

I glanced out my window. The side window of my bedroom looks right into the side window of Kristy's bedroom next door. Her light was off, the room dark.

I sat cross-legged on my bed and gazed around. No wonder Stacey had called me a baby. My room looks like a nursery. There's no pram or playpen, but basically the room hasn't changed since I was three. It's decorated in pink and white, which my father had just naturally assumed every little girl would like. The truth is I like yellow and navy blue. Pink is one of my least favourite colours.

The curtains, which are ruffly, are made of pink flowered fabric and are tied back with pink ribbons. The bedspread matches the curtains. The rug is pale pink shag, and the walls are white, with pink skirting boards.

Living in my room is like living inside a candy floss machine.

What bothers me most, though, is what's on the walls—or rather, what isn't on them. I've spent a lot of time in Kristy's and Claudia's rooms, and I've been to Stacey's room twice, and I've decided that you can tell a lot about the people who use those rooms just by looking at the walls. For example, Kristy loves sports, so her walls are covered with posters about the Olympics and pictures of gymnasts and football players. Claudia is an artist and her own work hangs everywhere. She changes it often, taking down old paintings or drawings and putting up new ones. And Stacey, who misses New York more than she'll admit, has tacked up a poster of the city at night, another of the Empire State Building, and a map of Manhattan.

Here's what you'll find on my walls: a framed picture of my parents and me, taken the day I was christened; a framed picture of Humpty Dumpty (before he broke); and two framed pictures of characters from *Alice in Wonderland*. They are all framed in pink.

Do you know what I would *like* to have on my walls? I've thought about this very carefully, just in case my father should ever lose his mind and say I can redecorate. I'm not allowed to put up posters because the thumbtacks would make too many holes in the wall. But assuming Dad was really bonkers and didn't care about holes, I'd put up a giant poster of a kitten or maybe several kittens, a big photo of the members of the Babysitters Club, a poster of New York City, and maybe one of Paris.

I would take down Humpty and Alice, but leave the picture of my family.

My gaze drifted from my walls to the window. I snapped to attention as a light went on in Kristy's room. Maybe I could wave to her and let her know that as far as I was concerned, the fight was over. But

Kristy pulled her shade down quickly, not even looking at the window.

I checked my watch. It was almost eight o'clock. In another hour, I could try signalling to her with my flashlight. I worked out a flashlight code so that we can "talk" at night without the telephone. One of us usually flashes to the other shortly after nine o'clock. At that time, my father has already said goodnight to me. I'm free to read in bed until 9.30, but I know he won't check on me. Kristy and I have been signalling to each other for a long time and we have never been caught.

I finished my homework and changed into my nightgown. By five minutes to nine I was in bed, reading a very exciting book called *A Wrinkle in Time*.

Dad stuck his head in the door. "Oh, good. I see you're all ready for bed."

I nodded.

"What are you reading?"

"*A Wrinkle in Time*. It's on Mr Counts' reading list." (Mr Counts is the school librarian.)

"Oh, that's fine. Well, goodnight, Mary Anne."

"Goodnight, Dad."

He closed my door. I could hear his footsteps as he went back downstairs.

I know my dad loves me, and I know the reason he's strict is that he wants to show everybody I can be a well-brought-up young lady even without a mother, but sometimes I just wish things were different.

I took my flashlight out of my desk drawer, turned off my light, and tiptoed to my window, waiting for Kristy to do the same. I planned to signal I'M SORRY to her.

I stood at my window for fifteen minutes, but her shade remained drawn.

I knew then that she was *very* angry.

3rd CHAPTER

The next morning I woke up feeling sad. Kristy had never stayed mad at me for so long. Then again, I had never called her the biggest, bossiest know-it-all in the world. As I got dressed for school, though, I tried to convince myself that the members of the Babysitters Club couldn't stay mad for long. After all, we had a business to run. Surely things would get straightened out in time for our meeting the next day.

When breakfast was over, I kissed my father goodbye and headed out the front door. I hoped he wouldn't see that I was walking to school alone. If he did, he would know that something was wrong.

I had walked to school alone only six times since kindergarten. Four of those times were days Kristy was home sick; once was when she and her family left for Florida the day before spring vacation started; and once was the day after the Thomases announced that they were getting divorced, and Kristy had been too upset to go to school.

Sometimes Claudia walked with us, sometimes she didn't. However, since just after we started the Babysitters Club, Kristy, Claudia, Stacey and I had been walking to and from school together almost every day.

I reached the sidewalk and paused in front of Kristy's house, trying to decide whether to ring her bell and ask to talk to her. In the end, I just kept on walking. Basically, I'm a coward. I didn't want to have a scene with her in front of her family.

I walked quickly to school, keeping my eyes peeled for Kristy, Claudia, or Stacey. But I didn't see them. A horrible thought occurred to me: "Maybe they'd all made up, and I was the only one they were still mad at." With a sinking feeling in my stomach, I entered school.

The very first person I saw was Kristy! She was not with Claudia and Stacey, so I began to feel a bit better.

I waved to her.

Kristy looked right at me. I'm sure she did. She saw me wave.

But she tossed her head in the air, turned around, and flounced down the hall. I followed her, since my classroom is next to hers, but I tried to keep a safe distance between us.

As I neared my classroom, I spotted Claudia coming down the hall towards Kristy and me.

"Hey, Kristy!" Claudia called.

Oh, no, I thought. They *have* made up.

But Kristy ignored Claudia.

"*Kristy*," Claudia said again.

"Are you talking to me?" Kristy asked icily. "Or to some other job-hog?"

Claudia's face clouded over. "No, you're the only job-hog I see at the moment."

"Then get a mirror," snapped Kristy.

Claudia looked as if she was preparing some sort of nasty retort, but before she could think of a really good one, Kristy walked into her classroom and slammed the door shut behind her.

I wondered whether it was safe to approach Claudia. After all, she had wanted to make up with Kristy. But just then, the bell rang.

Claudia disappeared into her classroom; I disappeared into mine.

The morning passed slowly. I couldn't concentrate. In my head, I wrote notes of apology to my friends. I realized that I must still be mad at them, though, because some of the notes weren't very nice.

Dear Stacey,

I'm really, really sorry you called me a

shy little baby. I hope you're sorry, too . . .

Dear Kristy,

I'm sorry you're the biggest, bossiest know-it-all in the world, but what can I do about it? Have you considered seeking professional help?

Dear Claudia,

I'm sorry I called you a stuck-up job-hog. You don't deserve that, and I didn't really mean it. I hope you can forgive me.

Love,
Mary Anne

Now *that* was a note I could send.

In English class, I finished my work early. I carefully removed a fresh piece of paper from the middle of my notebook, and took my special cartridge pen from my purse. The cartridge was filled with peacock-blue ink, and the nib on the pen made my handwriting look like scrolly, swirly calligraphy.

Slowly, making sure each word looked perfect and was spelled correctly, I printed the note to Claudia. Then I waved it back and forth to dry the ink, folded it twice (making the creases straight and even), and tucked it in my purse. I would give it to her at lunchtime.

My knees felt weak as I made my way to the lunch-room a few minutes later. I'd know right away whether Stacey and Claudia had made up, or if they were still mad, too. They always sat with the same kids—a sophisticated group that included *boys.*

The first thing I did when I entered the lunch-room was look around to see what was what with my friends. I found Claudia and Stacey's table. There was the usual bunch, or almost the usual bunch: Pete, Howie, Rick, Dori, Emily, and Stacey. But no Claudia.

So. Claudia and Stacey hadn't made up, either.

I scanned the lunch-room and finally found Claudia. She was sitting with Trevor Sandbourne. Just the two of them. Trevor is this boy she likes and goes out with sometimes. Claudia was leaning on her elbows, her hair falling over her shoulders, whispering to Trevor. He was listening with a smile on his face. They looked very private and very cosy.

I edged around a crowded table toward the one where Kristy and I always sit with the Shillaber twins, Mariah and Miranda. It was a round table with four chairs, perfect for our little group. But halfway there, I stopped. Kristy and the twins were already at the table. They had spread their lunches everywhere so that there wasn't an inch of available space. Furthermore, they'd removed the fourth chair, or lent it to a crowded table, or something. It didn't matter what. The point was that they hadn't saved a place for me.

I watched my friends for a moment. Kristy was facing me. She was talking away a mile a minute and Mariah and Miranda were giggling.

Kristy glanced up and saw me. She began talking even more earnestly. Then she gestured for the twins to lean towards her, and she made a great show of whispering in their ears and laughing loudly.

I turned around.

Suddenly I felt like a new kid at school. I didn't know who else to sit with. Ever since middle school began, I'd been eating with Kristy, Mariah, and Miranda.

I knew that if Kristy were in my shoes, she'd just join some other group of kids, even if she didn't know them very well. But I'd die of embarrassment first. I could never do that.

I walked around the lunch-room until I found an empty table. I plopped down in a chair and opened my lunch-box. Since I pack my own lunch, I never have to eat things I don't like, such as liverwurst sandwiches. On the other hand, there are never any surprises. Treats, yes; surprises, no.

I spread a paper napkin on the table and

arranged my lunch on it: peanut butter sandwich, apple juice in a box, potato chips, banana. I looked it over and realized I wasn't hungry.

I was still staring at it when a voice next to me said, "Excuse me, could I sit here?"

I glanced up. Standing uncertainly by my side was a tall girl with the blondest hair I had ever seen. It was so pale it was almost white, and it hung, straight and silky, to her rear end.

"Sure," I said, waving my hand at all the empty chairs.

She sat down with a sigh, placing a tray in front of her. I looked at her lunch and decided I was glad I had brought mine. I knew Stacey and Claudia think Kristy and I are babies because we still bring our lunches to school, but the macaroni casserole on the girl's tray looked really disgusting. And it was surrounded by mushy, bright orange carrots, a limp salad, and a roll that you'd need a chain saw to slice.

The girl smiled shyly at me. "You must be new, too," she said.

"New?" I blushed. Why else would I be sitting alone? "Oh," I stammered, "um, no. It's just—my friends are all . . . absent today."

"Oh." The girl sounded disappointed.

"Are—are you new?" I asked after a moment.

She nodded. "This is my second day

here. Nobody ever wants the new kid to sit at their table. And I feel embarrassed sitting alone. I thought I'd found the perfect solution—another new kid."

I smiled. "Well, I don't mind if you sit with me. Even if I'm not new."

The girl smiled back. She wasn't exactly pretty, I decided, but she was pleasant, which was more important. Especially considering three *un*pleasant people I could think of.

"My name's Dawn," she said. "Dawn Schafer."

"Dawn," I repeated. "That's such a pretty name. I'm Mary Anne Spier."

"Hi, Mary Anne Spier." Dawn's blue eyes, which were almost as pale as her hair, sparkled happily.

"Did you just move here?" I asked. "Or did you switch schools or something?"

"Just moved here," she replied. "Last week." She began to eat slowly and methodically, taking first a bite of macaroni stuff, then a bite of carrots, then a bite of salad. She worked her way around the plate in a circle. "Our house is still a mess," she went on. "Packing cartons everywhere. Yesterday it took me twenty minutes to find my brother for dinner."

I giggled. At that moment, I happened to look up and see Kristy across the cafeteria. She was watching me. As soon as I caught her eye, she began talking to Mariah and

Miranda again, making it look as if they were having the time of their lives without me.

Well, two can play at that game, I thought. Even though I have never been much good at talking to people I don't know well, I leaned across the table and put my head next to Dawn's conspiratorially.

"You want to know who the weirdest kid in school is?"

She nodded eagerly.

He happened to be sitting at the table next to Kristy's. I took advantage of that to point in her direction. "It's Alexander Kurtzman. The one wearing the three-piece suit. See him?" I whispered.

Dawn nodded.

"Don't ever try to butt in front of him on the lunch line. Don't even try to get in *back* of him, unless he's at the end of the line. His hobby is obeying rules."

It was Dawn's turn to laugh. "Who else should I know about?" she asked.

I pointed out a few other kids. We spent the rest of the lunch hour whispering and laughing. Twice I caught Kristy's eye. She looked absolutely poisonous. I knew I wasn't helping our fight, but I kind of liked the idea of getting even with her for not letting me sit at our table.

"Hey, do you want to come over to my house after school tomorrow?" Dawn asked.

"Well . . . well, sure," I replied. It felt so strange to be talking with somebody besides Kristy, Claudia, Stacey or the Shillabers. I wasn't sure that I had ever made a new friend all on my own. Mariah and Miranda had orginally been friends Kristy had made, Stacey had been a friend of Claudia's, and I had just grown up with Kristy and Claudia.

"Oh, that's wonderful!" exclaimed Dawn. She must have been really lonely.

I began to feel guilty. I knew full well that one reason I wanted to go over to Dawn's house was to make Kristy (and Stacey and Claudia) mad.

I hoped Kristy would see me leaving school with Dawn the next afternoon. I hoped she would be surprised. I hoped she would be mad (madder than she already was). I even hoped she'd be a little hurt.

"That would be fun," I added. "Where do you live?"

"Burnt Hill Road."

"That's not too far from me! I live on Bradford Court."

"Great! We have a video recorder. We can watch a movie."

"Okay!"

Dawn and I got up and cleared our places.

"Want to eat lunch again tomorrow?" asked Dawn. "Or will your friends be back?"

I paused. What if we'd all made up by the

next day? I decided to cross that bridge when I came to it. "I don't know," I answered.

"It doesn't really matter anyway," said Dawn quietly.

"Okay. Well . . . see you."

"See you."

We left the lunch-room.

I didn't see Kristy, Claudia or Stacey again until school finished that day. Just after the last bell rang, I was standing in the front doorway of Stoneybrook Middle School, looking out across the lawn.

Then I saw them, all three of them. They were walking home from school, each one alone, each one still probably mad.

I set out slowly after them. It wasn't until I got home that I realized I had never given Claudia the note I'd written.

4th CHAPTER

The first thing I thought when I woke up the next morning was, it's Wednesday. Today is a club-meeting day. We can't stay mad much longer or we won't be able to hold the meeting. And we've never missed a meeting. Suddenly, I was sure our fight was over.

I was so sure, that on my way to school, I stopped at Kristy's house and rang her doorbell. I thought we could walk to school together and apologize to each other.

Ding-dong.

David Michael answered the door. "Hi, Mary Anne!" he said.

"Hi," I replied. "Is Kristy still here?"

"Yup," said David Michael, "she's just—"

"I am *not* here!" I heard Kristy call from the living room.

"Yes, you are. You're right—"

"David Michael, come here for a sec," said Kristy.

David Michael left the front hall.

A few seconds later, I heard footsteps tiptoeing towards the hall. The front door slammed shut in my face.

I stood on the Thomases' doorstep, shaking.

Then I turned and crossed the lawn.

All the way to school I kept hearing Kristy's angry voice and the door slamming. Well, I thought, there's still Dawn. Dawn wasn't the same as Kristy or my other friends, but she was something.

We ate lunch together after all. "Your friends are absent again?" Dawn asked. She looked sceptical.

"Yeah," I replied. I decided not even to go into it.

I looked around the lunch-room for the other members of the Babysitters Club. Things were a bit different that day. Kristy was still eating with the Shillabers, but the empty chair had been filled by another friend of theirs, Jo Deford. Claudia and Trevor were sitting with Rick and Emily. At the opposite end of their long table were Dori, Howie, Pete and Stacey. Every so often, Stacey would look up and give Claudia the evil eye, or Claudia would whisper something to Trevor and then look in Stacey's direction and laugh. Once, she stuck her tongue out at Stacey.

Things were worse than ever. I wasn't surprised that Kristy was holding a grudge, but I had sort of expected Stacey and Claudia to make up, or at least to pretend to have made up. I never thought I'd see the day when cool Claudia would stick her tongue out at somebody in front of Trevor Sandbourne.

"Boy," I said under my breath.

"What?" asked Dawn.

I sighed. "Nothing."

When the bell rang at the end of the day, I made a dash for the front door of school. I was supposed to meet Dawn there and was having to figure just how to time things so that Kristy would be sure to see me walking off with my new friend. I decided that I should simply meet Dawn and dawdle. As it happened, things worked out better than I could have hoped.

Almost as soon as I reached the door, kids started streaming past me. I kept my eyes glued to the crowded hallway. After a few moments, I spotted Kristy. She spotted me at the same time and made a face that was a cross between a scowl and a sneer. So what did I do? I smiled. Not at Kristy, but at Dawn who happened to be right in front of her. I'm sure Kristy thought I was trying to make up with her again.

Boy, was she surprised when Dawn called, "Hi, Mary Anne!" and ran up to me.

"Hi," I replied. I flashed another smile. And as we headed out the door I looked over my shoulder in time to see Kristy standing open-mouthed behind me.

Dawn and I walked across the lawn, talking away nineteen to the dozen. We passed Claudia and Trevor on the way, which only made the afternoon more worthwhile, as far as I could see.

Dawn's new house turned out to be very old.

"It's a farmhouse," she told me, "and it was built in seventeen ninety-five."

"Wow!" I said. "You're kidding! Gosh, you were lucky to be able to buy such an old house."

"Yeah, I think so. Even though it needs a lot of work, and it's not very big. You'll see."

We walked through the front door. "If my dad were here," said Dawn, "he'd have to duck."

I looked up and saw that the top of the door frame wasn't far above my head.

"People were shorter in seventeen ninety-five," explained Dawn.

I stepped inside, pulling the door closed behind me. I was standing in the middle of a room strewn with packing cartons—some empty, some half-empty, some still unopened—mountains of wadded-up newspaper, and a jumble of, well, *things*. I think we were in the living room, but I could see dishes, toys, sheets and blankets, a shower curtain, a bicycle tyre and a can of peaches.

"My mother isn't very organized yet," said Dawn. "Actually ever. Mum!" she called. "Mum, I'm home!"

"I'm in the kitchen, honey."

Dawn and I stepped over and around things, and managed to reach the kitchen unharmed.

I could see what Dawn meant about the house being small. The kitchen wasn't even big enough for a table and chairs. And it was dark, the window being blocked off by some overgrown yew bushes outside.

A pretty woman with short, curly hair that was every bit as light as Dawn's was standing at the work-top slowly turning the pages of a large photo album.

Dawn took a look at the mess (the kitchen was as messy as the living room had been) and then at the photo album. "Mum!" she cried. "What are you doing?"

Mrs Schafer looked up guiltily. "Oh, honey," she said. "I keep getting side-tracked. I was working away, and I unpacked this album and an envelope full of pictures marked FOR PHOTO ALBUM, and I just had to stop and put them in."

Dawn smiled and shook her head. "I don't know, Mum. The way we're going, we might as well leave the house like it is. Then, if we ever move again, we could just throw the things back in the boxes."

Mrs Schafer laughed.

"Mum, this is my friend Mary Anne. We eat lunch together.

Mrs Schafer shook my hand. "Hi, Mary Anne. Nice to meet you. I do apologize for the mess. If you go up to Dawn's room, though, you'll find the one civilized spot in the house. Dawn had her bedroom cleaned, unpacked and organized the day after we moved in."

Dawn shrugged. "What can I say? I'm neat."

"Would you like a snack, girls?" asked Mrs Schafer.

"Is there actual food?" asked Dawn.

"Well," her mother replied, "there is actual grape jelly and an actual can of peaches."

"We've been eating out," Dawn told me, "in case you couldn't tell." She turned to her mother. "I think we'll skip the snack, Mum. But thanks."

Dawn and I went upstairs. Everything was little or low: a small dining room; a narrow, dark stairway leading to a narrow, dark hall. At the end of the hall was Dawn's bedroom, also small, with a low ceiling and a creaky floor.

"Wow, I like your room," I said, "but, gosh, the colonists must have been midgets."

"Maybe," said Dawn. "But there are two good things about this room. One is this."

She showed me a small, round window near the ceiling. "I don't know why it's there, but I love it."

"Kind of like a porthole," I said.

Dawn nodded. "The other thing is this." She flicked some switches and the room was flooded with brilliant light. "I can't stand dim rooms," she explained, "so Mum let me get lots of lamps and I put one-hundred-watt bulbs in all of them. I just hope the wiring in this old place can take it."

"Hey!" I exclaimed. "There's the video. It's in *your* room! Boy, are you lucky. Your own TV and video."

"They're only temporary, until the rest of the house is in order. Then they go downstairs to the living room. What movie do you want to see?'

"What do you have?"

"Practically everything. My mum's a movie nut. She scours the TV schedules and tapes things all the time."

"Well," I said, "you probably don't have *The Parent Trap*, do you?"

"Of course we do. That was the last thing she taped before—"

"Before what?" I asked.

Dawn lowered her eyes. "Before the divorce," she whispered. "That's why we moved here. Because Mum and Dad got divorced."

"Why did you move *here*?"

"Mum's parents live here. My mother

grew up in Stoneybrook."

"Oh! So did my dad. I wonder if they knew each other."

"What's your dad's name?'

"Richard Spier. What's your mum's name? I mean, what was her name before she got married?"

"Sharon, um, Porter."

"I'll have to ask my father. Wouldn't it be funny if they knew each other?"

"Yeah." Dawn was still staring at the floor.

"Hey," I said, "I guess it's awful when your parents split up, but there's nothing *wrong* with it, you know. Lots of kids have divorced parents. Kristy Thomas, my be— my next-door neighbour, has been a 'divorced kid' for years. And her mum goes out with this nice divorced man. And—" (I was about to tell her that the parents of the Shillaber twins were divorced, but I didn't really want to talk about the twins.) "And, I mean, I don't care that your parents are divorced."

Dawn smiled slightly. "Where did your mother grow up?" she asked. I guess she wanted to change the subject.

"In Maryland, but she's dead. She died a long time ago."

"Oh," Dawn flushed. Then she slipped the movie cassette in the video recorder. Soon we were wrapped up in *The Parent Trap*.

"What a great movie," said Dawn with a sigh when it was over.

"I know. One of my favourites." I looked at my watch. It was 5.15. "I better go," I said. "This was really fun."

"Yeah, it was. I am glad you came over," said Dawn.

"Me, too."

We clattered down the midget staircase.

"See you tomorrow!" I called as I left. I ran all the way to Claudia's house. My stomach was tied up in knots. It was time for a meeting of the Babysitters Club.

I had no idea what to expect.

5th CHAPTER

On the way to the Kishis' house, I told myself that if Claudia answered the door, it would be a good sign. It would be easy for her to let someone else answer it, so if she made the effort, then it probably meant she wasn't so mad any more.

I rang the bell.

Mimi opened the door. She looked worried. "Hello, Mary Anne," she said solemnly.

"Hi, Mimi." I hesitated. Usually, I run right upstairs. "Claudia's here, isn't she?"

"Yes, of course, Stacey is here, too . . ."

I knew she wanted to say something more, but was too tactful.

"Well, I'll go on up, too. See you later, Mimi," I walked up the stairs, dashed by Janine's room, and entered Claudia's.

There were Stacey and Claudia. Stacey was sitting cross-legged on the bed, staring at her hands. Claudia was seated stiffly in her director's chair, gazing out the window. Neither one spoke when I entered the room.

Remembering what had happened at Kristy's house that morning, I decided not to be the one to make the first move. I sat down tentatively on the floor.

The phone rang. Claudia was nearest to it, so she took the call. "Hello, the Babysitters Club . . . Oh, hi . . . Saturday morning? . . . Okay . . . okay. I'll call you right back . . . Goodbye."

Finally, I thought. Now someone will have to say something.

Claudia hung up the phone. "The Johanssens. They need someone for Charlotte on Saturday morning. Who's free?"

"I am," said Stacey to her hands.

"Mary Anne?"

I shook my head.

"I'm not, either," said Claudia. "I guess it's yours, Stacey."

"Fine." Stacey managed to look pleased through her anger. Charlotte is her favourite kid.

"What about Kristy?" I asked.

"She's not here," said Claudia shortly. "And she knows the rules. She *made* the rules. If she doesn't phone to tell us she'll be late or she can't make it, then she misses out on jobs. I'll call Dr Johanssen and tell her that *she*—" Claudia shot a dirty look at Stacey—"will be baby-sitting." When she turned to dial the phone, Stacey stuck her tongue out at her.

Claudia finished the call and hung up. No one said a word.

A few minutes later, the phone rang again. When it was on its third ring, Claudia said, "Somebody else get it this time. I'm not a slave."

I answered it. "Hello? . . . Oh, hi, Mrs Thomas. Is Kristy sick or something? . . . She's where? . . . Oh. No, it's not important . . . For David Michael? Sure. I'll call you right back." I hung up. "Kristy," I said, in case anybody was interested, "is over at the Shillabers' house, and Mrs Thomas needs someone to watch David Michael on Thursday afternoon . . . I'm free."

"So am I," said Claudia.

"So am I," said Stacey.

Uh-oh. When that happens, we usually start saying things like, "Well, I have two other jobs this week, so you can take this one," or, "I know you haven't had a chance to sit for David Michael in a while, so you take it."

Somehow, I didn't think anybody was going to say anything like that.

I was right.

Instead, Claudia cut out three scraps of paper, drew a star on one, folded them in half, tossed them in a shoebox, and said, "Everybody pick one. The person who gets the star sits for David Michael."

Claudia chose the star.

"Hey!" cried Stacey. "You knew which one it was!"

"I did not!" exclaimed Claudia. "How would I know that?"

"You made the scraps of paper."

"Are you calling me a cheat?"

"You said it, I didn't."

Oh, brother, I thought. Here we go again.

In the end, Stacey allowed Claudia to keep the job. The phone rang two more times before the end of our meeting and we managed to set up the baby-sitting jobs without actual violence.

At precisely six o'clock, Stacey stood up and marched out of Claudia's room without so much as a word. Claudia and I looked at each other, but Claudia didn't say anything, either, so I followed Stacey. Mimi watched us walk silently out the front door.

As we stepped onto the lawn, Stacey broke into a run but for some reason, I turned around and looked back at the house. Claudia was in her window. I hesitated. Then I waved to her.

She flashed me a hopeful smile and waved back.

On impulse, I ran up the Kishis' steps again, opened the door, called Mimi, and handed her the note I had written to Claudia. Then I ran across the street to my house.

My father hadn't come home yet. When

the numbers on the digital clock flipped to 6.15 and he still wasn't home, I took it as a sign and decided to call Claudia. If I didn't talk to her before supper, I'd have to wait until the next morning.

I dialled her private number.

"Hello?"

"Hi, Claudia," I said nervously. "It's Mary Anne."

"Oh. Hi."

"Well, I—"

"I got your note. Mimi gave it to me. Thanks."

"You're welcome."

"I forgive you. And I'm sorry I got mad, too," Claudia said rather stiffly.

"Well . . ." I didn't know what to say next. Was our fight over? "Well . . . one reason I'm calling is Kristy. Since she went to the Shillabers' today," I said, "and skipped our meeting, I guess that means she doesn't want to be part of the club. I mean, I don't know . . ."

"I guess for a while, anyway, she doesn't want to be part of it," agreed Claudia.

"What should we do about the club then? I mean, she *is* chairman."

"I know. I was thinking about that. We shouldn't *really* keep taking jobs without asking her whether she wants them."

"Yeah. On the other hand, she should come to the meetings."

Claudia didn't say anything.

"Claud?"

"I just don't know what to do. Stacey is almost as mad as Kristy is."

"What's strange," I said, "is that Kristy hasn't said she wants the club to go out of business. She's just ignoring it—and the club is *her* business. Why would she let us run it without her when we're the ones she's mad at?"

Claudia was probably shrugging her shoulders. "Maybe you and I should talk to Stacey and Kristy tomorrow and see what they want to do. We certainly can't keep having meetings like the one we just had. If you talk to Kristy, I'll talk to Stacey."

"All right," I agreed, "but it's not going to be easy." I didn't tell Claudia about Kristy and the door-slamming. I figured she was having just as much trouble with Stacey as I was having with Kristy.

How was I supposed to talk to Kristy? I didn't want to go to her house again, and I had a feeling that if I called her on the phone, she'd simply hang up on me. The only thing left to do was to surprise her.

I ambushed her at school the next morning as she came out of the girls' toilet. I stepped right in front of her.

"Ex*cuse* me," said Kristy haughtily.

My heart was pounding like a jack-hammer, but I stood my ground. "I have to talk to you," I said.

"No, you don't."

"Yes, I do."

"No."

"Yes."

"No."

"We have to decide what to do about the club. Are you out of it?'

"*Out* of it? It's my club."

"Exactly."

"What do you mean 'exactly'?"

"I mean, it's your club, but you didn't go to the meeting yesterday."

"It's my club so I didn't *have* to go to the meeting."

"But you missed out on a lot of good jobs."

Kristy kicked at a piece of screwed-up paper that was littering the hall.

"I mean," I went on, "we weren't going to call the Shillabers' house every time a job came in, to see if you wanted it."

"You should have," she said sullenly.

It was getting harder for me to argue with her. I was used to giving in on things. I drew in a deep breath. "Not according to the rules."

"Yeah."

"Anyway, Claudia decided that we'd better figure out how to run the club while"—I had started to say "while we're all mad at each other" and realized that that wasn't very tactful—"while . . ."

"While we're all mad at each other?"

suggested Kristy.

"Well . . . yes. I think Claudia and I are the only ones speaking to each other, so yest—"

"You and Claudia are speaking?"

"Yes."

"Brother. Whatever happened to faithful friends?"

"What *happened* to them?" I cried. "They had doors slammed in their faces, that's what!"

"Okay, okay, okay. Well, how about if we take turns answering the phone in Claudia's room at meeting times? You go one day, I'll go the next . . ."

"What about offering the jobs around? If we have to call each member of the club to tell her about each job call that comes in, we'll end up talking to each other more than ever that way."

Kristy looked to the ceiling for help. "When a club member is on duty, she takes on as many jobs as she can. Then the only jobs she has to offer around are the ones she can't take herself. How does that sound?"

"Fair," I said. "I'll tell Claudia."

Kristy nodded.

"Hi, Mary Anne!" called a voice from down the hall.

It was Dawn.

I turned around and waved. She ran towards me. "How are you? Yesterday was fun, wasn't it?"

"Great," I agreed. "And I was wondering. Do you want to come over on Saturday? We don't have a video but maybe we could make fudge or bake some biscuits." I glanced at Kristy. If she opened her eyes any wider, her eyeballs would roll out and land on the floor.

"Sure!" exclaimed Dawn.

"Good! See you at lunch?"

"See you at lunch," Dawn trotted happily down the hall.

Kristy was still staring at me. At last she managed to say, "You just invited her over to your house."

"Right."

"But you never ask anyone over except *me*. You don't usually even invite Claudia or Stacey over."

I shrugged. "Dawn's a good friend."

Kristy narrowed her eyes. I think she knew what game I was playing, because she chose that moment to say, "Oh, by the way, Mum extended my baby-sitting hours. Now I can stay out as late as Stacey: ten o'clock on weekends, nine-thirty on weeknights."

It was my turn to widen my eyes. *Ten o'clock?* Kristy could stay out until *ten*? That meant I had to be home earlier than any other club member.

I could feel my face flush. Kristy might just as well have pinned a sign to me that said BABY, because that's what I was. The only baby in the Babysitters Club.

Kristy walked off, smirking.

I hung my head, mad at Kristy and mad at my father.

I knew I had to do something—but what?

6th CHAPTER

According to our new emergency operating procedures, the Babysitters Club meetings were being handled by one club member at a time. Friday was my first day. Since Claudia and I were speaking, she stayed in her room with me, but we stuck to Kristy's new rules, and I took all but one of the jobs that afternoon.

The last call that came in was from a woman named Mrs Prezzioso. I knew the Prezziosos slightly. They lived on Burnt Hill Road not far from Dawn, and are friends with the Pikes, the eight-kid family our club members often sit for. I had met the Prezziosos several times at the Pikes'.

"Hello, the Babysitters Club," I said when I answered Mrs Prezzioso's call.

"Hello. This is Madeleine Prezzioso over on Burnt Hill Road. To whom am I speaking?"

To whom was she speaking? "This is Mary Anne Spier," I said.

"Oh, Mary Anne. Hello, dear. How are you?"

"Fine, thank you," I replied politely. "How are you?" I should mention here that the Prezziosos, all three of them, look extremely prim and proper—but Mrs Prezzioso is the only one who acts that way, too. She's fussy and fastidious, kind of like the neat half of *The Odd Couple*. She's always polite, and she usually appears to have stepped right out of the pages of one of those magazines that gives tips on getting out hard-to-remove stains and baking the perfect loaf of bread. She buys three-piece suits and monogrammed handkerchiefs for Mr Prezzioso. And Jenny, their five-year-old daughter . . . Well, Mrs Prezzioso dresses her as if every day were Easter Sunday. She puts ribbons in her hair and lacy socks on her feet. I've never seen Jenny in trousers. Mrs P. probably thinks *jeans* is a dirty word.

Poor Jenny doesn't seem to be the prim, fastidious type at all. Neither does Mr P. When I'm around him, I usually have the feeling that he'd rather be dozing in front of the TV in overalls, a T-shirt, and mismatched socks. And Jenny tries hard, but she just isn't what her mother wants her to be.

Mrs P. and I chatted for a minute or so

and then got down to business. "I know this is last-minute, dear," she said, "but I need a sitter for Sunday afternoon. Mr Prezzioso and I have been invited to a tea."

"What time does it start?" I asked.

"Four o'clock. I should think we'd be home by six or six-thirty."

"Okay, I'll be there."

"That's wonderful, dear. Thank you. I'll see you at four. Goodbye!"

I hung up the phone thoughtfully. The afternoon at the Prezziosos' could be pretty interesting.

On Sunday afternoon I rang the Prezziosos' doorbell promptly at 3.30. Jenny came flying to answer it. I could hear her calling hello and fiddling with the locks. After a few moments, she pulled it open—but the chain was still attached. CRACK!

"Jenny!" a voice exclaimed behind her.

"Did you ask who was there before you opened the door?"

"No, Mummy."

"Well, what are you supposed to do when the doorbell rings?"

"Say, 'Who is it?'"

"Then please do that." The door closed. The locks slid back into place.

"Mary Anne," Mrs Prezzioso called, "would you mind ringing the bell again, please?"

I sighed. *Ding-dong.*

"Who is it?" asked Jenny's voice.

"It's me, Mary Anne Spier."

"Are you a stranger?"

"No, I'm your baby-sitter."

"Now can I let her in, Mummy?"

"Yes, sweetheart. That was very good."

At last the door opened. I stepped inside and took off my coat. Both Mrs P. and Jenny were all dressed up. Mrs P. looked exactly as if she were off to a fancy tea. But Jenny seemed a bit overdressed for an afternoon of stories and games and fun. She was wearing a frilly white dress trimmed with yards of lavender lace and ribbons, matching lavender socks, and shiny black patent leather strappy shoes. Her hair had been curled, and was pulled back from either side of her face by combs from which long streamers flowed. Really, her mother ought to just pose her in a display case somewhere.

"Hello, Mary Anne," Mrs P. greeted me.

"Hi," I replied. "Hi, Jenny."

Jenny looked wistfully at the blue jean skirt I was wearing. "I like your skirt, Mary Anne," she said.

"Now, Jenny," Mrs P. said briskly, "it's a very pretty skirt, I'm sure, but not as pretty as my little angel in her brand-new dress!" She pulled Jenny to her and covered her with loud kisses. "Who's my little angel?" she asked.

Jenny's face was smushed up against her

mother's arm. "Mmmphh," she said.

Mrs P. tried again. "Who's my little angel?"

Jenny drew away from her. "I am, Mummy."

"And what are you made of?"

"Sugar 'n' spice 'n' all that's nice."

Gag, gag. I remembered another nursery rhyme. That one went, "There was a little girl who had a little curl, right in the middle of her forehead; when she was good she was very, very good, and when she was bad she was horrid."

"Isn't our angel pretty today?" Mrs Prezzioso asked me.

Our angel? "Yes, she sure is," I replied.

Jenny smiled sweetly.

"All right, I'm ready, Madeleine," boomed a voice from the stairs. Mr P. came thundering down from the second floor.

"Okay, angel, you be a good girl for your sitter. Will you promise me that?" He tossed Jenny in the air and she squealed with delight.

"Oh, be careful!" cried Mrs Prezzioso. "Her new dress . . . and your new tie. Nick, please."

Mr P. returned Jenny safely to the ground. "Well, let's go. Thanks for coming over, Mary Lou."

"Mary *Anne*." Jenny corrected him.

Mrs P. stood in front of her husband. She straightened his tie, adjusted his jacket, and arranged the handkerchief in his pocket so that it was absolutely straight and the monogram was perfectly centred.

Then she turned around and stood next to her husband. "How do we look?" she asked me.

I glanced at Jenny. Jenny was watching me.

I blushed. "You look . . ." Somehow "very nice" didn't sound like enough. "You look like a picture out of a magazine," I finally said. And they did, all posed and stiff.

Mrs P. appeared confused, but recovered quickly. "Why, thank you, dear."

There was a pause. "You're welcome," I said, to fill the silence.

"Now, we'll be at the Elliot Taggarts' this afternoon," said Mrs Prezzioso. "Their number is written on the message board in the kitchen, and the emergency numbers are right next to the phone. If we're not home by six o'clock, you can give Jenny a sandwich for supper."

"Okay," I said. Jenny and I walked her parents to the back door. "Have fun!" I called, as they climbed into their car.

I closed the door and leaned against it for a few seconds. "Well," I said to Jenny, "what do you want to do first?"

Jenny flopped on the couch in the playroom and pouted. "Nothing."

"Oh, come on," I said brightly, "there

must be something you want to do. We have two hours to play."

Jenny stuck out her lower lip and shook her head. "Unh-unh."

"Well, in that case," I said, "I'll just play with the Kid-Kit by myself."

Kid-Kits were something Kristy had dreamed up to make us baby-sitters as much fun as possible for our charges. Each of us had decorated a cardboard carton which we'd labelled KID-KIT. We kept the boxes filled with books and games (our own) plus activity books that we paid for out of our club subs. The kids we baby-sit for love the Kid-Kits and look forward to our visits because of them.

But Jenny had never seen one. "What's a Kid-Kit?" she asked.

"Oh, just something I brought with me." I'd left it on the front porch so I could surprise Jenny with it after the Prezziosos left. I retrieved it and sat down on the floor in the middle of the playroom. I opened the box and began pulling things out: three books, two games, a box of miniature toys, a sticker book, and a paint-with-water book. I turned my back on Jenny and began peeling balloons off the back page of the sticker book.

After a moment, Jenny left the couch and edged towards me and the Kid-Kit. She watched me put stickers in the book. Then she glanced at the things I'd pulled out.

She opened the box of toys. There was an old set of mine called Mrs Cookie's Kitchen. She touched the little plastic pots and pans and food. Then she put the lid back on the box.

"I can play with this stuff?" she asked.

"Sure. That's why I brought it."

"I can play with anything I want?"

"Of course."

"Is this a painting book?"

I glanced up. "Oh . . . yes. Here, how about the stickers? Don't they look fun?"

"I WANT TO PAINT!"

"Okay, okay." I looked at Jenny's pristine white dress. I looked at the paint-with-water book. Wasn't the point of painting with water that it wasn't messy?

I went to the kitchen and half-filled a paper cup with water. Then I brought it to Jenny, opened the paint book for her, and settled her on the floor. "Okay, go to it," I said. "All you have to do is brush water over the pictures, and the colour will appear. Make sure you rinse the brush off pretty often so the colours don't mix together. Okay?"

Jenny nodded.

"And . . . be careful," I added.

Jenny was sitting cross-legged, the book spread open in front of her. She dipped the paintbrush in the water and moved it slowly toward the book. Drip, drip, drip. Three wet spots appeared on her dress.

I closed my eyes. It was only water. Still . . .

"Jenny, wouldn't you like to put on playclothes while you paint?" I thought she must own *some*thing more casual than what she had on.

"No."

"No? Not even a smock? We could put it on over your dress."

"No."

"How about one of Mummy's aprons?"

"I DON'T WANT AN APRON!"

I watched Jenny smear the paintbrush over a big apple on the page. The apple turned red. Jenny lifted the brush and returned it to the cup. So far, so good.

I relaxed a little.

Then Jenny swung the wet brush back to the book. Two faint pink streaks appeared on her dress. Oh, well, I thought. It must come out with water.

But I wasn't sure. I decided that Jenny would have to wear an apron whether she liked it or not, and I dashed into the kitchen. I had just found one when I heard Jenny say, "Oops."

"Jenny?" I called. "What happened?"

There was a pause. "Nothing."

A nothing is usually the worst kind of something. I ran back to Jenny—and gasped. She had spilled the entire cup of water in her lap. A huge pinkish stain was spreading fast.

"Oh, *Jen*ny!" I exclaimed.

Jenny stared at me with wide eyes. She looked as if she were daring me to do something.

"Okay. Off with your dress. Right now."

'NONONONONONONO!" Jenny threw herself on her stomach and began kicking her legs on the floor.

I took advantage of that to unbutton her dress. "Off it comes," I said. "Then I'll show you some magic."

Jenny stopped kicking and yelling. "Magic?"

"Yeah." I hoped the trick would work.

Jenny let me take her dress off. She followed me into the kitchen and sat on the counter while I held the dress under a stream of water from the tap. She watched as the colour flowed out.

I breathed a sigh of relief. "Does your mummy have a hair dryer?" I asked.

"Yup."

"Come show me where."

So Jenny, giggling, helped me blow-dry her dress. Then I told her that she would *have* to wear playclothes if she wanted to finish painting. She took me to her room, pointed to a drawer in her bureau, and said, "That's where the playclothes are."

I opened the drawer and found myself looking at three piles of neatly folded, spotless, almost-new shirts, blouses, and slacks. "These are your playclothes?"

Jenny gave me a look that plainly said, "I told you so."

I closed the drawer. "Okay, Jenny-bunny," I said. "Do you want to finish painting?"

"Yes."

"All right. Come on." We went back down stairs and Jenny spent the rest of the afternoon painting in her underwear. I got her dressed just five minutes before the Prezziosos came home.

"How was she?" Mrs P. asked.

I glanced down at Jenny. "An angel," I replied. "An absolute angel."

Jenny smiled at me. Our secret was safe.

7th CHAPTER

I couldn't stand it any longer. I decided to ask my father if he would extend my baby-sitting hours. If all the other members of the club were allowed to stay out until ten o'clock, I ought to be able to as well. After all, I was the same age as they were, I was just as responsible as they were, and I had just as much homework as they did.

The one job that I had had to turn down when I was taking club phone calls the Friday after our fight, had been for a client who needed a sitter until ten o'clock on Saturday night. Kristy had taken the job.

I felt humiliated.

But I was nervous about facing my father. He wouldn't be angry; he just wouldn't see my side, unless I figured out exactly the right way to approach him. And I wasn't sure I'd be able to do that.

But by Monday night, I was ready to talk

to him—no matter what.

Unfortunately, he came home in a bad mood.

"We lost the Cutter case today," he told me. "I can't believe it. I thought it was open-and-shut. The jury was highly unreasonable."

I nodded. "Dad—"

"Honestly, sometimes people can be so unfair . . . No, not unfair, *unthinking*. That's it, unthinking."

We were setting the table, getting ready for dinner.

"Dad—" I said again.

"Can you imagine letting someone go who so clearly was guilty of grand larceny?"

I shook my head. "I guess not . . . Dad?"

"What is it, Mary Anne?'

Right then, I should have decided not to pursue the business of later hours, but I'd been planning on it all day. I'd rehearsed what I was going to say. I didn't know if it would work, but I was going to say, very rationally, "Dad, I've been thinking. I'm twelve years old now, and I feel that I could stay out until ten o'clock every now and then when I'm baby-sitting—not on school nights, of course, because I recognize that I need my sleep, but just on some Friday and Saturday nights."

"Dad, I've been thinking," I said.

The phone rang.

Dad leaped for it. "Hello? . . . Yes, I

know . . . I know. Yes. Definitely . . ." The conversation went on for ten minutes while our frozen pizza finished baking and then began drying out in the oven.

Dad finally got off the phone, and immediately it rang again. When he got off the second time, I practically threw the pizza down in front of him.

"Dad, I want to stay out until ten o'clock when I baby-sit at night," I blurted out.

My father looked at me blankly. "What? . . . Oh. Mary Anne, no. I'm afraid that's out of the question."

"But, Dad, everyone else gets to."

"I'm sure not *everyone* does. You can't possibly be the only twelve-year-old who has to be in by nine or nine-thirty."

"Dad, I'm the *only* member of the Babysitters Club who can't stay out till ten. You treat me like a baby, but look at me. In a year and a half I'll be starting high school."

For a moment, my father looked taken aback. Then a change came over his face. He rubbed his hands over his eyes tiredly. At last he said softly, "It's not easy for a father to raise a daughter alone. I have to be both a father and a mother. On top of that, I'm not home much. I'm doing the best I can."

"But Kristy and Claudia and Stacey—"

"What Kristy and Claudia and Stacey and their parents do is not our concern."

"That's not fair! Don't you think Mrs Thomas is a good mother? Don't you think

Mimi and the Kishis care about Claudia?"

"Those are not the issues," my father said. "The issues are you and me and your bedtime."

"Dad, I am old enough to stay out until ten o'clock. I'm twelve, and I'm very responsible and mature. Don't my teachers always write that on my report card? 'Mary Anne is a joy to have in class. She's responsible and mature.' "

"You don't sound mature at the moment."

I knew I didn't. I was whining. But it was too late to stop. I was on a roll. "I'm also too old to wear my hair in these dumb plaits, and my room looks like a nursery. It's a room for a five-year-old."

My father looked at me sharply. "Young lady, I do not like your tone of voice."

"You know, you're not the only parent who isn't around much," I went on, ignoring him. "Mrs Thomas is hardly ever home, either, and she has to raise Kristy *and* Kristy's brothers alone, and Sam and Charlie don't have Peter Rabbit all over their bedroom. I'd like to see a few changes around here. I'd like to be allowed to choose my own clothes. I'd like to take my hair out of these plaits. I'd like to wear nail polish and tights and lipstick. And if a boy ever asked me to go to the movies or something, I'd like to be able to say yes—without even checking with you first. You know what?

Sometimes you don't seem like my father to me. You seem like my gaoler."

It was at that exact moment that I knew I had gone too far.

Sure enough, my father turned his back on me. Then, in the calmest voice imaginable, he said, "Mary Anne, the subject is closed. Please go to your room."

I went. I felt horrible. I knew I'd insulted him, and I hadn't wanted to do that. But what did he think was going to happen if I wore my hair loose or took down Humpty Dumpty? Did he think I'd run away or start hanging around with the kids at the shopping arcade? And what could happen between nine o'clock and ten o'clock while I was baby-sitting, that couldn't happen before nine?

I didn't have any answers, but I knew someone who might—Mimi. She was a patient listener and I often talked to her about things that I might have talked to my mother about. At any rate, I talked to her about things I couldn't discuss with my father.

I paid her a visit after school the next day. I had apologized twice to my father that morning, and he'd said he accepted my apology, but things were a little chilly between us.

"Hi, Mimi," I greeted her, when she answered the bell.

"Hello, Mary Anne," she said solemnly. "How is your scarf coming?"

"Fine. It looks really nice. I hope my father will like it. If I work hard, I could finish it in time for his birthday."

"That would be a nice surprise for him." I shrugged out of my coat, and Mimi hung it in the closet. "Well," she went on, "are you here to see Claudia? She is not at home. I believe she is baby-sitting for Nina and Eleanor Marshall."

"Oh. No, actually I came to see you. I wondered if we could talk . . ."

"Of course. Please come in. Would you like some tea, Mary Anne?"

"Yes. Thanks." I don't really like tea, but I like drinking it with Mimi. She fixes it in a special pot and serves it in little cups that don't have handles. Then she lets me put in all the milk and sugar I want.

I followed her into the kitchen, and Mimi set the tea things on the table and began boiling water. She took some crackers out of a tin and arranged them on a plate.

When everything was ready, we sat down across from each other. Mimi poured the tea, straining the leaves out of my cup, but letting them flow into hers and sink to the bottom. I began adding milk and sugar. Mimi took hers plain—and strong.

"It is very dreary weather," Mimi commented, looking out at the barren trees being lashed about by the wind and soaked by the chilling rain that had fallen all day.

"Yeah," I agreed, feeling sad.

"In this weather," Mimi continued, "I always think of spring. Snowy weather makes me glad for winter, but raw, grey weather makes me wish winter were over. Perhaps we will be lucky and the groundhog will see his shadow."

I smiled. "That would be great."

"And how are you surviving this dreariness?"

I looked at Mimi. Her black hair, which had long been streaked with white, was pulled away from her face and fastened into a bun just above her neck. She wore no jewellery and no make-up, and her face was wrinkled and creased. I thought she was beautiful. Maybe it was because she always seemed so serene.

"I'm surviving the dreariness okay, I guess," I replied, "but I'm not surviving my father very well . . . Mimi, do you think I act like a normal twelve-year-old?"

"Tell me what you mean by normal."

"You know—like other twelve-year-olds. Am I about as responsible and mature and clever as other twelve-year-olds, and do I have pretty much the same interests they do?"

Now, most adults might have said something like, "That sounds like a loaded question," or "What are you *really* asking?" But Mimi put her teacup down, sat back in her chair, and considered me. At last she replied, "Yes, you seem like a normal twelve-year-old to me. You do not wear the clothes that Claudia does, but I do not think that means anything. You are very responsible, and you also seem very mature. But you are serious, too, and I know it is not wise to confuse gravity with maturity."

She had almost lost me, but all that counted was that she thought I seemed like any other kid my age. "So, Mimi," I went on, "how come I'm not allowed to make my room more grown-up? You know what's on my walls? Alice in Wonderland and Humpty Dumpty . . . Do you know who Humpty Dumpty is?"

"Oh, yes. He is the shattered eggman."

I giggled, then remembered the reason for our discussion and became serious again. "Right, but he's from a nursery rhyme. A *nursery* rhyme, Mimi. Nursery rhymes aren't for twelve-year-olds. They're not even for little kids. They're for *babies*. But Dad won't let me take Humpty down. He won't even let me leave Humpty where he is and put new posters up next to him. He won't let me wear my hair down or put on nail polish or stay out past nine-thirty at the absolute latest. And Claudia, Stacey, and even Kristy are allowed to do all those things—and a lot more. Every time I turn around, I'm facing another one of my father's rules: you can't ride your bike to town, you can't wear trousers to school, you can't do this or this or this."

I paused to catch my breath.

Mimi raised her eyebrows slightly. "I know it is not easy for you," she said slowly. She sipped her tea. "And I suppose you have heard people say that your father is doing the best he can."

I nodded. It seemed as if everyone in the *world* had said that at some time or other.

"Well, I will tell you something that I have often told my Claudia. If you do not like the way things are, you must change them yourself."

"But I've tried!" I exclaimed.

"Perhaps you have not found the right way yet. If this is truly important to you, then there is a right way to change it. And I know that you, my Mary Anne, will find that way."

At that moment, Claudia burst into the kitchen.

"What did you just say?" she asked accusingly.

"Claudia, you are finished baby-sitting already?" said Mimi.

Claudia ignored the question. "I heard you!" she cried, glaring at Mimi. "You called *her*," she switched her glare to me, "*my Mary Anne*."

"Why, yes, I did," Mimi said quietly.

"But I'm the only one you call yours. You don't even say 'my Janine' . . . I thought

I was the only one."

I had rarely seen Claudia so upset. Not when she got bad grades, and not when we thought the Baby-sitters Agency was going to put our club out of business. But she was standing in front of us with tears running down her cheeks.

Then she turned and ran. I could hear her feet pounding up the stairs and along the hall to her bedroom.

"Oh, no," I said to Mimi.

"Please do not worry," she told me. "That was my fault. I was not thinking. I will talk to Claudia and repair our misunderstanding." Mimi stood up.

I rose, too. "Thank you, Mimi," I said.

Mimi gave me a hug, then headed upstairs. I let myself out the front door.

What was the right way to change things? I wondered. I knew that I would have to discover it myself.

8th CHAPTER

Tuesday, January 20

I am so mad! I know this notebook is for writing up our sitting jobs so we can keep track of club problems. Well, this is not a sitting job but I have a club problem. Her name is Mary Anne Spier or as she is other-wise know MY MARY ANNE. Where does Mary Anne get off being so chummy with Mimi? It isn't fair. It's one thing for Mimi to help her with her ~~nittin~~ knitting but today they were sharing tea in the special cups and Mimi called her MY MARY ANNE.

NOT FAIR. So there.

Wow. Was Claudia ever mad. Mimi had apologized and tried to explain things to her, but Claudia stopped talking to me anyway, which meant that once again, not one of the members of the Babysitters Club was talking to the others.

Twice, recently, I had tried waiting for Kristy at my window with the flashlight after my father said goodnight to me. The first time, Kristy's room stayed dark, and the second time, she didn't bother going to the window. Her shade was up, and I could see her in her room—doing her homework, talking to her mother, and playing with Louie, the Thomases' collie. But she never once even looked towards her window. How long would our fight go on?

I considered telling Dawn about it, and decided not to.

The next time it was my turn to answer the Babysitters Club phone calls, I didn't have nearly as easy a time as I'd had before. For one thing, Claudia was at home, and she was not pleased to have me in her room. She put a tape in her tape deck and played it so loudly that the first time the phone rang I almost didn't hear it.

"Hello!" I shouted into the receiver. "Babysitters Club!"

I'm sure the person on the other end of the phone said something, but all I could hear was: 'DUM-DE-DUM-DE-DUM DUM. CAN'T LIVE WITHOUT YOU-OU-OU-OU-OU."

"What?" I yelled.

"DE-DOOOO. DE-DOOOO. MY LIFE IS YOU-OU-OU-OU-OU."

"CLAUDIA, CAN YOU PLEASE TURN THAT DOWN?" I shouted.

Claudia ignored me, She began singing along with the tape. "DE-DOOOO," she sang, "DE-DOP. IT'S LIFE AT THE TOP, THE TOP!"

I tried putting my finger in one ear "HELLO?"

Very faintly, I could hear a voice say, "Why are you shouting? Is everything all right?"

"MRS NEWTON? I MEAN, Mr Newton, is that you?"

"Yes. Mary Anne? What's all that noise?"

"Oh . . . just some music."

"Well, listen, I need a sitter Wednesday afternoon for Jamie. I'm going to visit a friend for a couple of hours and I'll be taking the baby with me. Is anyone available?"

Claudia's tape was between songs, so I could hear a lot better. "I'll have to check," I said. "I know I'm not free."

"Could you check with Kristy first? I think Jamie would like to see her."

"All right," I agreed—reluctantly.

Darn. I would have to phone Kristy.

"I'll call you right b—"

"OH, MY, MY. OH, MY, MY. MY

BABY'S SAD AND SO AM I." The next song blasted on.

Mr Newton and I hung up.

Just as Claudia's song was picking up pace, Mimi stuck her head in the room. I'm sure she had knocked, but of course we hadn't heard her.

She signalled to Claudia, who turned the volume down—slightly.

"Claudia," she said, "I must ask you to play your music more softly. It is much too loud. Also, I was wondering if you would like to come downstairs and have a cup of tea with me while Mary Anne is answering the phone."

Claudia considered the offer. At last she turned off the music and left with Mimi. On her way out the door, she stuck her tongue out at me.

I stuck mine out at her.

She slammed the door shut.

With shaking fingers, I dialled the Thomases' number.

Kristy answered the phone.

"Hello," I said, "it's Mary Anne Spier."

There was a pause. "Yes?"

I'd thought she'd at least say "hello" back.

"Mrs Newton needs a sitter for Jamie on Wednesday. She wants you. Can you make it?"

"Yup."

"All right, I'll tell her."

"Hey, don't hang up!"

No? Oh, boy. Kristy was going to make the big apology. I couldn't believe it. After all this time, bossy Kristy was going to be the one to give in first, while I, timid Mary Anne, had managed to wait the fight out. Our fight was finally over! I felt so happy at the idea, that I practically hugged myself. "Yeah?" I said.

"What time does she want me?"

"Ask her yourself," I said, and hung up. Then I called Mrs Newton back.

The next phone call was from Watson, needing a sitter for Karen and Andrew the following Saturday afternoon. "I know it isn't your club policy," said Watson, "but could you check with Kristy first? I'd sort of like Andrew and Karen to keep seeing her since she *is* going to be their stepsister soon."

"Sure," I replied dully. What else could go wrong? I dialled Kristy's number again.

David Michael answered. "Hello, this is David Michael speaking. Who's calling, please?"

"It's Mary Anne," I told him.

"Hi!" he cried. "When are you going to come over and baby-sit for me again? Remember the last time you came? We bowled paper cups down the stairs."

"Yeah, that was fun, wasn't it?"

"Yeah!"

"David Michael, can you call Kristy for

me, please? I have to talk to her."

"Sure."

When Kristy got on the phone, she didn't say a word. I just guessed that she was there because I heard light breathing.

"Kristy?"

"WHAT?"

"Watson wants you to sit on Saturday—from two-thirty until five," I added pointedly.

"Fine."

"I'll call him back. Goodbye."

We hung up.

The phone rang again. "Hello, the Babysitters Club," I said.

"Hi, Mary Anne. It's Mrs Newton again. I forgot to ask you whether you and Kristy and Claudia and Stacey want to come to Jamie's fourth birthday party. It's in about two weeks, and I'd like you girls to be there as helpers as well as guests. We've invited sixteen children, so I'm going to need lots of help."

"Sure!" I exclaimed. "I mean, if we can make it. It sounds like fun. I'll have to call the other girls."

Mrs. Newton gave me the information about the party, and I began to call the club members. Luckily, Stacey wasn't home, so I left the message with Mrs McGill for Stacey to call Mrs Newton.

One down, two to go. I didn't want to call Kristy a third time, but I didn't want to talk to Claudia in person, either.

I flipped a coin. Claudia.

I walked slowly downstairs and found her drinking tea from the special cups with Mimi.

"Claud?" I ventured.

Claudia put her cup down and covered her ears with her hands. "HMM, HMM, HM-HM." She closed her eyes and hummed loudly. "I CAN'T HEAR YOU."

I glanced helplessly at Mimi.

Mimi reached across the table and touched Claudia lightly on the arm. That was all it took for Claudia to act human again. She opened her eyes and uncovered her ears.

"Mrs Newton wants all the members of our club to be helpers at Jamie's fourth birthday party," I said. I told her when it was. "Do you want to go?"

"Yes," she replied coolly. "I'll go."

"Fine," I answered just as coolly.

But I was beginning to wonder how fine an idea it really was. How could the four of us help out at a party when we wouldn't even talk to each other? Nevertheless, I returned to Claudia's room to call Kristy for the third time.

"What *is* it?" she asked crossly.

I told her about Jamie's party.

Kristy sighed. "Oh, all right. I'll go, too."

"Don't strain yourself," I said. "I can call Mrs Newton and tell her you're busy."

"Don't you dare!"

"I was just trying to help out."

"Oh, sure."

We hung up again.

It was almost six o'clock by then, but I received two more Babysitters Club calls. The first was from Mrs Prezzioso, wanting me to sit for Jenny. I checked our record book, saw that I was free, and told her I'd be glad to sit.

The second call was from Mrs Pike, the mother of the eight kids. The Pikes are good customers, even though they usually just need a sitter for Claire and Margo and the younger children. The older ones can take care of themselves. However, Mrs Pike's call was not one of the usual ones.

"Hi, Mary Anne," she said. "Listen, Mr Pike and I have been invited to a cocktail party over in Levittown. It'll be an early evening—we'll be back by nine—but we don't want to leave the kids alone while we're out of town, so we need someone to sit for all of them. Actually, we need two someones."

"Okay," I said. We'd done that before—sent two sitters over to the Pike brood.

Mrs Pike gave me the information and I said I would call her back in a few minutes when I had found out who else was available. I checked our record book. I couldn't believe it.

The only person free was Kristy.

I didn't bother to sigh or get nervous. I just picked up the phone and dialled.

Kristy answered.

"Hi, it's Mary Anne again," I said in a rush. "The Pikes need two sitters on Friday while they go to a party in Levittown. You and I are the only ones free. We'd be sitting for all the kids. Do you want to do it?"

"With you?"

"Yes."

"Not really."

"Fine. I'll get Dawn Schafer to sit with me. I don't want to let Mrs Pike down."

"You wouldn't dare."

"I'll have to."

"Mary Anne Spier, for someone who's so shy, you sure can be—"

"What? I can be what?"

"Never mind. I'll sit with you."

"We'll have to be mature about it, you know."

"Look who's talking."

"I'm serious, Kristy. We don't want the Pike kids telling their parents that we were fighting or anything."

"I think that would be impossible."

"Why?"

"Because I'm not speaking to you."

"Good," I said. I hung up on her. Then I noted our job in the record book and called Mrs Pike back.

I was not looking forward to baby-sitting with Kristin Amanda Thomas.

9th CHAPTER

Saturday, January 31

Yesterday, Mary Anne and I baby-sat for the Pikes. I'm really surprised that we were able to pull it off. Hereby let it be known that it is possible: 1) for two people to baby-sit for eight kids without losing their sanity (the sitters' or the kids'), and 2) for the baby-sitters to accomplish this without ever speaking to each other. There should be a Baby-sitters' Hall of Fame where experiences like ours could be recorded and preserved for all to read about. To do what we did takes a lot of imagination.

Kristy's wrong. Imagination isn't all it takes. It takes a good fight, too. You have to be pretty mad at a person in order even to think about doing what we did at the Pikes' that evening.

Before I go into what happened, though, let me say a little about the Pike kids. The most interesting thing is that three of the kids are triplets—Byron, Adam, and Jordan—identical boys. (Kristy and I can tell them apart, though.) They're nine. The oldest Pike is Mallory, who's ten, and is usually a big help to baby-sitters. After the triplets come Vanessa, who's eight; Nicholas (Nicky), who's seven and Margo and Claire, who are six and four. They're quite a brood. Actually, they're really good kids but their parents have raised them liberally (according to my father), and without batting an eye, they do things I'd never *dream* of. For instance, Claire sometimes takes off her clothes and runs around the house naked. No one pays a bit of attention. After a while, she just puts her clothes back on. Also, although each of the kids has to be in bed at a specific time, none of them has to turn out the light and go to sleep until he or she feels like it. As long as they're in bed, they can stay up as late as they want. And they don't have to eat any food they don't like.

Kristy and I showed up at the Pikes' at five o'clock on Friday afternoon. We showed up separately, of course. Actually, I have to admit that I'd sort of been tailing Kristy all the way to the house. Since the

Pikes don't live too far from Bradford Court, we were walking to their house, and I wasn't far behind Kristy. I had to go very quietly so she wouldn't know I was there. Once she turned around suddenly and I had to duck behind a bush so she wouldn't see me. When we reached the Pikes', I hovered around the end of their driveway while Kristy went inside. I waited until the door had closed behind her. Then I rang the bell.

Mr and Mrs Pike were in a rush. Mrs Pike let me in hurriedly and she and her husband started giving Kristy and me instructions. They were gone almost before I knew it. As soon as they left, the kids surrounded Kristy and me. They like baby-sitters.

"What's for dinner?" asked Byron, whose hobby is eating.

"Cold fried chicken or tuna sandwiches," Kristy replied.

"Can I have both?"

"No," Kristy said.

"Yes," I said.

"I don't like chicken *or* tunafish," Margo complained.

"Then make yourself a peanut butter sandwich," suggested Mallory.

"Okay," agreed Margo.

"When do we eat?" asked Byron.

"Six o'clock," I answered.

"Six-thirty," said Kristy.

"Can I watch cartoons?" asked Claire.

"Can we make an obstacle course in the

living room?" asked Jordan, speaking for the triplets.

"Can I just read?" asked Vanessa, who's quiet. "I'm in the middle of *The Phantom Tollbooth.*"

"Can I colour?" asked Margo.

"Can we start a baseball game?" asked Nicky.

"Can I help make dinner?" asked Mallory.

"Yes, no, yes, yes, no, and yes," I replied.

The kids laughed. Kristy scowled.

"Let's do something together," said Adam. "There are ten people. We could do something with teams, five on a team."

"Hey, Kristy," I said, suddenly inspired. "How about putting on a play?"

Kristy pretended not to hear me.

It was my turn to scowl.

"Mallory," I said, "tell Kristy it would be fun to put on a play."

"Kristy," Mallory began, "Mary Anne says—Hey, how come she didn't hear you, Mary Anne? She's not deaf."

"I know." I tried to think of a way to explain what was going on. "We're . . . we're playing Chinese whispers."

"We are? Then wait. Okay, everybody," Mallory said to her brothers and sisters. "Let's sit down in a line, right here in the living room. And Kristy, you sit at that end, and Mary Anne, you sit at the other end. Now, start the game, Mary Anne."

Just for fun, I leaned over to Adam, who was next to me, and whispered, "Kristy Thomas is a nosy, bossy, busybody."

Adam giggled. Then he whispered to Jordan, Jordan whispered to Claire, and the game was underway.

By the time the message reached Kristy, she looked puzzled.

"What?" said Mallory. "What did you hear?"

"I heard, 'Cranky Tommy's nose is a bossy busy boy.'"

The Pike kids laughed hysterically.

"Okay, Mary Anne, now tell us what you really said," cried Mallory.

What I *really* said? I'd forgotten I'd have to do that. There was no way I could tell what I'd really said. I thought for a moment. "I said, 'Crystal tambourines—'"

"No, you didn't," interrupted Adam. "You said 'Critical—' I mean 'Christopher—' I mean . . . Oh, I don't know what you said!"

Everyone was laughing again. "Kristy, you start one this time," I suggested.

Kristy ignored me.

Oh, brother.

I whispered to Adam, "Tell Kristy to start the game."

By the time the message reached Kristy, she said, "Tired carrots take the blame?"

"No, *start* the *game*!" shouted Adam.

We played a while longer, letting

different kids take turns being on the ends. Luckily, Kristy and I never had to sit next to each other.

Promptly at six o'clock, Byron looked at his watch and announced, "It's time for dinner! Let's eat!"

"Okay," replied Kristy. "Into the kitchen, everybody!" She seemed to have forgotten that she'd said dinner was at 6.30.

I could see that she planned to take charge. "Wash your hands," I told the kids.

"No, we don't have to," said Nicky.

"Not unless we want to," added Margo.

Kristy smirked at me.

In the kitchen, pandemonium broke out. Ten people were scrambling around, getting out plates, forks, spoons, and glasses, and pulling food out of the refrigerator.

Kristy stuck her fingers in her mouth and whistled shrilly.

Silence.

"Now hold it!" said Kristy.

"We need some order," I added.

"What?" said Kristy. "Did somebody say something?"

"She said we need order," replied Mallory.

"We need order," Adam told Byron.

"We need order," Byron told Jordan.

"We need order," Jordan told Vanessa.

"We need order," Vanessa told Nicky.

"We need order," Nicky told Margo.

"We need order," Margo told Claire.

Claire hugged Kristy around the knees and grinned up at her. "We need order, Kristy," she said. "Whatever that is."

Kristy actually smiled. "Tell Margo to sit down."

"Sit down," said Claire, finding her place at the long table in the kitchen.

Margo sat. "Sit down," she told Nicky.

Nicky sat. "Sit down," he told Vanessa.

Vanessa sat. "Sit down," she told Jordan.

Jordan sat. "Sit down," he told Byron.

Byron was already sitting down, waiting for food to appear in front of him. "I am sitting," he said. "Sit down," he told Adam.

Adam sat. "Sit down," he told Mallory.

Mallory sat. "Sit down," she told me.

"No," I said, smiling. "*I* am going to serve you guys."

And that's how the rest of dinner went. Not once did Kristy and I have to speak to each other, and the Pike kids never realised anything was wrong. They thought we were playing a great game, and I could tell they were probably going to play it themselves for a long time. I felt slightly sorry for their parents.

By the time we finished dinner, it was after seven o'clock. The meal had taken an unusually long time because every word of conversation had to be repeated nine times and go all the way around the table, with much giggling. I finally put an end to the meal when Nicky, who was sitting between

Claire and Jordan, turned to Jordan and said, "Tell Claire she's a hot-dog-head."

"Claire, you're hot-dog-head," Jordan told Vanessa.

"Claire, you're a hot-dog-head," Vanessa told Adam.

By the time the sentence reached Claire and she said to herself, "Claire, you're a hot-dog-head," Nicky laughed so hard he spat his milk across the table.

"Okay, guys," I said. "Dinner's over. Help us clean up and put the dishes in the washer, and then we'll go and do something."

"Do what?" asked Mallory.

"Put on a play," I said firmly, not bothering to look at Kristy. I didn't care whether she wanted to or not, and I didn't want the question asked ten times before I found out.

When the kitchen was clean (part of being a good baby-sitter is leaving a tidy house behind you) I gathered the kids and a reluctant Kristy downstairs in the playroom. "Now," I began, "we're going to put on—"

"—whatever you want," Kristy supplied.

I tried not to look as angry as I felt. I'd been planning on suggesting a Winnie-the-Pooh story because there were so many Pooh characters and I thought that even Claire and Margo would know some of the tales.

But at Kristy's words, everybody started shouting.

"*The Phantom Tollbooth!*" cried Vanessa.

"Chuck Norris!" yelled Adam and Jordan.

"*Peter Rabbit*," suggested Claire.

After about ten minutes of arguing, we decided to put on two plays. Under Kristy's direction, the triplets and Mallory were going to put on a play called *Super-Girl Meets the Super-Nerds.* (A sound effects record was going to be involved.) Under my direction, Nicky, Vanessa, Claire, and Margo were going to put on *Peter Rabbit.* I took them upstairs to rehearse in the living room.

The Pike kids had lots of fun with their plays, and by the time I looked at my watch again, it was 8.30. Yikes! It was time for Margo and Claire to be in bed, and time for Nicky and Vanessa to start getting ready for bed. Furthermore, if Mr and Mrs Pike weren't home in about twenty minutes, I wouldn't be home by nine. But they had promised, and they usually kept their promises.

I took Margo and Claire upstairs and put them to bed, while Nicky and Vanessa changed into their pyjamas. Kristy stayed downstairs with Mallory and the triplets. When the littlest ones were settled, I closed the door to their room gently.

"You guys want a story?" I asked Nicky and Vanessa.

"Yes! Yes! We're in the middle of *Pippi Longstocking*!"

So we read a few pages. I looked at my watch. Five minutes to nine! What was I going to do? If I left early, the Pikes would be upset. After all, they were paying for two sitters. If I got home late, Dad would be upset.

Luckily, just as I was starting to panic, I heard the Pikes arrive. I shooed Nicky and Vanessa into their bedrooms. "Your mum and dad will say goodnight to you in a few minutes," I assured them.

Then I dashed downstairs. There was no time for dignity. "Mrs Pike," I said breathlessly, not daring to look at Kristy, "I've got to be home *right now*! It's almost nine."

"I know, Mary Anne. I'm sorry we're late. We got caught in a traffic jam on the way back. Hop in the car with Mr Pike, you two," she told Kristy and me. "He'll give you a lift home. Oh, and he'll pay you when he drops you off."

"Okay," I said. "Thanks. 'Bye."

When Mr Pike let us off in front of our houses, it was five minutes after nine. He paid us a little extra, since they'd been on the late side, which was nice of him. Then he drove off. I sprinted for my front door. Just as I reached it, I heard Kristy call from the darkness, "Baby, baby, baby!"

Humiliated, I let myself inside.

My father was waiting for me.

10th CHAPTER

"Hi, Dad," I greeted him apprehensively.

"Mary Anne, I was just starting to worry."

"I'm sorry I'm late. The Pikes got stuck in a traffic jam. They couldn't help it . . . I couldn't help it."

"That's all right. It's only five minutes after nine. I know things come up."

I was so relieved he wasn't upset, that I decided to bring up a touchy subject again. "You know, Dad," I began, "it would be a lot easier on my clients if I could baby-sit just a little later—say until ten. Or even nine-thirty. That would do."

"Mary Anne," Dad said gently, "we've been through that. If your clients need someone who can stay out late, then they should look for an older sitter."

"But Kristy and Claudia and Stacey—"

"I know. They're all allowed to stay out

later, and they're the same age as you."

"Right."

"But they're not you. And their parents aren't me. I have to do what I think is best for you."

I nodded.

"And the next time it looks as though you're going to be late—for whatever reason—give me a call to let me know, all right?"

"Okay."

Was Dad trying to tell me something? Was he saying that I hadn't been responsible? Maybe if I was more responsible, he'd let me stay out later. Maybe he made decisions based on responsibility, not age. It was something to think about.

I began thinking right away, on my way upstairs to bed. I felt that I was already fairly responsible. I always did my homework and I got good grades in school. I was usually on time for things. I usually started dinner for Dad and me. I did almost everything my father told me to do. Still . . . I supposed there was always room for more responsibility. I *could* have called Dad from the Pikes' instead of panicking. I could start facing up to things I was afraid of.

One of my biggest fears is confronting people and dealing with people I don't know—like picking up the phone to get information, or talking to sales assistants, or asking for directions. Dad knew all that.

Maybe when I stopped avoiding things, he would notice.

Even though my father didn't know about the fight everyone in the Babysitters Club had had, I decided that it was really time to do something about it. Whether the fault was mine or somebody else's (or everybody's), I was going to fix things. Now *that* was taking on responsibility.

I realized that the evening at the Pikes' could have been a disaster. If the kids had noticed that Kristy and I were fighting, it would have looked bad for our club. Luckily for us, the Pike kids are easygoing and have a sense of humour.

Luckily.

What if one of the kids had got hurt, and Kristy and I hadn't been able to agree on what to do about it? What if the kids had realized what was going on? They might have blabbed to their parents, and our club might have lost some of its best clients.

Besides, trying to run a club without meetings was stupid.

It was time to put the club back together before it fell apart completely. Since Kristy is the club chairman, I thought that the best way to do it was to make up with her. That was going to be a real challenge. It would take plenty of responsibility.

How to make up with Kristy? Long after I'd turned out my light, I lay in bed thinking. I could try to write her a note—one I could actually send her:

Dear Kristy,

I'm really sorry about our fight. I'd like to make up and be friends again.

Your best friend (I hope),
Mary Anne

That was good. Short but sweet.

And it was truthful. I really was sorry about our fight, no matter who had started it or whose fault it was. And I really did want to be friends again.

The next morning was Saturday, but I woke up early anyway. I ate breakfast with my father. Then I went back to my room and wrote the note to Kristy.

And *then*—how was I going to get the note to her? If I took it over personally, she'd close the door in my face. Maybe I could leave it in the mailbox, or give it to David Michael to give to her.

No. How could I be sure she'd read it? Maybe a note wasn't a good idea. But I couldn't think of another way to make up with Kristy.

I was still stewing about it when I heard the phone ring. A few minutes later, my father called up the stairs, "Mary Anne! It's for you!"

"Okay!"

As I ran to the phone, one teensy little part of me thought it might be Kristy, calling to apologize to *me*.

No such luck. It was Dawn. But I was glad to hear from her.

"Hi!" I said.

"Hi! What are you doing today?"

"Nothing. What are you doing?"

"Nothing."

"Want to come over?"

"Sure! Right now?"

"Yeah. I don't know what we'll do, but we'll think of something."

"Okay. I'll be right there."

"Good," I said. We hung up.

Dawn rode over on her bicycle, and she reached my house in record time.

I met her at the door and we ran up to my room. The first thing Dawn said was, "Mary Anne, I was thinking as I rode over here, and you know what we forgot to do?"

"What?" I asked.

"Find out if your father and my mother knew each other when they were young."

"Oh, that's right!" I exclaimed. "Did your mum go to Stoneybrook High?"

"Yup," replied Dawn. "Did your dad?"

"Yup! Oh, this is exciting!"

"What year did your father leave?" Dawn asked.

"Gee," I said slowly. "I don't know."

"Well, how old is he?"

"Let's see. He's forty-one . . . No, he's forty-two. Forty-two. That's right."

"Really? So's my mum!"

"You're kidding! I bet they did know each other. Let's go ask my father."

We were racing down the passage and had just reached the head of the stairs when Dad appeared at the bottom. "Mary Anne," he said, "I've got to go into the office for several hours. I'll be back this afternoon. You may heat up that casserole for lunch. Dawn is welcome to stay, all right?"

"Okay. Thanks, Dad. See you later."

Dawn nudged me with her elbow. I knew she wanted me to ask Dad about Mrs Schafer but it wasn't the right time. Dad was in a hurry, and he doesn't like to be bothered with questions when he's rushing off somewhere.

As soon as he left, Dawn said, slightly accusingly. "Why didn't you ask him?"

"It wasn't a good time. Believe me. Besides, I have another idea. His yearbooks are in the study. Let's go look at them. I used to go through them all the time when I was little, but I bet I haven't opened one since I was nine."

"Oh goody, yearbooks!" said Dawn.

In the study, we stood before a bookcase with a row of heavy old yearbooks in it.

"Why are there so many?" asked Dawn.

"They're my mother's *and* my father's—high school and college. So there are sixteen in all. Now let's see. Here are the Stoneybrook High yearbooks. These are Dad's, since my mother grew up in Maryland. Which one should we look at first?"

"His senior yearbook," Dawn answered immediately. "It'll have the biggest pictures. What year is this? Oh, this is the year my mum left, too! So they were in the same class. I bet they did know each other."

Dawn pulled the book off the shelf, and I blew the dust from the cover. "Yuck," I said. We stopped for a moment to look at the book. The year Dad had finished school was printed across the cover in large, white raised numbers.

We opened it gingerly, as if it would fall apart.

"Here are the seniors," said Dawn, turning to the front of the book. We peered at row after row of black and white photos, the students looking funny and old-fashioned. Under each picture was a little paragraph, words that meant nothing to Dawn and me. Inside jokes, I guessed. I wondered if the people who had composed them would know what they meant twenty-five years later. Under one boy's photo was written "Thumpers . . . Apple Corps. '61 White Phantom Chevy . . . 'Broc' junior Classroom. 'Rebel Rousers' & George." And one boy had written something that Dawn and I decided must be a code: E.S.R., A.T., DUDE, FIBES, G.F.R. .

"He spelled 'all right' all wrong," Dawn remarked.

Then we started laughing. "Look at that girl's hair!" I shrieked. "It looks like she blew it up with a bicycle pump!"

Dawn rolled over on the floor giggling. "It's called a bouffant or a pompadour or something."

"My dad has tons of old records," I said, pulling albums off a shelf and showing them to Dawn. "They're all girl singers. He's got Connie Francis, Shelley Fabares, and Brenda Lee, and here are some groups—the Shirelles, the Marvelettes, and Martha Reeves and the Vandellas. Look at that girl in the yearbook—her hair looks just like Shelley Fabares' hair on this album!"

Dawn started laughing again. "Now let's find your dad," she said at last.

The seniors were in alphabetical order. We flipped through until we reached the S's.

"There he is!" I cried, jabbing at the picture in the upper lefthand corner of a page. "There he is! Oh, wow, I forgot how weird he looks! He doesn't look like my father at all. He looks . . . like an alien!"

"He was seventeen, I guess, but somehow he looks a lot older," Dawn pointed out.

"He had a crewcut! Let's see what's under his picture . . . This is weird. It says: "To S.E.P.: Don't walk in front of me—I may not follow. Don't walk behind me—I may not lead. Walk beside me—and just be my friend.—Camus.' Who's Camus?" I asked.

"Beats me," Dawn replied, "but S.E.P.—those were my mother's initials before she got married."

Dawn and I looked at each other with wide eyes.

"Quick!" exclaimed Dawn. "Turn to the P's! We're looking for Sharon Porter."

Frantically, we flipped the pages back.

We went forward a few pages.

"Stop! We're in the M's!"

"There she is!" shouted Dawn. "Sharon Emerson Porter. That's all it says under her picture. Just her name. No quotes or silly stuff."

"But she signed Dad's yearbook," I said, looking at the scrawly message in blue ink that covered Sharon Porter's face.

We leant over.

"Dearest Richie,'" Dawn read.

"Richie!" I cried. "No one calls him *Richie*."

Mystified, Dawn read on. " 'Four years weren't enough. Let's start over. How can we part? We have one more summer. Hold on to it, Richie. (Love is blind.) Always and forever, Sharon.'"

"I guess they did know each other," said Dawn at last.

"I'll say," I said. "I'll say."

11th CHAPTER

Dawn and I practically suffered dual heart attacks after reading what was written in my dad's yearbook. We agreed not to mention our discovery to our parents, although we weren't sure why we wanted to keep the secret.

We spent the rest of the day talking about it. Then on Sunday we went through Dawn's mother's yearbook. The book was hard to find, since it was still packed away. We finally located it at the bottom of a carton labelled KITCHEN.

"Kitchen?" I said to Dawn.

She shrugged. "Don't ask."

We opened the book, knowing exactly where to look. Written across my father's picture in round, familiar handwriting was, "For Sharon, who knows what this means." (An arrow pointed to the quote from the person named Camus.) "Remember—the summer can be forever. Love always, Richie."

"People sure get poetic in high school," Dawn remarked. "What does 'the summer can be forever' mean?"

I didn't know. But far more interesting than what Dad had written was what was pressed between the "S" pages of Dawn's mother's book. It was a rose, brown and dried, with a stained, yellowing ribbon tied to the stem.

Although I had vowed to find a way to get the Babysitters Club back together, things kept coming up to take my mind off it. First, of course, was the discovery about Dawn's mother and my father. Dawn and I talked about it all week. We had a million questions, and we could only guess at the answers to them.

"What do you think the rose is from?" asked Dawn.

"A dance?" I suggested. "I bet they went to their high school dance together. I wonder what they wore."

"Hey," said Dawn. She crunched loudly on a piece of celery. Dawn refused to buy the school lunches, saying they were starchy and tasteless. As soon as her mother had got their kitchen in order, Dawn had insisted on bringing her own healthy lunches to school each day. "Don't parents *always* take pictures of their kids just before they go off to their high school dances?" she asked. "I mean, even back in those days, it was like a rule of parenthood. Your daughter's date arrives to take her to the dance. He's wearing a suit and your daughter is wearing her new dress and carrying a shawl. Then the parents *have* to make them pose in front of the mantelpiece in the living room for the ceremonial pictures, which they send to the relatives and to the boy's family."

I giggled. "But what does that have to do with our parents?"

"Well, there must be a high school dance picture of them somewhere. If we could find a picture, we could see if my mother was wearing a rose with a satin ribbon tied to it."

"Oh! Great idea," I said. But we couldn't find any dance pictures.

Another day we tried to guess what their notes to each other meant.

" 'Just one more summer,' " I repeated sadly. "I wonder why they knew they would have to break up at the end of the summer. Or maybe that's not what they meant at all."

"It must be what they meant. But why?"

"I don't know."

"I wonder what your mother meant by 'love is blind,' " I said to Dawn on Friday.

"Maybe someone disapproved of their relationship, but my mum and your dad were too much in love to see what was wrong."

"But what could have been wrong?"

"I don't know," Dawn replied. "But I bet someone disapproved of them."

"But we don't know for sure," I pointed out.

"No, that's true."

On Saturday, something else happened to keep my mind off the club. It was what turned out to be my scariest baby-sitting experience ever. Earlier in the week, Mrs Prezzioso had called needing a baby-sitter for Jenny all Saturday afternoon. Even though the Prezziosos are a bit strange, I rather like Jenny. So I took the job.

I arrived at the Prezziosos' house promptly at 11.30. I rang the bell.

A few moments later I could hear little feet run to the door. Then I heard the locks being turned. "Hey, Jenny!" I called. "Ask who it is first."

"Oh, yeah," I heard her say. "Who is it?"

"It's me. Mary Anne Spier, your baby-sitter."

"Are you a stranger?"

I sighed. "No. I'm Mary Anne. You know me."

The door was opened.

"Hi, Mary Anne," said Jenny. She was wearing a pale blue dress with a white collar and cuffs. Her tights were white. Her shoes were white. Her hair ribbon was white. I could tell it was going to be a long day.

Jenny's mother appeared behind her.

"Well," began Mrs Prezzioso, smoothing away a non-existent wrinkle in her black silk cocktail dress, "Mr Prezzioso and I are going to be up in Chatham for a basketball game." (Mrs P. was wearing a cocktail dress to a basketball game?) "My husband's college is playing their biggest rival. It's some sort of important championship or something. He's very excited about it, so we're going to drive up there, meet some friends, go to the game, and get out for an early dinner. We should be home by seven at the very latest.

"I'm a bit nervous, though, about being so far away," she added. (Chatham is an hour north of Stoneybrook.)

"I'm sure everything will be fine," I said.

"Well, I've left you a lot of phone numbers—Jenny's doctor, the number of the gymnasium where the game will be held, our next-door neighbours, and the usual emergency numbers."

"Okay," I said. I realised Jenny was being awfully quiet. I wondered what she had up her sleeve.

But I didn't have much time to dwell on it. At that moment, Mr P. ran down the stairs. He was wearing blue jeans and a striped polo shirt. I was willing to bet that there had been some battle over his clothing that morning. Maybe that was why Jenny was so quiet.

I looked at her. She was sitting in an

armchair in the living room, her legs sticking out in front of her, her head leaning back listlessly. She appeared to be listening to us.

I noticed that Mrs P. did not stand next to her husband and ask me how they looked. Frankly, I couldn't blame Mr P. for dressing the way he did, but I was sorry if it had caused a fight that had upset Jenny.

At last, after lots more instructions and cautions, the Prezziosos left. Jenny didn't even bother to wave goodbye to them.

"Well," I said to her, "what do you want to do today? We've got the whole afternoon to play."

Jenny stuck our her lower lip. "Nothing."

"You don't want to do anything?"

She crossed her arms. "No."

"Hey, come on. It's not that cold out. You want to see if Claire Pike can play?"

"NONONONONO!"

For such a little kid, Jenny certainly has a big set of lungs.

"Okay, okay," I said. What a fusspot. "I brought the Kid-Kit," I told her a few minutes later.

"I know. I saw."

What she didn't know was there was nothing even remotely messy in it. The paint-with-water book was at home on my bed.

I decided to try one more thing. "Do you want to read a story?"

Jenny shrugged. "I guess."

At last. That was a relief. I took *Blueberries for Sal, The Tale of Squirrel Nutkin,* and *Caps for Sale* out of the Kid-Kit. "Which one?" I asked.

Jenny shrugged.

I chose *Blueberries for Sal*. "Come sit by me on the couch." Wordlessly, Jenny got up, climbed onto the couch, and leaned against me. I began to read. When I reached the part of the story that I thought was the most exciting, Jenny didn't even make a sound. I glanced at her. She was sound asleep.

That's strange, I thought. Mrs P. had told me Jenny had slept late that morning and probably wouldn't take her afternoon nap. Yet there she was, asleep at twelve noon.

I eased myself up and laid Jenny on the couch. That was when I realized how warm she was. I put my hand on her forehead.

She was burning up.

I shook her gently. "Jenny! Jenny!"

"Mmphh," she mumbled. She stirred but didn't wake up.

My heart pounding, I raced upstairs to the bathroom off Jenny's parents' bedroom and looked frantically through the medicine cabinet. When I found a thermometer, I dashed downstairs with it.

Even though Jenny was still asleep, I stuck it under her tongue. I sat there with her for three endless minutes. Then I removed the thermometer and turned it until I could read it.

One hundred and four degrees!

One hundred and *four*. I'd never had a fever that high.

I began making phone calls.

First I called Jenny's doctor and got his answering service. A bored-sounding woman said the doctor would call back when he could.

That might not be fast enough. I called Pikes. No answer.

I called the next-door neighbours. No answer.

I called my dad, even thought I knew he was out shopping. No answer.

What to do? I didn't dare call the other members of the Babysitters Club, so at last I called Dawn.

"I'll be right there," she told me.

While I waited for her, I called the gym in Chatham and left an urgent message for the Prezziosos to be paged as soon as possible and told to call home. I knew they hadn't reached the gym yet.

When Dawn arrived, I showed her Jenny sleeping on the couch, and told her the people I'd tried to reach.

"And the doctor hasn't called back yet?" she asked.

I shook my head. "I guess we could just call for an ambulance, but really, she's only got a fever. I mean, it's not like she broke her leg or something."

"I know," said Dawn. "If Mum were home, she could drive us to the emergency room, but she took my brother out to Washington Shopping Center. Hey, try calling 999. Maybe someone could tell us what to do. At least they'd know whether it would be all right to call for an ambulance."

"Okay," I agreed.

Dawn sat with Jenny while I made the call. A man answered the phone, sounding calm and pleasant.

"Hi," I said. "I'm baby-sitting for a five-year-old and she fell asleep and I realized she has a fever and it's one hundred and four degrees. And," I rushed on, "I can't reach her parents or my dad or the neighbours, and I called her doctor but all I got was the answering service and he hasn't called back yet and I'm really worried."

"All right. Try to relax a little," the man said. "Young children often run fevers and it turns out to be just a sign of a simple infection. Sometimes it's nothing at all. However, a hundred and four is high and she should be looked at right away. I think the best thing to do is to get her to the emergency room of the hospital."

"But I'm only twelve," I said. "I can't drive."

"And you've tried reaching the neighbours?"

"Yes, several of them. And my dad."

"Well, then, I'll send an ambulance around."

"You *will*?" I said.

"Just tell me the address."

I gave it to him. Then he instructed me to get Jenny ready to leave the house and to keep cold compresses on her forehead until the ambulance arrived. I thanked him and we hung up.

"Okay, Dawn," I said, running into the living room. "An ambulance is on the way. I spoke to a man and he said to get Jenny ready to leave and to keep cold compresses on her head until the ambulance gets here."

"I'll make a compress, you get her coat," said Dawn.

Dawn dashed into the kitchen, while I found Jenny's coat and mittens in the closet. I laid them next to her on the couch, but didn't put them on her. I didn't want to make her hotter than she already was.

Dawn returned with a cold compress made from a dish towel. I held it to Jenny's forehead. "Oh, you know what?" I said. "In the kitchen by the phone is a number for Lewiston Gymnasium in Chatham. Call there and leave a message for the Prezziosos to turn around as soon as they reach the gym, and go right to the emergency room of the hospital here. I just left a message for them to call home, but if they do, no one will answer the phone."

"Okay." Dawn dashed off, then returned and stood looking out the front window. "Try to wake Jenny up," she said several moments later. "The ambulance is coming."

"Okay . . . Come on, Jenny-Bunny," I said. I shook her shoulder and sat her up. She fell to the side like a limp rag doll. "Naptime's over. Wake up."

Jenny opened her eyes a crack. "No," she said sleepily.

"Sorry, Jenny. I know you're not feeling well, so you have to see the doctor."

That woke her up—a little. "The doctor?" she repeated.

"Yup. He'll make you feel better. Come on, I want you to put your coat on."

Jenny allowed me to slip her coat and mittens on while Dawn let the ambulance attendants in. They were wheeling a stretcher through the front door.

"That the little girl?" asked one man, pointing to Jenny.

"Yes," I replied, "and she has a high fever, but she's not hurt. I don't think you need the stretcher.

They agreed. Dawn grabbed her jacket and mine as the man picked Jenny up gently and carried her out to the ambulance. I ran along behind him. "Lock the front door!" I called over my shoulder to Dawn as she dashed out with our jackets.

The attendants settled the still-sleepy Jenny in the ambulance, and I rode in the back with her while Dawn rode up front next to the driver. I'd never been in an ambulance before, but I was too concerned about Jenny to be nervous.

As we zipped along (no siren or lights, but plenty of speed) the attendants took Jenny's temperature (steady at 104), checked her pulse and blood pressure, listened to her heart, and looked at her ears. The man attendant kept talking to her and asking her questions. I looked at him, puzzled.

"Just trying to keep her awake," he told me.

I nodded.

We reached Stoneybrook General Hospital and pulled up to the entrance to the emergency room. One of the attendants carried Jenny inside, Dawn and I following, and spoke to a nurse. The nurse hustled us into a little curtained-off room. Then the attendant left and the nurse, clipboard in hand, started asking questions about Jenny. I answered them as well as I could. "Her parents will be here later, and they can fill you in," I told her finally.

She nodded. "A doctor will look in on her as soon as possible," she said. Then she parted the curtain and walked briskly down the the hallway. A few moments later she returned with a cold compress, then disappeared again.

Dawn and I looked at each other. "Now what?" asked Dawn.

"Now we wait, I guess." I adjusted the compress on Jenny's forehead. "How are you feeling?" I asked her. She seemed a bit more alert, but as hot as ever.

"Hot," she replied. "And my throat hurts. And my head."

"Yuck," I said. "I'm sorry. The doctor will be here soon, though, and he'll help you feel better. He or she, I mean."

"Look what I brought," Dawn spoke up.

"Hey, who's that?" asked Jenny, finally noticing her visitor.

"That's my friend Dawn. Dawn Schafer."

"Hi, Jenny," said Dawn.

"Hi . . . What did you bring?"

"This." Dawn held up *Blueberries For Sal*.

"Oh, goody," said Jenny.

I began to read. We were halfway through the story when a doctor poked her head through the curtain.

"Jenny Prezzioso?" she asked.

"That's Jenny," I said, pointing. "I'm Mary Anne Spier, her baby-sitter."

"Well, let's see what we have here."

The doctor examined Jenny gently.

"It looks like a nice case of strep throat," she said after a while. "I want to draw some blood and do a throat culture to be sure, but

I don't think it's anything more serious than that . . . Where are her parents?"

I explained. Then I looked at my watch. "If the people at the gym paged them right away, they could be at the hospital in a half an hour to forty-five minutes."

The doctor nodded. "Well, she can stay here until her parents arrive. While we're running the tests, I'll have a nurse try to bring her fever down. I'd like to talk to the Prezziosos before Jenny leaves."

"Okay," I said.

A nurse entered. She drew some blood from Jenny, which made her cry, and took a throat culture, which made her gag. But when she began bathing her in alcohol, Jenny said, "Oh, that feels good."

Her temperature dropped a degree and a half.

By the time the Prezziosos arrived, Jenny was on the verge of a temper tantrum. I took it as a good sign.

12th CHAPTER

Mrs Prezzioso was nearly hysterical. She flew into Jenny's cubicle in the emergency room, sobbing loudly, then hugged Jenny to her, pressing Jenny's face against her cocktail dress. "Oh, my baby!" she cried. "Angel, how are you feeling?"

"I feel better, Mummy," Jenny said. "Nice and cool."

Her temperature was still 101°. I could only imagine how Jenny had felt when it was 104°.

The doctor returned and spoke briefly to the Prezziosos, assuring them that Jenny was already on the mend. "I want to give you a prescription and make an appointment to see her again on Monday," she added. "And I need you to fill out some forms."

"Why don't you take care of that, dear," Mr Prezzioso said to his wife, "while I take

Mary Anne and Dawn home? Then I'll come back for you and our angel."

Mrs P. agreed, so Dawn and I said goodbye to the angel and her mother, and followed Mr P. out to his car.

"Actually, we need to go back to your house," I told him. "I left some things in the living room, and Dawn's bicycle is there."

"All right," he said.

On the way to the Prezziosos' Mr P. told Dawn and me over and over what a wonderful job we had done, and how proud of us he was.

"I hope you don't mind that I called a friend," I said apprehensively. "I really needed help and couldn't reach the neighbours or my dad."

"Or my mother," added Dawn.

"Not at all," said Mr P. "You did just the right thing. Leaving a message at the gym was clever, too. Apparently, they started paging us right away and just kept paging until we arrived. The first thing we heard when we entered the gym was our names being called over the loudspeaker . . . How did you get Jenny to hospital?"

"I called 999 and told the man I talked to how high Jenny's temperature was and said we couldn't find anyone to drive us to the hospital. He sent an ambulance over . . . Oh, and Jenny's doctor is probably going to call you back today. He was the first person

I called and I left a message with his service. He hadn't called back by the time we left for the hospital."

Again Mr P. looked impressed. "Thanks, Mary Anne," he said. "You, too, Dawn. I want you to know that I'll always feel at ease having Jenny in your competent hands."

Wow, I thought. Our competent hands. That was a real compliment.

When Dawn had got her bicycle from the Prezziosos' driveway and I had retrieved the Kid-Kit from the living room, Mr P. paid Dawn and me ten dollars—*each*. "For a job well done," he said.

"Thanks!" I exclaimed. "Thanks a lot!"

"Yeah," said Dawn. "You really didn't have to pay me."

"I know," said Mr P. "but you deserve it." He headed back to the hospital.

"Want to come over for a while?" I asked Dawn. The day had turned grey and drizzly. I thought we could spend the rest of the afternoon fooling around in my room. I had found two more old photo albums in the den, and through incredible willpower, had managed not to peek at them until Dawn was with me.

"Sure," said Dawn. "Just remind me to call my mum and tell her where I am."

Dawn rode slowly over to my house, and I trotted along next to her. I let us in the front door and called for my father, but he wasn't home yet. Then Dawn phoned her mother, who also wasn't home yet, and left a message for her on their answering machine.

"Are you hungry?" I asked. I had just realized that, with the excitement over, I was starving.

"Famished," replied Dawn.

We made sandwiches and ate them in the kitchen, discussing our adventure. "Isn't Mrs P. weird?" I said. "Did you see her fancy black dress? That's what she was wearing to a basketball game!"

"And she calls Jenny her angel."

I giggled. "Yeah. Mr P. does, too. But he's all right. I like him."

"He's generous," added Dawn. "Gosh, ten dollars."

When we were finished with lunch, I said, "Let's go upstairs. I want to show you something."

We ran up to my room and, with a flourish, I pulled the two old photo albums out from under my bed. "We haven't looked through these," I told Dawn. "I have no idea what's in them, but maybe we'll find high school dance pictures."

"Yeah!"

We sat side-by-side on my bed and opened one of the heavy albums. It was so big it spread across both of our laps.

"These pictures look *old*," Dawn said.

"Yeah, really," I agreed. They were yellowed with age. Not one face was familiar. "I don't recognize any of these people," I said.

"You know what would be funny? If these weren't your family's albums at all. If there'd been some kind of mix-up and they were, like, Joe Schmoe's albums, and we spent all afternoon trying to find pictures of our parents among the Schmoe family."

I threw my head back and laughed. And as I lowered my head, I looked straight in front of me—out my window and into Kristy's.

Kristy was staring back at me.

Since the day was dark, the overhead lights were on in our rooms and I knew that she had a perfect view of Dawn and me sitting side-by-side on my bed, laughing.

Kristy looked furious. (Good, she was jealous.) But she also looked . . . hurt? Or maybe betrayed. I couldn't tell. For some mean reason, though, I felt triumphant. I'd show Kristy. I was no longer the old Mary Anne who depended on her for friendship and who went along with anything she said or did. I could take care of myself. I could make my own friends.

To be certain that she got the point, I put my arm around Dawn's shoulders. Then I stuck my tongue out at Kristy.

Kristy stuck her tongue out at me.

And Dawn looked up from the album just in time to see me with my tongue out.

"Mary Anne, what—" she started to say.

Then she followed my gaze out the window and across to Kristy in her window.

She looked from me to Kristy and back to me again. "Who is that and what are you doing?" she asked.

Kristy crossed her eyes at us, then pulled her window shade down.

"What's going on?" Dawn demanded. "That girl looks familiar. I've seen her around school, haven't I?"

"Oh, that's just Kristy Thomas. She's nobody."

Dawn looked sceptical. "If she's nobody, how come you two are bothering to stick your tongues out at each other?"

I took a deep breath, but before I could say anything, Dawn went on, "And how come you put your arm around me just now? Was that something you wanted Kristy to see?"

"Well, the thing is," I began, "Kristy and I *used* to be friends." (The truth was going to have to come out sometime.)

"And you had a fight, right?" asked Dawn. She put the album aside and got to her feet.

"Yes . . ."

"Mary Anne, the first day we met—when we were eating in the lunch-room—you told me you were sitting alone because your friends were all absent. Was Kristy one of those friends?"

"Yeah . . ."

"And then you kept on saying your friends were absent," Dawn continued thoughtfully. "It seemed a bit strange, but I needed a friend of my own so much, I suppose I just tried to forget about your other friends. How come you said they were absent?"

"Well, see, we'd just had this big fight and we were all mad at each other . . ." I trailed off.

Dawn nodded her head. She looked really disgusted. "So you lied to me," she said.

"I guess," I replied uncomfortably.

"From the first day of our friendship you lied to me."

I didn't know what to say to that.

"You know, not bothering to tell a person the real truth," Dawn went on, "is just as bad as telling lies. You've been lying to me the whole time we were friends, you know that?"

"Hey, that is not true!" I cried, jumping up.

"Why should I believe that, coming from a liar? I'll tell you what I do believe, though. I believe I was pretty convenient when you needed a new friend . . . No, don't say anything, Mary Anne," she rushed on when I started to protest. "I know the rest of *this* story. See you later." Dawn stomped down the stairs.

I jumped up and ran after her. "Watch those steps," I said sarcastically. "Hope you have a nice *trip*."

"Have a nice *life*," Dawn shouted over her shoulder. She let herself out the front door. I ran back to my room and stood at the window that faced the front of the house.

I watched my last friend pedal her bicycle furiously down the street.

Then I flung myself on my bed and cried.

13th CHAPTER

I spent the rest of the afternoon moping around my bedroom. My father called to say that he'd stopped in at the office, wouldn't be home until six, and could I please start dinner?

I did, numbly.

When Dad came home, we sat down to hamburgers, peas, and French fries. Dad tried hard to make conversation, but I just didn't feel like talking. We were both relieved when the phone rang.

"I'll get it," said Dad. "I think it's a client." He reached behind him and picked up the phone. "Hello, Richard Spier . . . Pardon me? What antibiotics? . . . Oh, really? . . . No. No, she didn't . . . Well, I'm flattered to hear that. I'm proud of her, too. . . I'll give her the good news." Dad raised his eyebrows at me.

"What?" I mouthed.

He shook his head, meaning *I'll tell you in a minute*. "Yes. I certainly will," he said. "All right . . . Thank you very much. Goodbye."

Dad hung up the phone, looking somewhat puzzled. "Mary Anne?" he said. "Did anything . . . out of the ordinary happen today?"

I was so upset over my fight with Dawn (which was pretty out of the ordinary) that it was all I could think about. How could Dad possibly have heard about it, though? That couldn't have been Mrs Schafer on the phone. Dad had said he was proud of me. (He *had* meant me, hadn't he?)

Then in a flash I remembered Jenny Prezzioso. The trip to the hospital seemed like a million years ago. "Oh, my gosh!" I said. "How could I have forgotten to tell you? Yes, I—Who was that on the phone?"

"Mrs Prezzioso. She was calling to tell me what a good job you did this afternoon, and to let you know that Jenny does in fact have strep throat but is feeling much better. I was a little embarrassed to admit that I didn't know what she was talking about. I still don't think I know the whole story. Mrs Prezzioso was speaking very fast. She kept mentioning an angel."

I smiled. "That's Jenny. The Prezziosos call her their angel."

"Well, tell me what happened. It sounds rather exciting."

"It was, I guess, only I was so concerned about Jenny I hardly had time to feel excited or scared or anything. What happened was I was baby-sitting, and I noticed that Jenny seemed cranky and quiet, but at first I didn't think much of it. She gets cranky a lot. Then she fell asleep right in the middle of reading a book, and I realized she felt awfully warm, so I took her temperature. And, Dad, it was a hundred and four!"

"A hundred and *four*!"

"Yes. I couldn't believe it, either. So I called her doctor, but I only got his answering service. Then I started calling neighbours, trying to find someone who could drive us to the doctor or the hospital, but no one was home—"

"Including me," added Dad.

"Including you. And including Dawn's mother. But Dawn came over, and she suggested dialling 999, so I did, and I explained everything to the man who answered and he sent an ambulance over.

"You know," I went on, "now that I think about this afternoon, I'm surprised at everything I remembered to do. I remembered to call the gym in Chatham that the Prezziosos were driving to, so they could be paged to come home; I remembered all the instructions the man told me over the phone; and I remembered to lock the Prezziosos' front door as we left with the ambulance attendants."

Dad smiled at me. "Mrs Prezzioso said she was proud of you."

"So did her husband," I added.

"And so am I," said Dad.

"You are?"

"Very."

"Thanks," I said.

Dad sighed.

"What is it?"

"You're growng up," he said, as if it was some sort of revelation to him. "Right before my eyes."

"Well, I *am* twelve."

"I know. But twelve means different things for different people. It's like clothes. You can put a certain shirt on one person and he looks fabulous. Then you put the shirt on someone else and that person looks awful. It's the same way with age. It depends on how you wear it or carry it."

"You mean some twelve-year-olds are ready to start dating and other twelve-year-olds still need baby-sitters?"

"Exactly."

"But isn't that a double standard?" I asked.

"No, just the opposite. An example of a double standard would be that just because a boy or girl had turned fourteen he or she would automatically be encouraged to date, no matter how mature he or she was—but absolutely no thirteen-year-old would be encouraged to do so."

"Oh . . . Am I . . ." I hardly dared to ask the question. "Am I more mature than you realized?"

"Yes, yes, I think you are, Mary Anne."

"Am I . . ." Oh, please, please, *please* let him say yes, ". . . old enough to stay out a little later when I baby-sit?"

For a moment, Dad didn't answer. At last he said, "Well, ten o'clock seems a bit late for school nights. How about nine-thirty on school nights and ten o'clock on Friday and Saturday nights?"

"Oh, Dad, that's perfect! Thank you!" I started to get up, wanting to hug him, but we're not huggers. I sat down again. Then I had a great idea. "Dad, I want to show you something," I said. "I'll be right back." I ran upstairs to my room, pulled the rubber bands off the ends of my plaits, shook my hair out, and brushed it carefully. It fell over my shoulders, ripply from having been braided when it was still damp that morning. Then I ran down to the kitchen and stood in front of my father. "How do I look?" I asked.

I watched Dad's face go from serious to soft.

"Lovely," he finally managed to say.

"Do you think I could wear it this way? I mean just sometimes, not every day."

Dad nodded.

"And maybe," I went on, hoping I wasn't

pressing my luck, "I could take Humpty Dumpty off my wall and put up a nice picture of Paris or New York instead?" I could ask him about Alice in Wonderland some other time.

Dad nodded. Then he held his arms out. I crossed the room to him and he folded me into his arms.

"Thank you, Dad," I said.

Before I went to bed that night, I wrote two letters, one to Kristy and one to Dawn. Both were apologies.

14th CHAPTER

Monday, February 9

The members of the Baby-sitters Club have been enemies for almost a month now. I can't believe it. Claudia, Kristy, and Mary Anne — I hope you all read what I'm writing, because I think our fight is dumb, and you should know that. I thought you guys were my friends, but I guess not. I'm writing this because tomorrow the four of us have to help out at Jamie Newton's birthday party, and I think it's going to be a disaster. I hope you read this before then because I think you should be prepared for the worst.

P.S. If anybody wants to make up, I'm ready.

As it turned out, Stacey was both right and wrong. Jamie's party was *almost* a disaster, but something really good came out of it. I'm getting ahead of myself, though. Let me go back to Monday, the morning of the day Stacey wrote in our club notebook.

When I got to school, the first thing I did was find Dawn. I gave her the letter and stood next to her in the hall while she read it. I had been very honest in the letter, explaining that several times I *had* used her to make Kristy mad, but that I really liked her, and thought she was one of my best friends, Kristy or no Kristy. Then I apologized.

Dawn read the letter slowly. Then she read it again. Then she hugged me. I knew our fight was over.

A moment later, I realized that Dawn was staring at me. "What?" I asked.

"Mary Anne, your hair . . . Where are your plaits?"

I grinned. "Do you like it?"

"I love it! You look so pretty with your hair down!" Dawn made me turn around so she could see me from the back, too.

"Thanks. I plan to wear it this way often." I opened my locker, put my lunch away, pulled out some books, and slammed the locker shut again. "Now," I went on, "since I was able to make up with you, I ought to be able to make up with Kristy, too." I held up the other note I'd written. "This is for Kristy. I have to go find her."

I looked everywhere, but I couldn't find her. At last, just before the bell rang, I slipped the note into her locker. Several times that day I glimpsed her in the halls, and I knew she saw me, too, but she didn't say anything, and didn't act any differently than she had over the past few weeks.

Had she got the note? Maybe I'd stuck it in the wrong locker. Or maybe it had slid into a notebook and she hadn't seen it.

Or maybe she was just still mad.

Jamie's birthday party began at 3.30 that afternoon. I went to it with mixed feelings—excitement and dread. It could be a lot of fun. Or, as Stacey had pointed out, it could be a disaster. But the the members of the Babysitters Club had promised Mrs Newton we'd help out, so I knew we'd all be there.

I rang the Newtons' bell at 3.15, armed with a present for Jamie. I had arrived early so I could give Mrs Newton a hand.

"Hi-hi!" Jamie greeted me excitedly. "I'm four today! Four years old! That's this many." He held up four fingers.

"Hi, Mary Anne," Mrs Newton called from the kitchen when Jamie let me in. "I'm glad you're here early. I can really use you." She put me to work filling little baskets full of sweets for the table and making punch. By the time I finished, most of Jamie's guests had arrived.

The living room sounded like a school playground. Jamie's friends, all dressed up in their party clothes, were running around, screaming and shrieking, and wanting him to open his presents. Mrs Newton pulled Kristy, Claudia, Stacey, and me aside.

"Try to get them to sit down. We'll do presents first, because nobody can wait. It should go pretty fast."

The members of the Babysitters Club nodded. But we carefully avoided each other's eyes.

Mrs Newton clapped her hands. "Time for the presents!" she called.

Kristy rounded up four children and led them to the couch. "Sit over here," she told them.

Stacey rounded up four other children and led them to the floor in front of the fireplace.

Claudia guided several little girls to the floor by the piano.

Uh-oh, I thought. "Get everybody in one spot!" I directed.

Claudia, Stacey, and Kristy gave me the evil eye.

"Around the couch is fine," said Mrs Newton.

Kristy gloated.

After Jamie had opened his presents, Mrs Newton announced that it was time for Pin-the-Tail-on-the-Donkey. "Will three of you give me a hand, and somebody else go check on the baby?" Mrs Newton asked us.

The four of us made a mad rush for the stairs.

"*I'll* check on Lucy," said Kristy.

"No, *I* will," said Stacey.

"No, you won't. *I* will," I said.

"None of you will because *I'm* going!" Claudia exclaimed.

The four of us shoved each other around, trying to be the first to run up the stairs.

"Girls!" cried Mrs Newton.

We turned around guiltily. She was frowning at us.

"Stacey, would you please check on her?" said Mrs Newton. "I need the rest of you over here."

It was Stacey's turn to gloat. "Ha, ha," she said under her breath, and started up the staircase.

"Brat," muttered Kristy as we turned around.

Mrs Newton gave me the job of blindfolding the kids; Kristy, the job of guiding them if they strayed too far from the donkey; and Claudia, the job of watching the kids who were waiting their turn. Mrs Newton disappeared into the kitchen.

She hadn't been gone long when, just as I was tying the blindfold on Claire Pike, I felt something crunch down on my foot.

"Ow!" I cried.

"Oh, I'm *so* sorry!" I heard a voice say. "Was that your *foot* I stepped on?"

I straightened up and looked into Kristy's

eyes. I narrowed my own eyes at her. "Yes it was, Kristin Amanda Thomas," I said coldly.

"Do you have a problem?"

"Yes, I do."

"I could tell."

"My problem is that *your* foot is in *my* way."

I stuck my tongue out at her.

The game continued with no more "incidents". In fact, everything went smoothly until it was time for cake and ice cream. Mrs Newton had fixed up the table in the dining room. Streamers criss-crossed the ceiling and a huge bunch of balloons was tied in the middle. The table was decorated in a teddy bear theme: teddy bear plates and paper cups, a tablecloth with teddy bears all over it, and even tiny teddies for party gifts.

The children "oohed' and "aahed" as they came into the room, and Mrs Newton helped them find seats. "I want you girls to sit down, too," she told the members of the Babysitters Club. "Place yourselves strategically around the table so you can pass things and give the kids a hand if they need help."

After a little scuffle with Claudia, I sat down next to Jamie at one end. Kristy was sitting on one side, two places away from me. Stacey was across from her and Claudia was sitting across from me, at the opposite end of the table.

"Mary Anne, how would you like to pour the punch you made?" asked Mrs Newton when we were settled. "Then I'll bring the cake in."

"Sure," I replied. She handed me the heavy pitcher full of red juice and I walked around the table with it, carefully filling each cup halfway. When I reached Kristy I filled her cup to the top—and kept on going.

"Hey, watch what you're doing!" she exclaimed.

I watched.

"It's—that stuff's getting in my lap!" She jumped up.

"Oh, *so* sorry. My mistake," I said.

"You bet it's your mistake! What's the big idea?"

"What's the big idea? What's the *big idea*? That's what you get when you step on my foot and don't answer my note."

"What note?'

"You know what note."

"I do not." Kristy sat down and began mopping up her lap with a paper napkin.

At that moment, Claudia appeared with another napkin. She wiped up some of the punch by Kristy's plate, then walked around the table and flung the wet napkin in Stacey's face.

"Hey!" Stacey was on her feet in a flash. She ran after Claudia and smushed the napkin in *her* face.

The dining room was in an uproar.

"Mummy!" called Jamie. He looked as if he was about to cry.

Mrs Newton chose that very second to walk into the dining room with Jamie's birthday cake, five candles (four plus one to grow on) flickering cheerfully.

She came to a standstill before she reached the table. "Girls, what is going *on*?" She looked around. The room had grown silent. The members of the Babysitters Club were gathered around Kristy, whose lap was stained with the red punch. I was holding the pitcher over the mess on the table, and Stacey was smushing the wet napkin in Claudia's face. A lone tear ran down Jamie's cheek.

Nobody knew what to say.

After a moment, I took the napkin away from Stacey and put it and a dry one over the spilled punch. "Just a little accident," I said to Mrs Newton. "I'm sorry. We're *all* sorry." I looked meaningfully at the other girls. "Kristy, why don't you go in the kitchen and get cleaned up?" Kristy walked dazedly out of the dining room. "Come on," I said to Claudia and Stacey. "We're just going to help Kristy," I told Mrs Newton. "We'll be right back."

In the kitchen, the other girls stared at me.

"I don't care what any of you says or what any of you thinks," I told them boldly. "I am calling a meeting of the Babysitters Club for right after the party. *Be there,*" I added. Then I returned to the dining room to pass out the birthday cake.

15th CHAPTER

There was no more funny stuff during Jamie's party. The members of the Babysitters Club felt so guilty about almost ruining it, that we bent over backwards being nice to Jamie and helpful to Mrs Newton. Then, the end of the party was so hectic, trying to sort out all the prizes and baskets of sweets and find everybody's coats, hats, mittens, and boots, that by the time the guests were gone, Mrs Newton had forgotten about the trouble in the dining room and the argument over Lucy. At any rate, we hoped she had, since we didn't want her to think we were immature or irresponsible.

When Kristy, Claudia, Stacey, and I left the Newtons', we stood around uncomfortably in their front yard.

"Where should we have the meeting?" I asked. "Claudia? Your room as usual?"

She shrugged. "I don't care."

"Fine. We'll go to the Kishis'," I said firmly.

Kristy raised her eyebrows slightly, but she didn't say anything.

Mimi greeted us as we trooped through Claudia's front door. "Girls!" she exclaimed. "It is lovely to see you again."

I knew she meant, It's lovely to see you *together* again.

"Hi, Mimi," I said, and gave her a hug. "Guess what—I've finished the scarf for my dad except for the fringe."

"That is wonderful, Mary Anne," Mimi replied warmly. "I'll be glad to help you with it."

"We're just going to have a quick club meeting," Claudia told her grandmother. "We'll be done soon."

"All right, my Claudia. That is fine."

We climbed the stairs, ran by Janine's room, and took seats in Claudia's room. Everyone looked at me.

I swallowed hard, feeling nervous. Then I remembered how I had taken charge when Jenny was sick. I reminded myself that I'd made a new friend and had worked out some problems with my father.

I drew a deep breath. "We've been mad at each other for weeks now," I said. "And it's time we stopped. We almost wrecked Jamie's party today. I felt horrible. I know you guys did, too."

They nodded, looking somewhat ashamed.

"So," I went on, "we either make up or break up. Break up the club, that is. Because we can't run it when we're mad at each other. And I don't know about you guys but I don't want to break up the club. I had to work pretty hard just to be *in* it at first."

It was Stacey who spoke next. "I don't want the club to break up, either," she said softly. "You guys are my only friends here in Stoneybrook."

"Kristy?" I asked.

"I want to make up, I guess," she said. "But somebody owes me an apology. We all owe each other apologies."

"Who owes you one?" asked Claudia.

Kristy paused. "I can't remember!" she exclaimed finally. "I can't remember exactly who I'm mad at or why!"

I started to giggle. "Neither do I," I said.

We all began to laugh. Claudia laughed so hard she rolled off her bed.

"Just to make it official, though," I said, "why don't we apologize to each other? Right now. Ready? One, two, three—"

"I'm sorry!" the four of us shouted, still laughing.

Then I added, "I'm sorry I used to be such a coward and I would never stick my neck out or make decisions or take charge. And I'm sorry about Mimi, Claudia."

Kristy and Stacey exchanged puzzled looks, then shrugged their shoulders.

"That's okay. I'm the one who should be

sorry about that," replied Claudia. "And I'm sorry I'm careless and forgetful. I'm trying to change."

Stacey cleared her throat. "I'm sorry I'm conceited about having lived in New York. I like Stoneybrook ten times better, and you guys are much nicer than most of my old so-called friends."

"Well," said Kristy, "believe me, this isn't easy to say, but I'm sorry I'm so bossy. I mean, I *am* the club chairman, but I don't need to take charge *all* the time. And with Mary Anne around, it looks like I won't be able to any more. What's happened to you, Mary Anne? You've *changed* since our fight."

I blushed. "A million things have happened," I said. "It's hard to explain."

"You're wearing your hair differently," Stacey pointed out. "You look very pretty."

"Thank you."

"So your dad finally gave in?" said Kristy, looking awed. "Amazing."

"Not without a fight," I added, "but we have an understanding now. By the way, I can stay out until ten o'clock on Fridays and Saturdays, and until nine-thirty on week nights."

Kristy's mouth dropped open. "Gosh . . ."

Everyone began talking at once. While Claudia showed Stacey some new eye-shadow she'd bought, Kristy leaned over and said, "Mary Anne, there's something I don't understand. What was that note you were talking about at the party?"

"I left a note in your locker today. I decided our fight had gone on long enough, so I wrote a letter apologizing to you. I thought you'd at least say you'd received it."

"But I didn't," said Kristy. "My—"

"Oh, no!" I interrupted her. "I must have put it in the wrong locker!"

"No, you didn't. At least, I don't think so. What I'm trying to tell you is that my locker's broken. I couldn't get into it today. The janitor said he'd try to open it and put a new lock on it, but he probably won't be able to do that until tomorrow."

"Oh . . . Kristy, I'm sorry."

"So am I, but I think we've done enough apologizing today. Friends?"

"Friends."

She stuck out her hand and we shook on our friendship.

That evening I got home at 6.05 and heard the phone ringing. I unlocked the front door and rushed through the hallway and into the kitchen. The phone had rung about six times and was still ringing. I snatched up the receiver.

"Hello?" I said breathlessly.

"Hi, it's me, Dawn. Oh, I was *hoping* you'd be there."

"What's up?"

"Mary Anne, you won't believe this. You know how disorganized my mum is? Well, she's still unpacking a few stray cartons, and she came to one labelled SPORTS EQUIPMENT and guess what was inside."

"What?"

"A photo album. An old one. And guess what was inside that."

"What? *What?*"

"A *high school dance picture*."

"*Aughh!* Was it my dad and your mum?"

"*Yes!* And my mum did have a rose pinned to her dress, and a white ribbon was tied to the stem. So I asked her who the guy was, and her voice got all soft and sort of dreamy, and she said, 'Oh, that was Richie Spier . . . I wonder whatever happened to him,' and I said, 'Nothing.' I mean, not *nothing*, Mary Anne, just that he hasn't gone anywhere. And she said, 'Nothing? How do you know?' and I said, 'Because he's Mary Anne's father. He's still right here in Stoneybrook.' And my mum nearly fainted!"

"Wow!" I exclaimed. "I wonder—just a second, Dawn. I think my—Dawn, Dad's home! I've got to ask him! I'm dying to! I'll call you back after dinner. 'Bye!"

With my father, you can't just jump into things. I didn't say a word about Dawn's mother until dinner had been made and we were sitting at the table eating.

I asked how his day was.

He asked how mine was.

I asked how his cases were going.

He asked how school and the Babysitters Club were going.

Then I said, "Dad? Did you ever know someone named Sharon Porter?"

Dad choked on a mouthful of carrots and had to drink some water before he could answer. "Sharon Porter? . . . Yes. Yes, I did. Why do you ask?"

"Well, I just found out that Dawn's mother was Sharon Porter before she got married, and that she grew up in Stoneybrook. Dawn and I thought it would be really funny if you two knew each other in high school . . . Did you?"

"As a matter of fact, we did."

"Were you friends?"

Dad paused. "Yes," he said softly. "Very good friends. But we drifted apart. We didn't keep in touch. Her parents and I didn't get along very well . . . Sharon and I graduated from high school, we dated all that summer, and then we both went off to college. After college, Sharon moved to California. I lost track of her then . . . So Sharon got married!"

"And divorced," I pointed out. "She brought Dawn and her brother back here to Stoneybrook so they could all start over again . . . How come you and the Porters didn't get along?"

"Oh, it's a long story. Let's just say that they didn't think I was good enough for their daughter. My family didn't have much money when I was growing up."

"Grandpa was . . . a mailman?" I asked, trying to remember. Dad's parents had died at the time I was in first grade.

"That's right. And Mr Porter was—is—a big banker."

"I wonder if you'd be good enough for Dawn's mother now," I mused.

A faint smile appeared on Dad's lips. "Don't go getting any ideas, Mary Anne," was all he would say.

When dinner was over, I asked, "Dad, could I use the phone . . . just for a few minutes? I don't have much homework."

"All right," he said vaguely.

I ran to the upstairs extension and dialled the Schafers'. "Dawn!" I cried. "I got the story. Or part of it anyway. Dad went all sort of dreamy, too. He's still dreamy." I told her what I had learned.

"Hmm," she said. "We'll have to do something about that."

"Yeah," I agreed. "Wow, it's been some day. I made up with Kristy, too. In fact, the whole club has made up."

"You have?" Dawn asked wistfully.

"Yup. Gosh, I wish you could belong to the Babysitters Club, too. You were great with Jenny last Saturday. Did you do much baby-sitting before you moved to Stoneybrook?"

"Tons," she replied.

The wheels began to turn in my head. "Listen, Dawn, I have to go. I'll see you in school tomorrow, okay?"

"Okay. See you."

" 'Bye." I hung up the phone. I hoped Dad would let me make one more call. I had something important to discuss with Kristy.

16th CHAPTER

My father has lost his mind. Honest. I can't believe what he said to me the other day. He said, "Yes." The amazing thing is that he said yes *after* I said, "Dad, may I have a Babysitters Club party at our house?"

So yesterday, Friday, I gave a special party. It was special because, aside from Kristy, Claudia, and Stacey, there was one guest who wasn't a club member—yet. Dawn. I'd told the others all about her, and they wanted to meet her. They knew that I'd like her to become a club member. I wasn't sure how they'd feel about that. We'd had to look for new club members once before, and that was a disaster. But Dawn was different.

My party was held from five to eight. Dad and I ordered a large pizza, and my father even came home from work early to help me toss a salad. (We made a hamburger patty for Stacey, since she can't eat the processed cheese in pizza, because of her diabetes.)

At quarter to five, the doorbell rang.

"Yikes! It's starting," I said to Dad. "And they're early! Well, I think everything's ready." We were going to hold a getting-to-know Dawn meeting in my room first, then eat in the kitchen (*with* Dad—he insisted) and then go back up to my room to fool around.

"Don't worry, your party will be fine, I'm sure," Dad told me. "You better go to let your guests in," he added, as the doorbell rang a second time.

"Okay," I replied, and it was then that I tripped over the empty pizza box (the pizza was warming in the oven), and fell against the kitchen counter, spilling a glass of diet soda and knocking a pile of carrot peelings to the floor.

"Oh, no!" I cried. My jeans skirt was covered with soda.

"Relax, Mary Anne," said Dad calmly. "I'll get the door. You clean up."

I sighed. "All right. What a way to start a party."

Dad adjusted his glasses and headed for the front door. I got out the paper towels and started mopping up.

It took me a moment to realize that after I'd heard the door open, there had been absolute silence. I waited a few more moments, then peeped into the front hall.

What I saw nearly took my breath away. Dawn was in the hall, taking her coat off—and her mother and my father were standing at the door, staring at each other. Dawn saw me, grinned, and gave me the thumbs-up sign.

I opened my eyes wide. Then I grinned, too. Despite the fact that my hands were sticky and little pieces of carrot were clinging to my soda soaked skirt, I joined the others in the hall.

"Dad," I said, "this is Mrs Schafer, Dawn's mother. Mrs Schafer, this is my dad, Mr Spier." I waited for a reaction. "I think you two know each other," I added.

My father recovered himself. "Yes. Yes, of course we do. Sharon, it's wonderful to see you. It's been years."

"It's good to see you, too, Richie," replied Dawn's mother.

Richie! I had to put my hand over my mouth to keep from giggling.

"Please come in," my father went on.

"Oh, I'd love to, but I can't stay," said Mrs Schafer. "I've got to pick up Dawn's brother at hockey practice."

"Dawn," I said quickly, "there's a huge mess in the kitchen. Come help me clean it up."

"Oh, sure," she replied. We hustled into the kitchen. But we didn't clean up. We hovered by the door, trying to hear what was going on in the hall.

"I'm glad you're back in Stoneybrook," my father said. "Would you like to have dinner sometime?"

"I'd love to. When?" was the fast answer.

"When?" Dad repeated, sounding flustered. "Well, how about tomorrow night?"

"Wonderful."

"I'll see you tomorrow, then," said my father.

Dawn and I looked at each other. We gripped hands excitedly. A *date*! Our parents were going to go out on a *date*!

"Oh, and I'll drop Dawn off tonight," added Dad. "No need for you to make another trip."

Mrs Schafer thanked my father and left. Dad returned to the kitchen, looking dazed.

Dawn and I were pretty dazed ourselves. I thought I'd never be able to concentrate on the party after what had happened, but by the time the mess had been cleaned up, I'd changed my skirt, the members of the club had arrived, and we were sitting around in my room, I felt much calmer.

I'd introduced Dawn to the other girls as they'd arrived. Now Dawn and Kristy looked at each other warily.

"Mary Anne says you've done a lot of baby-sitting," Kristy said.

"Oh, yes," replied Dawn. "In California—that's where we used to live—I baby-sat all the time. We lived in a neighbourhood where there were tons of families and kids. I started sitting when I was nine. I bet I took care of every kid on my street at one time or another."

"Have you ever had an emergency?"

I could see that Kristy, as our chairman, was really going to grill Dawn. Then again, that was her job.

"An emergency?" said Dawn. "Well . . ."

"She was terrific when Jenny Prezzioso was sick," I interrupted. I had told the others about our hospital adventure.

Kristy nodded.

"And once," added Dawn, "there was a fire in a house when I was sitting. It was a problem with the wiring. I got the kids outdoors and called the fire department."

"Wow," exclaimed Claudia, looking impressed. "Then what happened?"

"The firemen came really fast and put the fire out. The kitchen was all wet and smoky and black, but none of the other rooms were hurt."

"That was a pretty good emergency," said Stacey, looking hopefully at Kristy.

I smiled at Stacey, saying a silent thank you.

Kristy wasn't finished, though. "Have you ever taken care of a baby? I mean, a *real* baby—a newborn?"

Dawn paused. "No, not a newborn," she said slowly. "I think the youngest baby was Georgie Klein. He was about seven months."

"How late can you stay out?" (That was Kristy's favourite question.)

"Gosh, I'm not sure," said Dawn. "I'd have to check with my mother. Maybe ten o'clock? I don't know about school nights, though. It's been a while since I baby-sat for anyone besides my brother. The last kid I took care of was in California, since I don't know many people here. Mum's probably changed the rules since we moved."

Kristy looked satisfied.

"How come you moved, Dawn?" asked Stacey. "Did your father get transferred?"

Dawn glanced at me, then lowered her eyes. "Divorce," she replied.

"Your parents got divorced?" said Kristy. She sounded sympathetic. "Boy, I know all about that. Mine are divorced, too. It stinks."

"And I know all about moving," said Stacey. "My parents and I moved here from New York last summer. That wasn't so great at first, but it's a lot better now."

"Yeah, that's because she met all these wonderful friends!" Claudia waved her hand around the room, indicating the club members.

"And now Dawn's meeting us," I said pointedly. I looked at Kristy and raised my eyebrows.

She smiled at me. "We sure have a lot of clients now, more than we know what to do with. We could use some help." She turned to Claudia and Stacey, who nodded their heads ever so slightly.

"Mary Anne?" said Kristy. "Do you want to say it?"

I grinned. "Sure. Dawn Schafer, would you like to join the Babysitters Club?"

The smile that spread across Dawn's face was one of the brightest I'd ever seen. "*Really?*" she cried. "I mean, yes! Yes, I want to join. More than anything! Thanks, you guys."

I jumped up. "Well," I said, "the pizza's warming up and I'm hungry. I think the Babysitters Club should go pig out."

Kristy, Stacey, Claudia, Dawn, and I thundered down the stairs and into the kitchen. Kristy and Claudia attacked the pizza with our pizza cutter.

"Dad?" I called. "We're going to eat now!"

My father came into the kitchen. He looked as if he were moving underwater. Dawn and I glanced at each other. We both knew what my dad was thinking about, and we absolutely could not wait until Sunday morning to find out about our parents' date.

I was glad I had the Babysitters Club—the *five-member* Babysitters Club—to help keep my mind off Saturday night.

I took a piece of pizza and held it in the air. "Pizza toast!" I cried. Kristy, Claudia, and Dawn raised their pizza, too, and Stacey raised her hamburger. (Dad didn't know *what* was going on.)

"To our new member," I said.

"To our new member," said Kristy, Stacey and Claudia.

"To *me*!" cried Dawn. "Thanks for letting me join the Babysitters Club."

The Babysitters Club

DAWN AND THE IMPOSSIBLE THREE

1st CHAPTER

The Babysitters Club. I didn't start it and I don't run it, but I am its newest member. I'm Dawn Schafer, baby-sitter number five. The other girls in the club have titles, like Mary Anne Spier, secretary, or Claudia Kishi, vice-chairman. But I'm just me.

The club is the most important thing in my life. If it weren't for the club, I wouldn't be riding my bicycle off to another baby-sitting job at this very moment. And if it weren't for all the baby-sitting jobs I've had, I wouldn't know so many people here in Stoneybrook.

See, I've only lived in Connecticut a few months. Until January, I lived in California with my parents and my younger brother, Jeff. But last autumn Mum and Dad split up, and Mum decided to move back to the place where she grew up. Her parents still live here. So right after Christmas, Jeff and

I were uprooted from hot, sunny California and transplanted to cold, sloppy Connecticut, where (so far) it's never been warm enough for me.

I hate cold weather. On the days when the temperature slips down a few degrees, I yell at the weatherman. On the days when it creeps up, I congratulate him and apologize for yelling. I'm still not sure what the big fuss about New England winters is all about. Back in California, we had one season: summer. I thought it was wonderful. I loved the beach, I loved sunshine, I loved eighty-degree Christmases. Why, I wondered, would anyone want to interrupt all that warmth with three other seasons?

The family I was baby-sitting for that afternoon was the Pikes. There are eight Pike children — and three of them are triplets! However, I wasn't going to sit for all of them. The triplets, who are nine-year-old boys, would be at ice hockey practice (my brother Jeff was there, too), and eight-year-old Vanessa would be at her violin lesson. That left Nicky, who's seven; Margo (six); Claire (four); and Mallory, who's ten and usually a big help.

When I reached the Pikes', I parked my bicycle at the side of the drive and rang the doorbell.

"I'll get it! I'll get it!" cried a voice from inside.

The door was flung open by Claire, the

youngest Pike. She loves answering the door and the phone.

"Hi, Claire!" I said brightly.

Claire suddenly turned shy. She put her finger in her mouth and looked at the floor.

"Hi," she replied.

"I'm Dawn. Remember me?"

Claire nodded.

"Can I come in?"

She nodded again.

As I was opening the door, Mrs Pike ran down the stairs. "Oh, it's you, Dawn. Terrific! You're right on time. How are you?"

"Fine, thanks," I answered.

I really like Mrs Pike. She has lots of energy and she loves kids. (She'd have to, I suppose.) She's patient and funny and hardly ever shouts. She and Mr Pike have been really nice to our family ever since we moved here.

"I'm just going to be at a meeting of the trustees of the public library. The library number is on the notice board by the phone. If you need to call me, ask for the Prescott Room and say that I'm in the board meeting, okay?"

"Okay."

(Mrs Pike is always organized. She's a baby-sitter's dream.)

"The emergency numbers are in their usual spot, and the kids can have a snack — a small one — if they're hungry. I'll be home a little after five. Is that all right?"

"Perfect. We have a Babysitters Club meeting at five-thirty."

Our club is run very professionally. We meet three times a week to go over club business and take job calls. (We get tons of jobs.) The chairman is Kristy Thomas. She's the one who had the idea for the club.

The vice-chairman is Claudia Kishi, who's really great and sophisticated. She lives across the street from Kristy. We hold our meetings in Claudia's room because she has a phone. Claudia is Japanese and beautiful. She hates school, but loves art and mystery stories. She's a little bit hard to get to know.

The club treasurer is Stacey McGill. Stacey moved to Stoneybrook just a few months before I did, so we have something in common. She came from New York City, and I know she had trouble getting adjusted to small-town life. Sometimes we talk about that.

Then there's Mary Anne Spier. She's the one who introduced me to Kristy, Claudia, and Stacey. She's the secretary of the club and responsible for the Babysitters Club Record Book, which is where she records our job appointments, as well as the phone numbers and addresses of our clients and stuff like that. (Also in that book is a record of the money we earn. Stacey's in charge of that section.)

We keep a Babysitters Club Notebook, too, which is like a diary. Kristy insists that we write up *each* job we take and that we all read the book every few days. That's so we know what's going on in the families the club sits for.

The most important thing about Mary Anne (to me, anyway) is that she's my new best friend. (My old best friend was Sunny Winslow in California.) Mary Anne lives next door to Kristy Thomas, and for a long time Kristy was her only best friend. Now I'm Mary Anne's other best friend.

The strangest thing happened right after Mary Anne and I got to know each other. It turned out that her father and my mother went to high school together. Not only *that*, they dated — for a long time. They were really serious about each other. Mary Anne and I found all this romantic stuff they'd written to each other in their senior yearbooks.

Even more amazing is that they've started dating each other *again*! (Mary Anne's mother died when Mary Anne was really little.) Mary Anne and I can hardly believe that our parents are going out. It's so exciting! Mr Spier is this stern, lonely guy who needs some fun in his life (and something to think about besides Mary Anne, who's his only kid.) And my mum has been so sad since the divorce. She needs some fun, too.

Mrs Pike was putting on her coat and hat, and tossing things in her bag. "Mallory's upstairs doing her homework," she told me, "but she'll be down soon. She wants to see you. Margo's in the playroom, and Nicky's at the Barretts' playing with Buddy. Do you know the Barretts?"

I shook my head.

"They live a few doors down — towards your house. Our kids and their kids are back and forth all the time. Nicky'll probably bring Buddy over here at some point today. You won't need to call Mrs Barrett. She's very relaxed, and she'll probably know he's here, anyway."

"Okay," I said.

"I guess that's it." Mrs Pike stooped down to kiss Claire. "See you later, pumpkin," she said. "Wear your jacket if you go outside. It's chilly today." (Was it ever!) Then she called upstairs to Mallory and downstairs to Margo to let them know she was leaving — and she was gone.

I looked at Claire. "Let's go and see what Margo's doing, okay?"

Claire nodded and I led her down to the playroom.

What Margo was doing was performing. She had put on a big floppy straw hat and a long filmy dress with some beads and scarves, and was dancing around to "Puff, the Magic Dragon," which was playing at full volume on the children's record player.

When she knew the words, she mouthed them.

Claire and I plonked ourselves down on the couch and pretended we were the audience. When the song ended, Margo made a sweeping bow and Claire and I clapped loudly.

"Bravo!" I shouted.

"Bravo!" Claire shouted.

Margo took another bow.

I heard a clatter of footsteps in the kitchen and Mallory called down, "Hi, Dawn. What's eight times seven?"

"Hi, Mal," I called back. "You know that one."

"Fifty-six?" she asked.

"Right!" I said.

"Thanks!"

She returned to her homework.

Margo put "Old MacDonald Had a Farm" on the record player and began another performance. Claire joined in on the animal sounds. They were just finishing when I heard Mallory in the kitchen again.

"Homework's done," she announced. "Can I have a snack, Dawn?"

"Sure," I replied. "Claire and Margo and I will have one, too."

The four of us sat around the Pikes' kitchen, eating nut bars.

"So, Dawn," said Mallory, "how's your new-old house?"

Claire and Margo giggled. Mallory had

christened our house "new-old", and the little girls think it's funny, but Mallory's right. I do live in a new-old house. It's new to Mum and Jeff and me, but it was built in 1795. I love it, even though it's dark inside, and the stairs are narrow, and the doorways are low because people were a lot shorter in 1795. I like to think that I live in a house that so many other people have lived in — people who saw the War of 1812 and the Civil War and the Emancipation Proclamation and the Gay Nineties and the first aeroplane and the Depression and the first rocketship. It's exciting.

I bet our house has a secret passageway somewhere. Mary Anne and I are going to explore it thoroughly one day. We'll tap on walls and press the wood panelling, hoping for something to spring out or swing open. We plan to explore the attic, too. Maybe we'll find an old diary or something.

I smiled to myself, thinking that Mum would want to be in on a search of the house. She loves things like that. She thinks they're romantic, and Mum is a very romantic person. That's one reason Mr Spier liked her so much when they were in high school. Guess what she did? She saved the rose tied with a white ribbon that he gave her the night of their high school dance. She pressed it between the pages of her yearbook. It's still there. Mary Anne and I found it.

"The new-old house is fine," I replied.

Mallory grinned at me and raised her eyebrows. "And how's your *mum*?" she asked meaningfully. Mallory knows about my mother and Mr Spier, and loves to hear about them. She likes most of all to hear about when they were in love in high school and what had happened to drive them apart. I'd told her as much as I knew, which wasn't much. Several times I had asked Mum why she and Mary Anne's father ended their relationship. It had something to do with Mum's parents not approving of the Spiers because they didn't have much money (Mum's parents have *tons* of money), but I didn't know the whole story.

"Honey," she said, "it's not really very interesting."

"I think it is. You two were in love, but you went off to college and never saw each other again. I think it's romantic . . . and sad."

"Our paths just never crossed. Our holidays usually came at different times. During the summers, I stayed in California and worked. And at Christmas-time, Granny and Pop-Pop would take me to the Bahamas."

"Didn't you think about Mr Spier, though?"

"Sometimes, yes. But we were young. We had new lives and new interests. We were both busy with college. And then I met your father, and Mr Spier met Mary Anne's mother — and you know the rest of the story."

I certainly did. The rest of the story is that my mother and father got married, got unhappy, and got divorced. They just weren't right for each other. Dad is super-organized. And Mum is a crazy person — not nasty crazy, just an absentminded-professor type.

Jeff and I are actually *used* to finding the mixing bowls carefully put away in the linen cupboard, or finding her mending clothes we outgrew two years earlier. And although we've been living in our new-old house for several months, there is still a gigantic pile of unpacked boxes in the dining room. Every now and then I start to go through one, and each time Mum runs in and says, "Dawn, you don't have to bother with that, honey. Let me do it." And then she doesn't do it.

My mum is really terrific, but her habits are what drove her and Dad apart. I'm not saying the divorce was her fault. I'm just saying that she's disorganized and Dad couldn't live with that.

I didn't tell Mallory all that, though. What I said was, "Mum's okay. She's still going out with that Mr Spier."

"Yea!" cried Mallory.

"And she's started looking for a job. She's always off on interviews —"

We were interrupted by a thump and a

wail that seemed to come from the front porch. Mallory and I looked at each other. "What was that?" I asked.

We raced to the door. There was Nicky Pike with a boy about his age, and a round-faced, pigtailed little girl who was crying.

"Suzi!" Mallory exclaimed. "It's Suzi Barrett," she informed me. "And this is Buddy, her brother."

"She fell coming up the steps," Buddy said. "I think she grazed her knee."

I braved the cold weather to dart outside and roll up Suzi's trouser legs. Sure enough, one knee was bleeding, but it didn't look bad. "I'm Dawn, Suzi," I told her. "Why don't you come in and I'll wash your cut and find you a plaster."

"Thanks," said Suzi tearfully.

"We have plasters with dinosaurs on them," Nicky said helpfully.

We found one and I put it carefully over Suzi's scrape. She liked it so much that she rolled up the leg of her trousers and left it that way so everyone could see the plaster.

Suzi and Buddy stayed at the Pikes' for the rest of the afternoon. Suzi watched *Sesame Street* with Claire and Margo, and Mallory helped Nicky and Buddy make a dinosaur village. (I never did work out what that was.)

When Mrs Pike got home it was 5.15 and time to make tracks to the Babysitters Club meeting. I said good-bye to the children, got on my bike, and rode off in a hurry, deciding to go to Mary Anne's house and pick her up beforehand.

When I reached the Spiers', I guided my bicycle into the driveway and pulled to a stop. While I was fiddling with the kick-stand, Mary Anne burst through her front door and dashed across the lawn.

"Hey, guess what!" she cried. "Great news!"

2nd CHAPTER

Mary Anne's brown hair flew behind her as she ran to me.

"What? What is it?" I asked excitedly.

"Dad just called. He said not to expect him for dinner tonight."

"So?" I prompted.

"He said not to expect him because he's taking your mum out!"

"Another date!" I squealed. "Fantastic! This is really exciting."

Mary Anne closed her eyes and sighed. "Yeah. The date was spur-of-the-moment, too, which is a good sign. Dad never used to just rush off and do things. He'd plan them for weeks. But he said he got the idea about five minutes ago, called your mother, asked her to join him for a quick dinner, and then called me. I can't believe it."

I checked my watch. "It's almost five-thirty," I said. "We'd better get to Claudia's."

Mary Anne started across the street with me, but she didn't say anything, just sighed again. It was a sigh of pleasure.

I knew one reason Mary Anne was so happy about her father and my mother. It was because my mother took Mr Spier's mind off Mary Anne. Mr Spier used to make all these rules for Mary Anne: she had to fix her hair in plaits and wear the clothes he bought for her; she couldn't talk on the phone after dinner; she had to be in by nine; she had to put half of her baby-sitting money in the bank, etc etc. It was awful.

He was already beginning to change when he "re-met" Mum, but now he's a completely different father. He let Mary Anne get contact lenses to replace her reading glasses. He allows her to spend her baby-sitting money if she saves her allowance, and since he no longer buys her clothes, you should see what Mary Anne gets with her money. She doesn't look like Claudia or Stacey, who wear these really wild outfits such as tight black pants and Day-Glo shirts, but, well, for instance, at that very moment as we walked across the Kishis' lawn, Mary Anne had on her first sweat shirt and her first pair of jeans ever. She looked terrific!

"You know what I'm going to start

doing?" Mary Anne asked me with a giant grin.

"What?"

"Re-decorating my room."

"No! Really?"

"Really. I used to think that the only way I'd be able to re-decorate was if my father lost his mind. I guess he did lose it — over your mother."

"Thanks a lot!" I said.

"Oh, you know what I mean. I think it's great."

"Great that he and Mum are going out, or great that he's lost his mind?"

Mary Anne giggled. "Both," she said.

"What are you going to do to your room?"

"I'm going to take all the babyish stuff off my walls and put up posters and photographs. That's all I can afford to do. Then I'll have to work on my dad a little. I have to see if he'll help me do anything expensive. I want a new bedspread and a new rug and new curtains and new wallpaper. Everything in my room is pink, and I can't stand pink!"

We reached the Kishis' front door. I rang the bell.

Claudia's sister Janine answered the door.

Mary Anne and I glanced at each other. Janine is fifteen years old. She's a genius. Mary Anne and Kristy don't like her because she's so clever, and she's always correcting whatever they say. But I don't mind Janine. I think she's all right. You just have to know how to handle her.

"Hi, Janine!" I said.

Mary Anne hung back. She's shy around some people.

"Hi," Janine answered. "I suppose you're here for a meeting of your club."

"Yup," I said.

"You know," Janine began, "the expression 'yup' —"

"Janine," I interrupted her, "did you notice Mary Anne's clothes? She has new jeans and a new sweat shirt. She bought them with her own money — money she earned baby-sitting."

"The club must be doing awfully well," Janine commented.

"Oh, it is. Extremely well." I decided to toss out a few big words. "Thanks to the foresight of our chairman it's both profitable and proficient . . . profusely proficient," I added. "Well, we must continue on."

We ran past Janine and up the stairs, but I could hear Janine yell after us, " 'Continue on' is redundant!"

I didn't know what *redundant* meant, and I didn't care.

We entered Claudia's room. Claudia was sitting cross-legged on her bed while her grandmother, Mimi, brushed her hair.

Claudia's hair is absolutely beautiful. It's long and jet black and always shiny. She uses special stuff in it.

Claudia and Stacey have suddenly taken great interest in their hair. One night a week they muck it up with an egg rinse. On Wednesdays and Sundays they squeeze lemon juice on it — from real lemons. They keep telling me I should use eggs and lemons in my hair, too. I have long, l-o-n-g hair (almost down to my bottom). It's thin and fine, and so blonde it's white. Mum says it's like cornsilk. Claudia says the egg would give it body. Stacey says the lemon would make it shiny. I say it's my hair and what I do with it is my business. (I plan to try an avocado paste on it. If Claudia and Stacey and I put our heads together, we'd have a salad.)

"Hello, girls," Mimi greeted us in her gentle accent. "Is it time for your meeting?"

"Yes," Mary Anne replied, leaning over to kiss Mimi on the cheek. She and Mimi are special friends.

"Well, then, I will leave you to your work." Mimi rose and left the room, just as Stacey thundered up the stairs. She was followed a few moments later by Kristy.

"Hi, everybody!" called Kristy. "We're all here! Great. It's subs day. Did you guys bring your money? Did you bring the treasury, Stacey?"

Kristy never wastes a second. She's a

take-charge, rushing-around kind of person. Sometimes she's bossy, but not too often. Mary Anne says she used to be a lot worse, but now she tries to watch herself.

"Here's the treasury," said Stacey. She dumped the contents of the treasury (a manila envelope) onto the bed. Several dollar bills and a whole mess of quarters fell out. "Seven-fifty," she said, after counting the money quickly.

We each put in another fifty cents — our weekly subs — which brought the total to ten dollars.

"Not bad," said Kristy. "Maybe we should buy some stuff for the Kid-Kits."

Kid-Kits are boxes that we baby-sitters sometimes take along on jobs. Mostly they're filled with our old games and toys and picture books (which are new to the kids we sit for), but we also keep them stocked with colouring books, sticker books, puzzle books, and other stuff that we have to replace from time to time. We pay for those things out of club subs. The stuff we buy is worth it. Kids love our Kid-Kits, so they ask their parents to use the Babysitters Club and we end up getting more jobs. My dad always used to say, "You have to spend money to make money." He's a good businessman. And I guess Kristy is a good businesswoman.

Ring, ring.

Our first phone call. Claudia answered it.

"Hello. Babysitters Club . . . Oh, hi . . . Saturday, from three to five? I'll check around and call you right back. 'Bye." She hung up the phone.

Mary Anne had already opened the record book to the calendar section. "This Saturday?" she asked.

"Nope, the next one," replied Claudia. "That was Mrs Prezzioso. She needs someone for Jenny for two hours that afternoon. Who's free then?"

The Babysitters Club rule for calls that come in during meetings is that every member has a chance at each job. If someone calls one of us at home some other time, that's a different story. We can take those jobs on the spot, of course. But club calls are for the group.

Mary Anne checked the calendar. "We're all free then," she said.

"Well, don't worry about me," said Claudia quickly. "I — I think I might have to go shopping that day."

"Yeah, me, too," said Stacey. "With Claudia." You could tell that the idea had just occurred to them.

"And I think that . . . that I promised David Michael I'd take him to the new Disney movie then," Kristy said in a rush. David Michael is Kristy's little brother. (She also has two big brothers in high school.) As far as I know, she has never taken David Michael to a movie.

Mary Anne looked at me.

"You take the job," I said grandly.

The truth is, nobody really likes Jenny Prezzioso except Mary Anne. The rest of us think Jenny is a spoiled brat. And that her parents are weird. But Mary Anne handles the Prezziosos well, and for some reason she quite likes Jenny.

Claudia called Mrs P. back to tell her who would be sitting, and Mary Anne noted the job in the record book. Two more calls came in. The first was from Mrs Newton, needing a sitter for four-year-old Jamie (one of our all-time favourite little kids), and the other was from Watson Brewer.

Mr Brewer was calling so far in advance that once again all five of us were free, but we very generously gave the job to Kristy. That's because Mr Brewer (Kristy and the other girls call him Watson) is going to become Kristy's stepfather this autumn!

Kristy's parents got divorced a few years ago, and sometime last year Mrs Thomas started seeing this really rich man, Watson Brewer, who lives in a mansion (no kidding, a real mansion) across town. Mr Brewer is also divorced. He has two little kids, and since she's about to become their stepsister, we always let her take Mr Brewer's jobs if she's free.

Ring, ring.

This time I answered the phone. "Good afternoon. Babysitters Club."

"Hello?" said an uncertain voice on the other end of the line.

"Hello?" I said again.

"Hello, I — Mrs Pike gave me your number. I need a baby-sitter. Actually, I'm going to be needing a lot of sitters. And your organization was very highly recommended. I live on Slate Street, just down from the Pikes."

"Well," I said briskly. "Thank you very much. May I ask you some questions?" Kristy and the other club members had trained me on handling new clients.

"Never take them on without finding out certain important information first," Kristy had told me.

"How many children do you have?" I asked.

"Three," she replied. "Buddy, my oldest, is seven. He's Hamilton, Junior, actually. Suzi is four, and Marnie is the baby. She's a year and a half."

"Buddy and Suzi?" I said. "Is this Mrs Barrett?"

"Why, yes, it is."

"I met Buddy and Suzi over at the Pikes' today." I told her about Suzi's knee. Then I asked a few more questions, and after that Mrs. Barrett said nervously, "I suppose you should know that my husband and I have just got a divorce. This is a hard time for my children. I've got to find a job and they're used to having their father around, and I'm not a terribly organized person."

Wow. I could sympathize with that.

When it turned out that I was the only one available on the afternoon Mrs Barrett needed a sitter, I was secretly glad. I barely knew her kids, and already I felt close to them.

3rd CHAPTER

"Hi, I'm home!"

"Honey, I'm leaving!"

I got back to my house that evening just as Mum was on her way out to meet Mr Spier for dinner.

She kissed my forehead and ducked under the low doorway. "I should be back in a couple of hours," she told me from the front porch.

"Okay," I said. "Have fun." I started to close the door. We were letting cold air in.

"Dinner's ready for you and Jeff."

"Okay." I started to close the door again. I was freezing.

"It's in the double boiler on the stove."

"Okay —"

"And there's salad in the fridge."

"Okay." Just when it looked like I really might be able to close the door, I suddenly had to open it wide. "Mum, come back here," I said.

She ducked back inside. "What?"

"Look," I said, pointing. "Only one earring, a rubber band around your wrist, and a price tag on your skirt. Mum, for heaven's sake."

Mum laughed sheepishly. "What would I do without you, Dawn?" She pulled off the rubber band, removed the price tag, and started out the door.

"Earring!" I yelled.

"Oh, *darn*!" exclaimed Mum. "I don't know where the other one is. Does this one look too funny by itself?"

"Well, it looks sort of punk."

"*Punk!*" Mum spat the word out as if it tasted bad. She yanked off the earring and handed it to me. "I'll do without earrings," she said. "You and Jeff behave yourselves. I'll be back soon."

"Say hi to Mr Spier for me," I called.

"I will!" Mum dashed off, waving over her shoulder, and climbed into her car.

I closed the front door and stood around in the hall with my jacket on, trying to warm up. Then I walked through the living room and collected the things that didn't belong there: a can of hair spray, a bicycle pump, a jar of instant coffee, and a ladle. Sometimes I thought our entire house (except for my room) was like one big game of "What's Wrong with This Picture?"

I put the hair spray, the pump, the coffee,

the ladle, and Mum's earring away. In our dark little kitchen, I lifted the lid on the double boiler and peeked inside. I sniffed. I poked at the stuff with a fork.

"Hey, Jeff —" I started to shout.

"It's leftover stew," he called from the sitting room, before I had even asked the question.

Oh, yuck. Ew, ew, ew. Leftover Stew.

I checked our freezer. "Hey, Jeff!" I shouted again.

"There's all-natural frozen meatless pizza," he replied. "Couldn't we have that?"

"Definitely." I popped the frozen pizza in the oven. Then I wandered into the living room.

My brother was sprawled on the sofa, watching a cartoon show. "What're you going to do with the stew?" he asked.

"Put it back in the fridge. Maybe Mum will eat it."

"I wish we had a dog," Jeff said. "Dogs love leftovers." Jeff's eyes never left the TV screen.

I returned to the kitchen table and checked the pizza. Then I sat down at the table and tried to begin my homework, but I couldn't concentrate. I got up and walked slowly through our house.

I didn't care that it was dark or that the rooms were small or that everything was low down. I thought it was cosy. I was glad, however, that the kitchen and the bathrooms had been modernized. Actually, I was glad to have bathrooms at all. The old outhouse was still in our back garden, at the edge of the property. I had looked in it once. Yuck. Dark, dusty, and full of cobwebs. A Colonial kitchen might have been fun — but not very practical. I wondered how long it would take to bake a pizza in a fireplace.

Ding! The oven timer went off.

"Hey, Jeff, it's pizza!" I yelled.

Jeff dragged himself away from the TV while I went back to the kitchen. I returned the leftover stew to the refrigerator. Jeff got out plates, napkins, forks, and the salad.

We sat down across from each other. I was starving.

No sooner had I lifted a piece of steaming, spicy, melty pizza to my mouth than the phone rang.

I looked at Jeff. He was faster than me. He already had the pizza *in* his mouth. He looked at me.

"Would you puh-*lease* get the phone?" I pleaded. The pizza smelled so good it was making me dizzy.

"Mphhhyrst?" Jeff asked. He'd taken the biggest bite in the history of the world.

"Never mind." With a gigantic sigh I put the pizza back on my plate. I answered the phone on the fourth ring.

"Hi, it's me," said Mary Anne's voice.

"What are you doing?"

"Eating dinner," I replied. My mouth was watering.

"Oh. I just ate. I had a sandwich. What are you eating?"

"Pizza. Hey, I should have asked you over so you wouldn't have to eat alone."

"That's okay. Maybe next time. Listen, I had a great idea. Do you want to help me re-do my room?"

"Sure! That would be fun. Hey! You know what?"

"What?" asked Mary Anne.

"We've got some stuff I bet you could use. Our house in California was bigger than this one, and we've got boxes of things up in the attic that we don't have room for. I know there are a few posters somewhere. And there's this great reading lamp that used to be in my room. And probably some cushions, too."

"Doesn't your mum want those things?" asked Mary Anne, sounding worried. Honestly, she's the biggest worrier.

"Nah. We were going to have a garage sale, but Mum realized there wasn't really enough stuff for sale, and then she couldn't decide what to do with it, so she piled it into the downstairs bathroom and left it there. I moved it into the attic last week and she never noticed. I'm sure she's forgotten about it."

My pizza was getting cold, but I didn't

care. I was too excited about becoming an interior decorator.

"We-ell," said Mary Anne.

"Why don't I come over on Saturday?" I suggested. "I'll bring some stuff with me. If you like it, you can use it. If not, we'll think of other things to do to your room."

"Okay!" Mary Anne was beginning to sound more enthusiastic. And I understood how she felt. I love starting new projects.

Later, as I ate my pizza, I made a mental list of things to take to the Spiers' on Saturday: posters, picture frames, reading lamp, scatter cushions. Was there a bed-spread somewhere? I'd have to check.

By Saturday morning, I'd gathered so much stuff together that Mum had to drive me over to the Spiers'. This was pretty sneaky on my part, since it served three purposes: 1) I got a ride; 2) When Mary Anne saw my mother, she'd know it was okay to use our things; 3) It would give my mum and Mary Anne's dad a chance to see each other.

Unfortunately, Mary Anne's father wasn't home when we got to her house. At least I had been given a lift, though. And as Mum helped me carry the boxes inside, she said to Mary Anne, "I hope you can use these things. We don't have room for them, and I'd rather see them go to someone we know than to strangers or to the dump."

Mary Anne looked relieved. "Thanks a

lot, Mrs Schafer. Really," she said, "this is so nice of you. The cheaper we can redecorate my room, the happier Dad will be."

My mother smiled. "I remember that about your dad," she said fondly. "Kind of tight with a penny."

"Pretty tight with dollars, too," said Mary Anne. "In fact, the more dollars, the tighter he gets."

We laughed. Then Mum left, and Mary Anne and I carried the boxes up to her room. We put them on her bed and settled ourselves next to them.

Mary Anne pulled three rolled-up posters out of one box.

"Let's see what those are," I said. "I don't even remember."

Mary Anne slipped off the rubber bands. Carefully she unrolled one poster. "Oh!" she cried. "London at night!" (That's what was written under the picture.) "How pretty. Look at all the lights. I had wanted to put up a poster of New York or Paris, but London is just as good. Was this yours? I mean, did it used to be in your room?"

"Nope," I said. "That was in the kitchen, believe it or not. Our kitchen in California was huge."

Mary Anne set aside the poster of London and reached for another poster. She unrolled it and stared at it. She turned it upside down and stared some more.

"Let's see," I said.

Mary Anne turned the poster around. "It's some kind of chart —"

"Hey! That was my dad's astronomy chart. I guess he didn't want it. Those are all the constellations and stars and planets. Do you like it?"

"Yeah," she said slowly. "It's interesting, but I don't know if it's really *me*."

"Well, you don't have to decide about anything just yet."

We continued going through the boxes. After about fifteen minutes we heard a voice shout, "Hey, you guys! What are you doing?"

We looked out Mary Anne's open bedroom window — and right into Kristy's open bedroom window next door.

"Hi, Kristy!" called Mary Anne. "We're redecorating my room." She glanced at me. "Okay if I ask her over?" she whispered.

"Sure," I replied.

"Want to come over?" she yelled.

"Okay."

"Let yourself in," Mary Anne told her. "Dad's not home."

Kristy disappeared from her window. A few minutes later, we heard the Spiers' front door open and close, and then the sound of feet running up the stairs. "Hi," said Kristy. "Gosh, what's all this stuff?"

"Dawn brought it over," Mary Anne replied. "It's from their old house in

California. They don't need it any more. Dawn thought I could use it here. Dad's letting me take the baby stuff — Alice in Wonderland and Humpty Dumpty — off my walls and put up things I want — posters, a photo of the club members, if I could get one."

"He's letting you put drawing pins in the walls?" asked Kristy incredulously.

"I suppose so."

Kristy brushed her messy brown hair out of her eyes. "How come you didn't tell *me* you were going to start redecorating?"

"I don't know," Mary Anne answered hesitantly.

Kristy turned to me, but she continued to talk to Mary Anne. "You know, I might have some things you could use, too. Remember last year when we made that poster for art class and it won the prize? You could put that up. I still have it."

"You *do*?" cried Mary Anne. "That would be great! We had fun making that."

"And you know that stencil kit Watson gave me?" she went on.

"Yeah?" said Mary Anne excitedly.

"We could paint those awful pink picture frames and then stencil designs on them."

"Oh, great!"

Kristy smirked at me.

I felt completely left out.

After that, the three of us worked on Mary Anne's room for hours. We talked and planned and giggled. But I noticed two things: 1) Kristy only spoke directly to Mary Anne; 2) Kristy never laughed at my jokes. (Even though Mary Anne did.)

I was beginning to worry. I didn't think Kristy liked me very much, and that was not a good situation, since I was a member of the Babysitters Club — and she was the chairman.

4th CHAPTER

The first time I met Mary Anne Spier, she was sitting at a table all by herself in the lunchroom. It was my second day at Stoneybrook Middle School, my fourth day in Connecticut. The members of the Baby-sitters Club had just had a huge fight and were mad at each other. They weren't even speaking. They were all sitting with other friends — except for Mary Anne, who didn't have any other friends.

Ordinarily, Mary Anne sat with Kristy and the Shillaber twins. Now that she and Kristy are friends again, they're back to their usual lunch group. Sometimes I join them, sometimes I join Claudia and Stacey, who sit with a different crowd — girls *and* boys. Kristy and Mary Anne think boys are stupid. Stacey and Claudia love them. I'm deciding.

The Monday after I helped Mary Anne

redecorate her room, I sat with her, Kristy, and Mariah and Miranda (the twins), even though Kristy was giving me some pretty chilly looks.

The four of us spread our lunches out. The twins had bought the hot lunch. Ew, ew, ew. It was a greyish tuna salad, chips, limp green beans, ice-cream, and milk.

Kristy and Mary Anne and I had brought our lunches. Kristy's and Mary Anne's were the same. They had each brought a peanut butter and jam sandwich, an apple, a bag of crisps, and a carton of fruit juice. They brought that lunch almost every day. It must be the Connecticut state lunch or something.

It was nothing like what I'd brought.

"What's that you've got?" asked Kristy, pointing to my lunch.

I opened a tupperware container. "Tofu salad." I unwrapped some foil pouches. "And dried apple rings, a nut bar, and some grapefruit."

I saw Kristy and Miranda exchange looks.

Mary Anne saw it, too. She glanced at me and shrugged.

"It's very healthy," I added.

"I know," said Kristy. "Your lunches always are. They're very California, too."

"And yours are quite Connecticut," I said.

I decided to change the subject. If Kristy

wanted me to feel left out for some reason, I could do the same to her. I sighed dreamily.

"What is it?" asked Mariah.

"Oh . . . Mary Anne's dad and my mum went out on another date this weekend. On two, actually."

That got the twins' attention. "They *did*?!" they squealed at the same time.

Mary Anne and I nodded. We looked at each other and smiled.

Kristy scowled.

"Where'd they go?" asked Miranda.

"Out to dinner and the movies on Saturday night, and then out to brunch the very next morning."

"You know something?" said Miranda suddenly. "If your parents got married, you two" — Miranda nodded at Mary Anne and me — "would be *stepsisters*."

A hush fell over the table. Nobody could speak.

Mary Anne and I looked at each other. We were agape. I knew my eyes couldn't be open any wider than hers, because if they were, they'd be stretched up to the moon.

Stepsisters! Why hadn't that occurred to us?

"I never thought of that," I said softly.

"Me, neither," said Mary Anne.

"I did," Kristy mumbled.

"It would be almost as good as being twins," said Mariah.

"I'd have a brother *and* a sister!" I exclaimed.

"I've always wanted a sister," said Mary Anne.

"I thought *I* was like your sister," said Kristy.

Everyone ignored her. Everyone but me. I watched Kristy carefully for a few moments. She looked small and hurt. And suddenly I *knew*.

Kristy wasn't mad at me. She didn't dislike me. She was *jealous*. She used to be Mary Anne's best and only friend, but now Mary Anne had me, too. She didn't need Kristy so much any more. Kristy was trying to make me feel left out because she already felt left out.

I remembered how I had taken over when Mary Anne wanted to re-do her room. I had jumped in and organized things. We hadn't even asked Kristy over. And, of course, before I came to Connecticut, Kristy would have been the one in charge. No two ways about it.

I felt terrible. What could I do to make Kristy feel better? And if she felt better, would she be nicer to me?

Without knowing it, Mariah gave me a hand.

"Maybe they'll get married and have a big, beautiful wedding. Everything will be white and beautiful. And there'll be flowers all over the place," she said.

"Your mother's going to get married soon, isn't she, Kristy?" I asked.

Kristy shot me a surprised and grateful look. "In the autumn, probably," she replied.

"And then you'll have a little stepsister and a little stepbrother, right?"

"Right. Plus my three real brothers."

"Gosh, you're going to be a big family," I commented.

"Yeah," added Mary Anne, jumping in. "Four brothers and your first sister."

Kristy nodded happily. "Karen and Andrew are great."

"How's everybody going to fit in your house?" asked Miranda.

It was a good question. The Thomases' house isn't all that big. There *are* four bedrooms, but David Michael's room is more like a cupboard. In fact, it used to be a storage cupboard off the hall upstairs.

"Oh," said Kristy, "Karen and Andrew won't live with us. They live with their mother. Watson just gets them every other weekend, every other holiday, and for a couple of weeks each summer."

"But where will they stay when they're visiting?" asked Miranda.

"Actually," Kristy replied, "we don't have to make room for them. We're sort of moving."

"To a mansion," I said.

"A real mansion?" asked Miranda.

"A real mansion," said Kristy.

"I've been there," added Mary Anne. "It really is gigantic. Are you each going to get your own bedroom?"

"Sure," replied Kristy. "There are nine bedrooms in Watson's house."

"Do you get to re-decorate? I mean, can you choose the curtains and wallpaper and all?"

Kristy shrugged. "I suppose so. What I really want is exactly what's in my room right now."

Kristy was beginning to look less than thrilled, so I made one more stab at being friendly. "Kristy and I are helping Mary Anne re-decorate her room," I said.

The twins didn't seem to have heard. "How come you want what's in your room right now?" Mariah asked Kristy. "You've had that for years."

I poked at my tofu salad. "Just think," I said. "You could probably do anything you wanted to your new room. High tech or —"

Kristy was eating her sandwich. (She looked more like she wanted to kill it.) Very slowly, she put the crusts down on her paper napkin.

She brushed the crumbs off her hands.

Then she turned to look at me. "What I want," she said coolly, "is what I've got — where it is. So lay off, okay?"

"Okay," I said, frowning.

"Good." With that, Kristy stood up,

stuffed her rubbish in her brown bag, scrunched up the bag, and left. "See you guys later," she said over her shoulder.

"Later," said Mariah and Miranda.

I looked at Mary Anne. I wanted to say, "What'd I do?" but before I could ask the question, Mary Anne said simply, "She doesn't want to move."

"Oh," I replied. I had made another mistake. And then, "*Oh.*" Kristy was letting me know that I was still an outsider, at least at *her* lunch table.

After school that day, I went over to Mary Anne's house. The sunshine was warm on my shoulders as we walked along.

"Almost like California," I told her. "Like California in December. But that's okay. It's better than nothing."

"You really miss it, don't you?" Mary Anne said. "California, I mean."

"Yeah, I really do. I suppose if I'd grown up here in Stoneybrook, I'd be happy here and love the weather. But I didn't and I'm not, so I don't."

"You're not happy?" Mary Anne asked. She looked disappointed.

"Oh," I said, "I'm not *un*happy. I just miss things, that's all. Think how you'd feel if your father suddenly moved to California. You'd probably hate it. At least at first."

"I guess you're right. But I want you to be happy here."

"Hey!" I said. I smiled. "I'm not

complaining — about anything except the weather. You're great, your friends are great, the Babysitters Club is great. And between us, you and I might end up with a whole family again. What more could I ask for?"

"A million bucks?" Mary Anne suggested.

"That'd be nice. And maybe a swimming pool."

"And no more school."

"And eighty-degree weather all year round."

"And a lifetime supply of ice-cream."

"And a pet baboon."

Mary Anne giggled. "And . . . and . . . Hey, there's Kristy! Just up ahead. Kristy! Kristy!" she called.

Kristy turned around. "Yeah?"

"Wait!" Mary Anne shouted. We ran to catch up with Kristy.

Even as we were running, I could see that Kristy was not pleased to see us. At any rate, she wasn't pleased to see me. I'm sure she thought I was hogging Mary Anne again.

"Hi," said Mary Anne, as we reached Kristy. "Are you baby-sitting this afternoon?"

"Yeah, for Jamie. What are you guys doing?"

"We're . . ." Mary Anne started to say. "We're . . ." She didn't know how to finish the sentence.

The problem was that we were going to work on her room some more, and she had realized that that was a touchy subject.

"Going to work on your room?" asked Kristy.

Mary Anne nodded.

"I thought so."

I shifted from one foot to the other. "Too bad you're baby-sitting," I said. "If you weren't, you could help us."

"Yeah, too bad," Kristy said sarcastically.

I glanced at Mary Anne.

She looked at me and shrugged.

"Want to help us tomorrow?" I asked.

"Can't. I'm sitting for David Michael."

Mary Anne looked at the ground.

"Well," I said, after a pause, "we'll see you at the meeting this afternoon. Have fun."

"Okay. See you." Kristy turned into the Newtons' driveway, leaving us behind.

I looked at Mary Anne. She looked at me.

"Is she mad?" Mary Anne asked, nodding toward Kristy.

"Nope," I replied. "She's jealous."

5th CHAPTER

On the afternoon of Tuesday, April 28, I let out a cheer and congratulated the weatherman from WSTO (the local radio station). He was the one who said the day before that the weather would turn sunny and the temperature would rise to seventy-eight.

He was right.

Maybe there would be summer in Connecticut after all.

I took the beautiful weather as a sign that things would go well when I baby-sat for the club's new clients that afternoon. It was my day to take care of Buddy, Suzi, and Marnie Barrett, and I was looking forward to it.

When I rang the Barretts' bell that afternoon, the door was opened by Suzi, looking timid.

"Hi, Suzi," I said. "I'm Dawn. I fixed your knee. Do you remember?"

She nodded.

"Well, I'm going to baby-sit for you today. Is your mum here?"

Suzi nodded again.

At that moment a small, curly blonde head peeped around Suzi.

"Marnie?" I guessed.

Suzi nodded.

"May I come in?" I asked finally.

Suzi nodded.

I stepped into the hallway. "Hello?" I called.

"YAH! YAH! Bang-bang-bang!"

I jumped a mile as Buddy, wearing a cowboy hat and swimming flippers, galloped out of the living room. He was pointing a ray gun at me.

"Shpoof! You're burned! You're a goner!" he cried.

I raised an eyebrow. Then, ever so casually, I leaned over and took the gun from him. "Hello," I said. "I'm Dawn Schafer. I met you at the Pikes'. And I'm your baby-sitter. I don't like guns. So no guns when I'm around. That goes for you guys, too," I told Suzi and Marnie.

Suzi nodded.

Marnie stared at me with wide blue eyes.

I noticed that Suzi's jumper was coming unbuttoned, and that Marnie's nappy was drooping and the hem was falling out of her overalls. A grubby bandage was wrapped around one of Buddy's fingers. All three kids needed to have their hair brushed.

I looked in the living room. It was a sight. Newspapers and toys were scattered everywhere. A plateful of crumbs sat under a lamp. Something red had been spilled on the coffee table and was never wiped up. Our house might have been disorganized, but the Barretts' house was a pigsty.

I dared to glance in the kitchen. What a mistake. The sink was overflowing with pots and dishes, napkins and lolly wrappers, and about a million TV dinner trays. The breakfast dishes were still on the table. I could tell exactly what Mrs Barrett had served because the remains were in plain view. Soft-boiled eggs (the yolks, now crusty, glued to the plates), orange juice (dried pulp in the glasses), bananas (peels on the table), and toast (crusts stuck in a glass).

Yuck. Ew, ew, ew.

I was still looking around when I heard footsteps on the stairs. I turned and saw an absolutely gorgeous young woman rushing toward us. She looked like a model. Honest. She was wearing a silk blouse, a sleek linen suit, brown heels, and gold jewellery — not too much, but enough so you noticed it. Her hair fell away from her face in chestnut curls and she smelled of a heavenly perfume.

"Dawn?" she asked breathlessly.

"Yes. Hi, Mrs Barrett."

"Thank you for coming." She flashed me

a warm smile, then quickly kissed Marnie, Suzi, and Buddy in turn.

"So long, darlings. Be good for Dawn." She rushed to the front door.

"Wait!" I called. "Where are you going to be?"

"On a job interview. And I'm late. Buddy, be a sweetheart and let Pow in the back door. I can hear him whining." Mrs Barrett was halfway down the pathway.

"Hey, what am I supposed to do this afternoon?" Where were the special instructions? Snacktime at four o'clock or help with homework, or *some*thing.

Mrs Barrett paused. For a moment her beautiful face looked confused. "Just . . . sit," she said.

"What if — what if there's an emergency?" I asked. "How do I reach you?"

"I'll be at Mason and Company. It's on Spring Street. Or call the Pikes, okay?"

"Well . . ." (Mrs Barrett's car zoomed backwards up the driveway.) ". . . all right," I finished, as she waved to us from the window and sped away.

I looked at the Barrett kids. They looked at me.

"You guys ever see *Mary Poppins*?" I asked.

They shook their heads.

Darn. I'd thought I could get them to tidy up the living room by pretending we were Mary Poppins and Jane and Michael

Banks, cleaning up the nursery.

"Well, how'd you like to surprise your mother?"

"Okay!" said Buddy. I could tell he'd do anything for her.

"We're going to surprise her with a clean house."

"We are?" asked Buddy suspiciously.

"Yup. First go and let Pow in, then I'll tell you what we're going to do."

"All right."

Buddy disappeared. While he was gone, I buttoned Suzi's jumper and rolled up the cuffs of Marine's overalls. Then I pulled a brush out of my purse and ran it through Marnie's curls. "We'll do your hair later," I told Suzi. "We'll have to take the plaits out first."

Suzi nodded.

Buddy returned, followed by a sleepy-looking basset hound. "This is Pow," he announced. "The meanest dog that ever lived."

Pow's eyelids drooped. He rolled over on his side.

"Are you sure?" I asked.

"Yup," replied Buddy.

"This must be an off day," I said as Pow fell asleep. "Okay, you guys, are you ready for a game? I'm going to time us to see how fast we can clean up the living room. Take anything that doesn't belong in there and put it where it does belong. Tidy everything else up. But be careful. Don't work so fast you break something. We'll have to add time to our score if we break anything." I looked at my watch. The second hand was approaching the twelve.

"Take your marks." Suzi and Buddy and I crowded into the doorway to the living room. Buddy removed the swimming flippers. (Marnie didn't know what was going on.)

"Get set." We crouched down.

"GO!"

We ran into the living room and a flurry of activity began. Buddy found three plates and ran them into the kitchen.

"Bring the sponge back with you!" I yelled.

Buddy returned and threw me the sponge. I wiped up the coffee table while Suzi collected newspapers.

"Does your mum save the papers?" I asked.

Suzi shook her head.

"Then stack them up," I told her. "We'll make a bundle for the rubbish collector."

Suzi stacked, I straightened cushions, Buddy rounded up toys, and Marnie helped him.

Within minutes the room looked as if it belonged in a different house, or maybe even in a TV commercial. I checked my watch. "Six minutes and seventeen seconds!" I announced.

"Is that a record?" exclaimed Buddy.

"It might be," I said. "But not if we break it cleaning up the kitchen. Shall we try to break our record?"

"Yes, yes, yes!" shouted Buddy.

Suzi smiled shyly at me. Her eyes were shining.

Marnie scrunched up her face and wrinkled her nose.

"That's the ham face," Buddy informed me. "She only makes it when she's happy."

I grinned. "All right, everybody, here are the special instructions for the Kitchen Race. I'm in charge of putting dishes in the dish-washer. You guys bring dirty dishes to me and I'll take care of them. Rubbish goes in the dustbin, and anything that doesn't belong in the kitchen goes to the room it belongs in. Got it?"

"Got it," said Buddy.

"Got it," said Suzi.

Marnie made the ham face.

"Take your marks," I cried. "Get set, go!"

The kitchen was tougher than the living room. It took longer than I had thought it would to rinse the plates and glasses and put them in the dishwasher, but we worked hard, anyway. Suzi cleaned the rubbish out of the sink and put it in the dustbin. Buddy swept the floor. Marnie found a bag of M&M's and began eating them. I stopped her, gave her a paper towel, and showed her how to mop up the floor around Pow's water bowl.

When we had finished, I looked at my watch again. "Well, we didn't break our record, I'm afraid. That took eleven minutes and forty-eight seconds."

"Darn," said Buddy.

"Yeah, darn," said Suzi.

"Let's clean up the playroom," Buddy suggested. "That's a real mess. If we break the record in there, it'll be a miracle."

So we straightened up the playroom, too. (We did not break our record.) Mrs Barrett wasn't going to recognize her own house when she got home.

The Barrett kids and I flopped on the couch in the playroom. Pow wandered in. Buddy aimed a finger at him. "Blam, blam!" he shrieked.

I covered Buddy's hand with my own. "Hey, remember what I said about guns," I warned him. "Not while I'm around."

"So? Who says you're the boss?" Buddy asked defiantly. He leaped up and stood in front of me, legs spread, cowboy hat askew. Very slowly, he raised his gun finger and aimed it at me.

"Buddy," I said calmly, "while I am baby-sitting, I am the boss. I'm in charge. And I say no guns."

"Why?"

"Because real guns are very dangerous. They are not toys. And I don't think we should ever pretend they are toys. There are plenty of other things we can pretend instead."

"Like what?"

"Like I'm a hairdresser, and you're a father, and Suzi and Marnie are your kids and you decide to take them to get their hair fixed."

Buddy considered this. "I'm the daddy?" he asked.

"Yup."

"I'm the boss of them?" He pointed to his sisters.

"Yup."

"Okay."

So I accomplished two things. I replaited Suzi's hair (and even brushed Buddy's), and I took Buddy's mind off guns. Buddy wasn't going to be playing with guns while I was around.

By five o'clock, the kids were getting tired and irritable. Buddy yelled at Pow. Marnie stopped making the ham face. Suzi stopped talking and started nodding again.

"Do you have a daddy?" Buddy asked me suddenly.

We were sitting on the floor in the playroom. I looked at him in surprise. "Well, yes," I replied. "But not here. I mean, he doesn't live with us."

"Really?" said Buddy.

I sighed. "Yeah. He's in California. Three thousand miles away."

Buddy nodded knowingly. He looked like a little old man. "We don't have our daddy, either."

"My mum and dad are divorced," I explained.

"So are ours," said Buddy.

"I know."

Suzi had been helping Marnie build a tower of paper cups. She looked up with interest. "I wonder how long divorce lasts," she said.

"It's for ever," I replied, surprised.

"That's what Mummy said, but . . ."

"But you keep hoping your dad will come back?"

"Yeah," said Buddy and Suzi at the same time.

"Me, too," I said, "except I know he won't."

"Do you miss your dad?" asked Buddy.

"Very much."

"Me, too."

Buddy moved over until he was sitting next to me. I put my arm around him. Then I held my other arm out to Suzi, but instead of joining us, she jumped to her feet.

"You. Are. A. Liar!" she cried, pointing her finger at me. "A *liar*." Then she ran out of the playroom and upstairs.

"What did I say?" I asked Buddy.

Buddy frowned. "I think it was the part about daddies not coming back. She *really* thinks ours is going to come home for good one day."

"Hmm," I said. "Well, we'll leave her alone for a while."

Buddy turned on a cartoon show and settled down to watch. After a while I decided to take Marnie upstairs to change her nappy. Marnie shared a room with Suzi, but Suzi wasn't in the room. The door to the bathroom was closed, however.

As I was finishing with Marnie, the bathroom door opened a crack. Suzi peeked through. "Dawn?" she asked.

"Yeah?"

"I – I had an accident." Suzi scrunched up her face and began to cry.

"Hey, that's okay," I said. "Accidents happen." I put Marnie in her cot, and stepped into the bathroom, closing the door behind me.

"I wet my pants," Suzi moaned.

"It's really all right," I told her. I grabbed some paper towels and mopped up the puddle on the tile floor.

"Do we have to tell Mummy?" asked Suzi.

"Not if you don't want to. Here, we'll rinse out your trousers and your underwear, and get you some clean ones. Then you'll be all set."

By the time Suzi and Marnie and I were on our way downstairs, Suzi was smiling again. A few minutes later, Mrs Barrett came home. I wish I'd had a camera so I could have recorded the look on her face when she saw the clean house.

"You're a wonder, Dawn!" she exclaimed.

"She's the best baby-sitter we ever had," said Buddy.

"She's our favourite," Suzi chimed in.

"I hope you'll come back," said Mrs Barrett as she paid me.

"Any time," I told her cheerfully.

If I had only known then how often "any time" was going to be, I might not have spoken so quickly.

6th CHAPTER

Saturday, May 2

I baby-sat for Karen and Andrew for four hours this afternoon. Karen invited a friend over and the four of us played "Let's All Come In." We had a scary encounter with Mrs Porter and she did some witchy things, but nothing happened. Boo-Boo is terrified of her now and stays inside, so there weren't any problems. He slept in one of the second-floor bedrooms most of the afternoon. Karen says he used to go on the third floor, but that their attic is haunted, so he won't go any higher than the second story. Karen's got a real thing about this haunted attic, which you guys should be aware of when you sit at Watson's. I'm trying to convince her it's not haunted— without actually having to go in it myself.

Kristy is so lucky. I wish Andrew and Karen were going to be *my* little stepsister and stepbrother. I baby-sat for them once and they were lots of fun and really cute, even if Andrew is a bit shy and Karen talks too much.

I asked Kristy lots of questions about her afternoon there because I was trying extra hard to be friendly to her. Kristy always opens up where Andrew and Karen are concerned. This is what she told me.

As soon as Mr Brewer left, Karen pulled Kristy into the living room and said, "Let's play 'Let's All Come In'. *Please*."

"Okay," said Kristy, "but I don't think we really have enough people. Wouldn't the game be better with four?"

"Let's All Come In" is a game Karen invented herself. Karen has just turned six and she's very clever. She started out in kindergarten last autumn and was skipped into junior school after Christmas. She didn't have a bit of trouble, and now she reads like crazy and can add and subtract almost as fast as I can.

Her game is about the guests who come to a big, fancy, old-fashioned hotel. Karen always makes Kristy (or the oldest person) the bell captain. Then she and Andrew and her friends take turns entering the lobby as hotel workers or exotic guests — wealthy old women in furs, sea captains, famous people. Karen and Andrew have an amazing collection of "dressing up" clothes, so they can put on a good costume for just about every character. And Mr Brewer's living room is perfect for a lobby.

As I've mentioned, Mr Brewer is rich and his house is a mansion. It's full of expensive things, but he hasn't turned it into a museum. What I mean is that Karen and Andrew are allowed in the living room, the dining room, the study, etc, even though there are antiques and breakables everywhere. As far as I know, they're always careful. Maybe it's because they know their father trusts them.

Anyway, Mr Brewer's living room is gigantic — big enough for a grand piano, and even a little tree, which stands in a brass tub near the fireplace. There are three couches, five armchairs, a long glass coffee table, several end tables, and a crystal chandelier. Instead of carpeting, Mr Brewer has put small Oriental rugs down and keeps the wooden floor polished. The room does look like a hotel lobby, if you squint your eyes and use your imagination, which Kristy and Karen and even Andrew (although he's not quite four) can do just fine.

"I know who the fourth person for our game could be," Karen told Kristy that Saturday afternoon.

"Who?'

"Hannie Papadakis."

Hannie is one of Karen's new junior school friends. She lives across the street and two mansions down from the Brewers. Kristy had met Hannie a couple of times and liked her.

"Okay," said Kristy. "Let's call her. You invite her over, but I'll have to talk to her mother or father."

(A good baby-sitter always includes parents in plans for younger children. Kristy knew that Mr and Mrs Papadakis might not want Hannie going to a house with a baby-sitter in charge instead of a parent.)

But Mr Papadakis said it was fine for Hannie to come over, and a few minutes later, Hannie was ringing the Brewers' front bell.

Karen and Andrew ran to answer it.

"See who's there before you open the door," Kristy cautioned them. (You can't be too careful.)

Karen peered out of the left window, Andrew peered out the right. "It's Hannie!" they called at the same time.

"Okay, let her in."

Karen hauled open the door and led Hannie into the living room. "Are you ready for 'Let's All Come In'?" Karen asked her excitedly. "That's what we're playing today." Sometimes Karen can be bossy. I'm surprised she and Kristy get along so well.

"I'm all ready," replied Hannie, who has played often. "First I'm going to be Mrs Noswimple."

"Okay," said Karen. "Kristy, you go behind the desk. Andrew, you be the bellboy."

As the youngest, Andrew often gets stuck with parts like lift operator or bellboy, or less important characters such as somebody's little boy. Once, Karen made him play a pet cocker spaniel.

Kristy sat on the floor behind the coffee table. Karen had placed a pencil, a writing book, and a bell in front of her.

"Hannie, come and put on your Mrs Noswimple outfit. Andrew, get your cap and jacket."

The kids ran up the stairs to the playroom on the second floor. A few minutes later, they ran back down. Andrew was wearing a red cap and a blue jacket decorated with gold braid. Hannie was wearing a skirt that reached to the floor, large, sparkly high heels with no toes, a fur stole, and a hat with a veil. In one hand, she carried a pair of spectacles attached to a diamond-studded stick. Behind her, Karen was dressed as Mrs Mysterious, all in black, including a black eye patch and a black wig.

"Places, you guys!" Karen directed.

Andrew ran to stand next to Kristy's "desk", Karen waited in the foyer since guests only come into the hotel one at a time, and Hannie made her entrance.

She walked into the hotel lobby as grandly as was possible, considering she was clumping around in shoes that were six sizes too big for her. "Hell*oo*," she called in a high, thin voice.

"Good day," replied Kristy. "Won't you come in, Mrs Noswimple. How nice to see you."

"Why, thank you," replied Hannie. "I'm just staying for one night this time, Mr Bill Capstan." (Hannie has never once pronounced "bell captain" properly.) "I'm meeting my husband in Canada tomorrow. We're going to go to a party with the Queen. And the Emperor."

"How lovely," said Kristy. "Does the Emperor have new clothes?"

"Oh, yes. He has a new suit of silver," replied Hannie, not getting the joke.

"Oh," said Kristy. "Well, why don't you sign the registration book and then the bellboy here will help you to your room."

"Okay." Hannie bent over the writing book, pencil poised. "Kristy," she whispered, "how do you spell 'Noswimple'?"

Kristy spelled it out and Hannie printed the name painstakingly. She straightened up. "Ready, bellboy? I have two trunks and a hatbox, so I need lots of help."

"Ready, Mrs Noswimple," said Andrew.

Andrew and Hannie left the living room and Karen entered.

"I don't believe it!" cried Kristy. "Mrs Mysterious! What a surprise! How nice to see you. You haven't stopped by in ages."

"Heh, heh," cackled Karen. "I've been at a Mysterious Meeting in Transylvania. All the witches and warlocks and ghosts and spooks and mysterious people got together."

"Well, you're looking especially mysterious today," said Kristy.

"Thank you," Karen answered politely. "I do look mysterious, don't I." It was a statement, not a question. Karen stepped over to one of the floor-to-ceiling windows that look out on the Brewers' front lawn. "This is a mirror," she told Kristy. "I'll just —"

Karen stopped midsentence. She shrieked.

So did Kristy.

Andrew and Hannie ran into the living room to see what was happening. Andrew gasped and hid behind an armchair. Hannie opened her eyes and mouth wide, but couldn't make a sound.

Kristy told me later that she was so surprised she thought she was going to faint.

What everyone had seen when Karen stepped in front of her "mirror" was another scary, black-clad figure. Only it wasn't Karen's reflection. It was someone outside the window — Mrs Porter from next door.

The thing about Mrs Porter is that Karen is convinced she's a witch whose real name is Morbidda Destiny. Karen's got everyone — Andrew, Hannie, Kristy, and all of us baby-sitters (especially Mary Anne) thinking she's a witch, too. So it was no wonder everyone panicked.

Mrs Porter gestured toward the front door with a wave of her cape.

"Yipes," said Kristy, heart pounding. "I wonder what she wants."

"Probably frogs' noses or the hair from a mole or something. I bet she's cooking," Karen offered.

"Don't be silly," said Kristy.

With legs that felt as heavy as lead, Kristy opened the front door — just a crack.

Mrs Porter was standing on the front steps. She was leaning over so that her nose poked into Kristy's face.

Kristy jumped back.

"I rang your bell," Mrs Porter said in a croaky voice, "but you didn't answer."

"Sometimes it doesn't work," Karen spoke up timidly from where she was hiding behind Kristy.

"Can — can I help you?" Kristy asked. The last time Mrs Porter had come to the door, it was to dump poor fat old Boo-Boo, the Brewers' cat, inside after he had left the remains of a mouse on Mrs Porter's front porch.

"I'm cooking. I need to borrow something."

Kristy noticed that Mrs Porter had a little scar near the corner of her mouth that jumped around when she spoke.

Karen nudged Kristy's back. "I told you so," she whispered. "Morbidda Destiny is *cooking*."

Kristy nudged Karen back. "What do you need, Mrs Porter?"

"Fennel and coriander."

"Aughh!" screamed Karen.

"Aughh!" screamed Andrew and Hannie, who were watching from the safety of the living room.

"Shh," said Kristy. "They're just herbs, you guys." She turned back to Mrs Porter. "I'm really sorry, but I'm sure Mr Brewer doesn't have those things. He's not much of a cook."

"Well, it never hurts to ask." Mrs Porter turned abruptly and dashed down the front steps and across the lawn towards her house. Her black cape and dress flapped in the breeze.

Karen, Andrew, and Hannie found the courage to run to the front door and watch her leave. Kristy watched with them. They saw her pause at her herb garden and examine the new green shoots. They saw her flap up the steps to her own front porch. And they all saw her take up a broom and carry it into the house, talking to it.

Kristy closed the door before the kids could panic again. As she did so, something occurred to her. "Karen," she said, "where's Boo-Boo?"

"Well," replied Karen, "I'm not sure. But he's probably upstairs. I'll show you where." Karen ran up the stairs, the others at her heels.

She ran down the long hallway past the playroom, past her room, past Andrew's room, and past two guest rooms to a room at the end of the hall.

Kristy looked inside. Curled up at the foot of the bed was Boo-Boo, the world's fattest cat.

"Oh, good," said Kristy with a sigh. "I was afraid he might be out in Mrs Porter's garden again."

"Nope," said Karen. "He's scared of her now. He stays inside all day. Mostly he stays right here. And he never goes up to the third floor any more. You know why?"

"Why? I'm afraid to ask."

"Because the attic is haunted."

"Karen . . ." Kristy warned.

"It is?" said Hannie in amazement.

Karen nodded solemnly. "Animals know those things. Our attic is haunted. It's haunted by the ghost of old Ben Brewer, Daddy's great-grandfather, who —"

Kristy cut Karen off. Karen's imagination frequently ran away, and when it did, it took Andrew and Hannie along with it.

"Come on, you guys. Let's go back to 'Let's All Come In'."

So the kids returned to the living room and took up the game again. They were still playing when Mr Brewer came home.

Kristy sighed as she left. She'd had fun. But she was pretty sure she hadn't heard the last about old Ben Brewer.

7th CHAPTER

I had to do something about Kristy. I was trying my hardest to be nice to her, but things were no better between us. So one day at school, out of the clear blue, I said to her, "Want to come over to my house this afternoon?" I didn't even know I was going to say it. It just slipped out. I was as surprised as Kristy was.

And we were both pretty surprised when she replied, "Okay. Sure."

What had I got myself into? What would Kristy and I do? Every time we talked, it turned into an argument. Well, I thought, we could always watch a movie on the video. I hadn't seen *The Sound of Music* in a while.

After school that day, I met Kristy and we walked to my house together. Mary Anne didn't walk with us. She was baby-sitting for Charlotte Johanssen, and the

Johanssens live in the opposite direction from me. That was just as well, since Mary Anne is sort of the cause of our problems. Kristy and I needed some time alone together.

At first we walked along in silence. Kristy stared at the ground. She didn't look mad, but I felt uncomfortable being silent with her.

"We live in an old farmhouse," I told her, just to make conversation. "It was built in seventeen-ninety-five."

"Oh, yeah?" said Kristy.

Was she interested, or did she think I was bragging?

"Yeah," I replied uncertainly.

"Do you like it?"

"Mostly. It's great living in a place that old. But the rooms are kind of small and the doorways are low. The first time Mary Anne came over, she said the colonists must have been midgets."

Kristy burst out laughing. Then she caught herself and scowled. She pressed her lips into two straight lines. Thin lips are never a good sign.

I cringed. How could I have mentioned Mary Anne? I really hadn't meant to.

I went on about the house some more. "When the house was first built," I said, "there was nothing but farmland for miles around it. But Stoneybrook kept growing, and the people who owned the house kept selling off land until finally there was just one and a half acres left, with the house, a shed, a barn, and an old smokehouse. It sort of got rundown. By the time my mum bought the place, nobody had lived on the property for two years. We got it cheap."

"You have a barn on your property?" Kristy asked with interest.

"Mm-hmm."

"Do you play in it?"

"Well," I said, "we're not supposed to go in it too much, but sometimes my brother and I play there."

"Why aren't you supposed to go in it?"

"Because it's so old. Mum's afraid the roof will come crashing down sometime. She may be right."

"You don't have any animals, do you?" asked Kristy.

"You mean in the barn?" I shook my head. "But the people who lived there before us must have. There are still bales of hay sitting around, and there's tons of hay in the hayloft. Sometimes Jeff — that's my brother — and I go up in the loft. There are great places to hide, and we rigged up a rope so that we can swing down from this beam way high up under the roof, and land in the hay."

"*Really*?" said Kristy.

"Yup."

She paused. Then she said, "I guess you

and Mary Anne play in the barn all the time."

"Mary Anne?" I exclaimed. "Not a chance. She won't jump off the beam into the hayloft. She won't even go inside because of what Mum said about the roof. She may have changed this spring, but not that much."

Kristy looked at me and grinned.

When we got home, the front door was locked, so I let myself in with the key. Back in California, I never needed a key. Mum was always home. Now I'm in danger of becoming a latchkey kid.

I almost said so, but luckily remembered just in time that Kristy has been a latchkey kid for years. Instead I said, "I wonder where my mum went."

We found out as soon as we walked into the kitchen. Stuck to the fridge with a magnet shaped like a pair of lips was a note that said:

Hi, kids! I've gone on two interviews. Back at five. Love, Mum. P.S. Do not, under any circumstances, touch the tofu-ginger salad in the refrigerator.

Kristy looked at me wide-eyed. "You mean there's a chance someone would?"

I tried to glare at her, but it turned into a smile. "Yes," I replied. "We all happen to love tofu-ginger salad. It's good . . .

Really," I added, as Kristy made gagging noises.

I looked helplessly around the kitchen. "You're probably hungry, aren't you?"

"Starved," Kristy said, "But – but not so starved I'd eat tofu or sunflower seeds or something. I don't suppose you have any peanut butter."

"Sugar-free and unsalted, made from organically grown peanuts."

"That'll do. Any jam or honey?"

"Raw honey. We've already scooped the comb out."

"Wonder Bread?"

"High-fibre wheat-and-bran."

Kristy made do with the peanut butter, honey, and bread. I ate some yoghurt with wheat germ in it.

Jeff came home, ate a banana, and went over to the Pikes' to play with the triplets.

When he was gone, I looked at Kristy. "Well," I said, "what do you want to do? We could watch a movie on the video. Or I could show you my room. Or we could search the house for a secret passageway."

"Could we go in the barn?" asked Kristy.

"Sure," I said. "As long as we're careful."

We ran out the back door and across the yard to the barn. We didn't even need our jackets since the hayloft gets pretty warm on a sunny day.

The main entrance to the barn (which, I

should say, is not a very big barn) is a pair of sliding doors on one end. We leave one of the doors partway open all the time. We've stored some stuff in one of the horse stalls, but nothing that's worth stealing.

Kristy and I stepped through the opening. "Ooh," said Kristy. "It smells . . . like a barn. I mean, even without the animals."

"I know," I said. "Isn't it great? You could almost imagine you were on a big old farm out in the middle of nowhere."

(I think the barn-smell comes mostly from the hay.)

We walked down the aisle between two rows of stalls. The stalls had long ago been cleaned out, and the harnesses and tools that had once hung on the walls had been removed, but here and there a nameplate remained.

Kristy read a few of them aloud. "Dobbs, Grey Boy, Cornflower."

Aside from the stalls and some old feeding troughs, there wasn't much to see.

"How do you get to the hayloft?" asked Kristy.

"This way," I said. I led her to the end of the barn. A ladder was leaning against the loft, which was just a couple of feet above my head.

We climbed up and Kristy walked around in the hay. "Mmm," she said. "It's soft — sort of. And it smells good." She looked up. The roof was high above us. The sun shone through the cracks and caught the dust motes in its light.

"Great," said Kristy. "It's so *quiet* in here."

"You want to swing from the rope?" I asked.

"Sure. I mean, I think so. How high up is it?"

"I'll show you." A series of wooden blocks were built into the wall above the loft. They went up and up and up. I climbed them until I reached a beam that was twelve feet above the hayloft. (Jeff and I measured once.)

"Swing that rope up to me," I called to Kristy.

Kristy looked doubtfully at the rope, then at me. "All the way up there?" she said.

"Sure, it's easy. Just try it."

Kristy took hold of the end of the rope and swung it over and up.

I missed it by inches.

We tried again and I caught it. "Watch this!" I yelled. Holding onto the knot that Jeff had tied near the bottom of the rope, I pushed away from the wall and sailed out and down. When I had almost reached the outer wall of the barn I let go and landed with a thump in the hay. "*Oof*. Oh, that was great! Do you want to try?" I stood up, brushing the hay off my jeans.

"I guess so." Kristy began her ascent. She was climbing the wall awfully slowly.

"You don't have to go all the way to the beam, if you don't want," I told her.

"No — I can do it."

Kristy sat shakily on the beam. I tossed the rope to her. The expression on her face as she flew through the air changed from sheer horror ("Let go! Let go!" I screeched as she approached the opposite wall) to amazement to joy (when she landed).

She sat in the hay for a moment, then leaped up and exclaimed, "Oh, wow! That was terrific!"

We each took five more turns, Kristy looking cockier every time. Then we lay on our backs in the loft, gazing at the roof and watching the sunlight grow dimmer.

We began to talk. We talked about divorces. (They should be against the law," said Kristy. I agreed.) We talked about moving. ("Across town is nothing compared to across the country," I pointed out. Kristy agreed.) We talked about the Baby-sitters Club. ("It's more important to me than school," I said. Kristy understood.)

Then we talked about Mary Anne. After saying some boring things like how good she looked in her new clothes, Kristy said, "I'm glad she made a new friend."

"Really?" I asked.

"Yes. She needs new friends."

"Well, I'm glad she still has her old friends."

"You know, I've been thinking," said

Kristy. "We should have an alternate officer for our club. Somebody who could take over any job if one of us can't be at a meeting. Someone who understands each office. Would you like to be Official Alternate Officer?"

"Definitely!" I replied. And that was how, all in one day, I patched up my problems with Kristy and became Official Alternate Officer of the Babysitters Club.

8th CHAPTER

The spring was growing warmer and warmer. For several days in a row, the temperature reached eighty degrees. Mary Anne said that this was abnormal, which I took as both good news and bad news.

The good news was that maybe we'd continue to have abnormally warm weather, which would be a kind way to ease me through my first spring in Connecticut. The bad news was that maybe next year we would have an abnormally cool spring (to make up for this year), which would be cruel to my system.

I think I'm cold-blooded.

One of those eighty-degree days was a Saturday, and I had a baby-sitting job with the Barretts. I had been there several times by then. I was looking forward to the day not only because it was going to be warm (hot!) and because I liked the Barrett kids, but because Stacey and Claudia were going to be sitting down the street at the Pikes', and we had plans to get together with our charges.

The reason both Stacey and Claudia were going to be sitting for the Pikes was because all eight children were going to be there.

Mrs Barrett had asked me to show up at 8.15 on Saturday morning. Yuck. I like to sleep late. But Mrs Barrett had found a seminar she wanted to go to that would help her with her job search. It was an all-day affair that started at eight-thirty in the morning.

Despite the fact that I had sat at the Barretts' on Thursday — just two days earlier — the house was in its usual messy state when I got there on Saturday. Furthermore, although Mrs Barrett came downstairs looking stunning, Buddy, Suzi, and Marnie were still in their pyjamas. Their beds were unmade, they had not eaten breakfast, their hair was a fright and Marnie's nappy badly needed to be changed.

Mrs Barrett didn't mention any of this, though. She didn't give me any instructions, either, just dashed out of the house, saying that the number where she could be reached was taped to the phone. At least she had remembered to do that.

The kids gathered around me in the kitchen, and looked at me expectantly.

"How long are you staying?" asked Buddy.

"All day," I replied, feeling less than enthusiastic.

"Yea!" cried Buddy and Suzi. They jumped up and down.

Marnie made the ham face.

I felt better.

I changed Marnie's nappy. Then I asked the kids if they were hungry.

"Yes!" chorused Suzi and Buddy.

Well, first things first. I decided to give the kids breakfast. After breakfast I would get them dressed and help them make their beds and clean up their rooms. The day began to take shape. They could play outside until about twelve-thirty, then have lunch. Around one-thirty the girls would go down for naps, and maybe, I would have a quiet time with Buddy. After that, more playtime, then some races to clean up the living room and playroom.

I made a mental schedule as I settled the kids at the kitchen table. The only thing I forgot to figure in was playing with Claudia, Stacey, and the Pike kids.

My mental schedule called for breakfast to be over at 9.15.

At 9.20, Buddy asked for more cereal.

At 9.22, Pow whined to be let in.

At 9.25, Marnie spilled Suzi's orange juice.

At 9.28, Suzi was still yelling at Marnie.

At 9.31, Pow whined to be let out.

At 9.34, I was still cleaning up the table. (The schedule called for the kids to be dressed by 9.45. I revised the schedule, deciding that the kids could be dressed by 10.15, and chopped half an hour off their morning playtime.)

At 9.50, Claudia called and suggested having a picnic lunch in the Pikes' backyard with all the kids. She asked if we could bring sandwiches for ourselves and bake brownies for everyone. She said she thought the picnic should start at one o'clock.

One o'clock! I'd never get Marnie and Suzi down for naps by one-thirty. I revised the schedule, shortening playtime again, then adding brownie-making time. If the kids were dressed and their rooms straightened by ten thirty, we might be ready for the picnic by one o'clock.

"How would you guys like to have picnic lunch at the Pikes'?" I asked.

I got a yeah from Buddy, a yeah from Suzi, and a ham face from Marnie.

"Okay," I told them. "Then we have a lot to do this morning. You've got to get dressed and tidy up your rooms, and — guess what — we're going to make brownies for the picnic!"

"Oh, boy!" cried Buddy. "Can we start right now?"

"Nope," I told him. "Not until you and your sisters are ready for the day."

"We're ready for the day," he said.

"Not in your pyjamas you aren't. Come on, everybody."

Dressing, bed-making, and room-straightening went much more slowly than I could have imagined. I thought about having cleaning races, but decided not to over-use the activity. If I did, it would lose its appeal.

An hour and a half after we'd gone upstairs, the Barretts were "ready for the day". It was eleven-thirty. The picnic started at one o'clock. We had an hour and a half to make brownies. I hoped Mrs B. had brownie mix somewhere, because the kids and I were going to do a lot better working with a kit than working from scratch.

I assembled Buddy, Suzi, and Marnie in the kitchen. (I put Marnie in her high chair and gave her a wooden spoon to play with.)

"Aprons for everybody," I announced, pulling three out of a cupboard.

"Not me," exclaimed Buddy. "Aprons are for girls."

"Aprons are for *cooks*," I corrected him. "See? Here's a plain white one like the master chefs wear." I tied it on him. It came to the floor.

"Now," I continued, "does your mum buy cake mixes?"

"Yup," said Buddy.

"Where does she keep them?"

Buddy pointed to a cupboard. I opened it

and looked inside. I found flour, sugar, baking powder, boxes of cake and frosting mix, and (thank goodness), way in the back of the cupboard, two boxes of brownie mix.

"Here we go!" I said. I decided we'd better make both boxes, a double batch, since there would be fourteen people at the picnic. Mrs Barrett would probably appreciate the left-overs.

Buddy and I looked at the instructions on the back of the box.

"What do we need to add to the mix?" I asked him.

He frowned. "An egg and . . . and some o-*oil*," he finally pronounced triumphantly.

"Good. Okay, you get out the eggs and the bottle of oil, and I'll get the pans and mixing bowls."

"What should I do?" asked Suzi.

"You can, um, get some dish towels," I replied. They were the first unbreakable things that came to mind. Luckily, she didn't ask me what they were for. I didn't know at the time, but I figured we'd use them for something.

I was right. We needed the towels when Buddy dropped an egg on the floor, and again when Suzi turned on the electric mixer just as Buddy was lowering the beaters into the batter.

The brownies finally went into the oven at 12.35. They had to bake for a half an hour.

We would only be five or ten minutes late to the picnic.

We spent that half hour cleaning the chocolate batter off the wall around the mixer, and washing the bowls and spoons. At 1.05 I removed the pans from the oven and tested the brownies with a knife. They were done. And they smelled divine!

I remembered just in time that you're not supposed to cut brownies into squares before they're cool, so I carried the pans over to the Pikes' with hot mitts. I had to make two trips: the first with one batch of brownies, Pow, and the Barrett kids (Suzi took our sandwiches), the second with the other batch after the Barretts had been left at the Pikes'.

The Pikes' garden looked festive but crowded. Claudia and Stacey had spread blankets on the ground and laid out paper plates, cups, and napkins, and plastic spoons and forks. The Pike kids had been busy decorating the yard with flags and balloons left over from a recent birthday party.

I took a quick head count to make sure we were all accounted for, and came up with fifteen.

"Hey, Stacey," I said. "Come here."

"What is it?" Stacey trotted over to me, looking as fabulous as always. She was wearing a simple pink T-shirt under a baggy jumpsuit with big pink and red flowers all over it. Her permed hair bounced over her shoulders. I was wearing blue jean shorts and a white T-shirt that said GENIUS INSIDE. I looked ordinary next to Stacey.

"How many Pike kids are there?" I asked.

"Eight," Stacey replied. "You know that."

"Right, and there are three Barrett kids. That makes eleven. Plus you and Claudia and me — fourteen.

"Yeah?"

"Now count the people in the garden."

Stacey counted. ". . . thirteen, fourteen, fifteen . . . *Fifteen*?"

"That's what I just realized," I said.

"Well, let's see who doesn't belong here."

"All right," I replied. "There are Buddy, Suzi, and Marnie."

"And there are Mallory, Byron, Adam, Jordan, Vanessa, Nicky, Margo, Claire, and Jenny."

"You just counted nine Pikes," I informed Stacey.

"Jenny!" cried Stacey. "What's Jenny Prezzioso doing here?"

"Oh," I groaned. Jenny the brat. She lived right around the corner. "I wonder why we didn't notice her earlier." Jenny was the only kid in the garden who appeared to be dressed for a wedding. She had on a pink pinafore over a spotless white dress, white tights, and pink shoes. Her mother had plaited her hair and tied pink ribbons at the ends.

Claudia was carrying food out of the house and setting it on the blankets. The picnic was almost ready. "We might as well ask Jenny to stay," said Stacey.

I made a face, but said, "I guess you're right."

"I'll go inside and call Mrs Prezzioso," Stacey offered. She returned a few minutes later saying, "It's okay."

Claudia and Stacey and I settled the kids on the blankets. We passed out sandwiches and poured cups of lemonade and milk. For two and a half minutes, the twelve children were good as gold. Then something very small happened. Jordan put his sandwich down, turned to Nicky, aimed his index fingers at him, and went, "Bzzz."

The result was astonishing. Nicky yelped and said, "Claudia, Jordan gave me the Bizzer Sign!"

"What's the Bizzer Sign?" I whispered to Stacey.

"Something the Pike kids made up. It's like an insult or something. They use it when they want to annoy each other. Or their friends."

"Ignore him," Claudia told Nicky.

"But he gave me the *Bizzer* Sign!"

"*Ignore* him."

"But he *gave me the Bizzer Sign*!"

Claudia sighed. She glanced at Stacey and me. I shrugged.

The next thing we knew, Adam was

giving Jenny the Bizzer Sign, and Buddy was giving Suzi the Bizzer Sign.

Both Jenny and Suzi began to cry.

Then Mallory, who is usually quite well behaved, gave Byron the Bizzer Sign, and *he* began to cry.

Within the next thirty seconds, seven kids were crying and seven were bizzing and grinning. (Marnie was making the ham face.)

This may be how a war gets started. One day, a world leader pokes another world leader in the ribs and says, "Nyah, nyah, nyah." The second world leader begins to cry, and suddenly their countries are fighting each other.

Our picnic had gone from a dream to a disaster in under five minutes.

Luckily, I had a brainstorm. In the midst of the pandemonium, I stood up and shouted, "Who wants brownies?"

"I do!" shouted every single kid, except Marnie.

"Great," I said, "but you can't have any until you stop teasing each other, finish your sandwiches, and behave yourselves. And the next person who gives somebody the Bizzer Sign will have to go inside."

Silence reigned. Then laughter. Then some elephant jokes. Fifteen minutes later, the sandwiches were gone and I was passing around brownies. I broke off a piece of one and handed it to Marnie, wondering whether she would eat it.

"Hey!" shouted Mallory. "Don't give

her that!" She dived over Vanessa and Buddy and snatched the brownie out of Marnie's fist.

"What do you think you're doing?" I said crossly. "You'll get a brownie in a minute, Mallory."

Mallory looked at me with wounded eyes. "She's allergic," she said quietly. "Marnie can't eat chocolate. She'll get sick."

"Are you sure?" I exclaimed. "Mrs Barrett never told me that."

"I'm positive. You can ask my mum."

I apologized to Mallory four times. Then I began to feel angry. The Barrett kids were great and they needed me, but their mother was a problem. She never gave me instructions. She hardly paid any attention to her children. She was totally disorganized. Plus, I was doing all her housework, and she was only paying me regular baby-sitting wages.

I planned to talk to Mrs Barrett about every single one of my grievances, but when she blew through the front door late that afternoon, her perfume trailing behind her, she started praising me right away. She looked around at the tidy house, the tidy children, and the plate of leftover brownies, and said, "Dawn, I swear, you're a wonder. I don't know how you do it. Thank you so much. Mrs Pike said you were a real find, and she was right."

What could I say? All my complaints flew out of my head. So I kissed the kids goodbye and left.

9th CHAPTER

Wednesday, May 27

This evening I babysat for Dawn Shafer's brother Jeff. I could tell he thoght he was to old for a baby-sitter but Dawn was sitting at the Barretts and her mum had suddenly gotten tickits to a Concert and Mrs Shaffer didn't want to leave Jeff alone at night. She called me at the last minute and luckly I was free. Sitting for Jeff was an easy job.

But! Dawn I noticed this is the second night in a row you've sat at the Barretts. And I looked in our apontment book and you were their four times last week. Maybe you are over doing it?

I am telling you this as a freind.

And I listened to Claudia as a friend. I knew she wasn't jealous because I had so many sitting jobs. The truth was that I was practically living at the Barretts'. Mrs Barrett constantly needed someone to watch the kids, and she constantly called me. A couple of times I hadn't been available, so Kristy or Mary Anne had gone, but Mrs Barrett said the children, especially Buddy, liked me best.

It was flattering — but I was so busy! Once I had even missed a meeting of the Babysitters Club. Mrs Barrett had promised me she would be home by 5.30, and she didn't get back until 6.05. If she'd been somewhere important, say a job interview, I wouldn't have minded so much. But she'd just been out shopping with a friend.

On the Monday after the picnic at the Pikes', I finally asked Mrs Barrett about Marnie's chocolate allergy. I waited until she'd returned for the evening, so she couldn't rush off.

After she'd paid me, I said, "Mrs Barrett, could I talk to you for a sec?"

Something passed over her eyes then. It was a look — just the briefest look — of fear? Annoyance? I couldn't tell.

Anyway, we sat down in the living room and before I could lose my nerve, I said, "How come you didn't tell me Marnie's allergic to chocolate?"

"Oh, dear," said Mrs Barrett. Sitting

cross-legged on the couch in her beautifully tailored suit, she looked chic and fashionable and oh-so-put-together — from the neck down. From the neck up, she looked weary and worried. There were lines around her eyes and at the corners of her mouth, and I caught sight of a few grey hairs. But I knew that she was only thirty-three years old.

She rubbed her eyes tiredly. "I didn't tell you about Marnie's allergy?"

"No," I replied. "And I almost gave her a piece of brownie the other day. Mallory Pike stopped me just in time."

"Thank goodness," said Mrs Barrett. And then she added, "Poor baby," as Marnie toddled into the living room and held her arms out to be picked up. Mrs Barrett pulled her into her lap and rocked her back and forth.

"Does she have any other allergies?" I asked.

"Not that we know of." Mrs Barrett kissed the top of Marnie's head.

"What about Buddy and Suzi? I mean, is there anything else I should know?"

Mrs Barrett's face softened and I thought I was going to hear all about nightmares and childish fears and favourite foods. Then it hardened again, and she said crisply, "Just one thing. If my ex-husband ever calls, don't let him talk to the children, don't tell him he can see the children, and don't tell him I'm out. Say you're a mother's-help and I'm busy."

Mrs Barrett looked as if she was going to say more, but a crash sounded in the playroom, followed by a shriek from Suzi.

"Uh-oh," said Mrs Barrett. She hoisted Marnie onto her hip and hurried into the playroom. I followed.

A horrible sight met our eyes. When we had left Buddy and Suzi, they'd been watching a re-run of *The Brady Bunch* on TV. But while Mrs Barrett and I had been in the living room, they had transformed the playroom into a disaster area. A bowl of water sat in the middle of the floor, surrounded by half-full paper cups and jars — and bottles of food colouring. They had been experimenting with colours, but it had got out of hand. Little puddles of pink and blue and yellow water were everywhere. The kids' clothes were streaked, and several stuffed animals now had greenish fur. The shriek had occurred when Buddy had spilled pink water over Suzi's head.

He said it was an accident.

Suzi disagreed.

Mrs Barrett looked ready to fall apart. She hugged Marnie to her, and closed her eyes. I thought she might even cry. Since my mother is a big crier, I know the signs well.

"I'll take care of it," I told Mrs Barrett. "Why don't you dry Suzi off? Buddy, go get the paper towels. We'll clean up."

"How come Suzi doesn't have to clean up?" whined Buddy. "She made a mess, too."

"I know, but she's all wet. Besides, if you get the towels, I'll show you a trick."

Buddy hesitated for just a second. "Okay!" he agreed.

Mrs Barrett took the girls upstairs, and Buddy returned with the towels. I placed one square over a puddle, soaked it up, and held the towel out for Buddy to see.

"It's pink!" he exclaimed. "Let me try!" So Buddy went around wiping up puddles, and I emptied the jars and cups into the bowl and returned everything to the sink in the kitchen. Then I scrubbed at the stuffed animals, but even after several minutes they still had a greenish cast to them.

Buddy finished with the puddles and we hung several of the colourful paper towels up as artwork. Then Mrs Barrett returned with Marnie and a smiling Suzi, and peeped into the playroom.

"Oh, thank goodness, Dawn," she said. "It looks wonderful in there. I don't know what I'd do without you." She began to usher me towards the front door. As I put my sweat shirt on, she handed me another dollar. "For averting a crisis," she explained. "You're a lifesaver. Each time you sit, the house looks better when you leave than it did when you arrived. I used to be such an organized person, but since the divorce, everything seems overwhelming. Money is a little tight, too. If the children's father would — Oh, well. Anyway, I hope you know how much I appreciate you. I think you're the glue that's holding us together."

The glue that was holding them together? That was a little scary. It sounded like an awfully big responsibility.

At that moment, the phone rang. "I'll get it!" Mrs Barrett yelled, but she was too late. We could already hear Buddy on the extension in the kitchen saying, "Hello?"

"Buddy, I told you, you are not to answer the phone!" Mrs Barrett shouted.

"It's Dad, Mum," Buddy shouted back.

Mrs Barrett clenched her teeth.

"He says where are we? He says you were supposed to drop Suzi and me off at his apartment by five-thirty, and he's been waiting for half an hour."

"Oh-my-goodness-I-completely-forgot!" exclaimed Mrs Barrett. "Dawn, I'll see you on Wednesday afternoon, right?"

"Right," I replied. "At three o'clock." But Mrs Barrett didn't even hear my last words. She was already rushing for the phone.

Over the next couple of weeks, I baby-sat for the Barretts an awful lot. This did not escape any member of the club. They didn't mind, of course, except when it cut into meetings.

But I minded a few things. Mrs Barrett's disorganization caused a number of problems. One afternoon when I was sitting, Suzi said she didn't feel well — and immediately threw up all over the kitchen floor. I cleaned up the mess, then held my hand to her forehead and realized she had a fever.

I dialled the number Mrs Barrett had left by the phone. It was for an employment agency where she had got a temporary afternoon job.

The gruff voice that answered the phone said, "Hurley's Garage."

Hurley's Garage? "I suppose you don't have a Mrs Barrett working there, do you?" I asked.

"Sorry, kid," replied the man.

"Great," I said to no one in particular as I hung up the phone. "Mrs Barrett left the wrong number."

At that moment, Suzi threw up again.

As I cleaned up the second mess, I racked my brain trying to remember whether Mrs Barrett had mentioned the name of the agency where she was working. I didn't think she had.

Just in case, I opened the yellow pages of the phone book and scanned the firms listed under EMPLOYMENT AGENCIES, but nothing sounded familiar. Then Suzi began to gag again. That time I managed to rush her to the kitchen sink before she was sick.

I put Marnie in her playpen, sent Buddy over to the Pikes', rolled up the rug in the bathroom, and spent the rest of the afternoon there with Suzi, reading to her, and holding her head over the toilet every time she had to throw up.

She was miserable. I was angry at her mother.

When Mrs Barrett came home, I told her, rather crossly, about the mixed-up phone number. She apologized, but it was a little late for that. If Suzi hadn't needed her so badly, I might have said more to her.

Two days later, I came down with Suzi's bug and spent hours in the bathroom. Mum and Jeff caught the bug from me, and the Pike kids caught it from Buddy, who had been spreading it around the afternoon I sent him to their house while I was taking care of Suzi.

Another day, as Mrs Barrett rushed out the door, Buddy called plaintively after her, "Hey, Mum my homework . . ."

"I'll look at it tonight," she called to him, and continued down the walk.

Buddy burst into tears and ran to his room.

I ran after him, pausing in his doorway. "Hey, old Buddy. What's the matter? Can I come in?"

He was lying face down on his bed, but I

saw him nod his head.

I sat next to him and patted his back. "Can you tell me what's wrong?" I asked.

He hiccupped. "My homework."

"Do you need help with it?"

"I need *Mum's* help." He rolled over and looked at me mournfully.

"Are you sure I won't do? I'm pretty clever," I told him. "I'm in seventh grade."

Buddy managed a smile. "It's not that. We're studying families. We're supposed to make a family tree tonight, starting with our grandparents. You won't know their names. I don't know them. They're just Gram and Gramps and Gee-ma and Gee-pa. And I have to take it to school *tomorrow* and it's our first homework ever and I want it to be good."

"Oh, I see."

"And Mum said she'd help," Buddy moaned, "but she won't. Not really. She's always too tired at night to do anything."

"Well, let's make it easy on her," I suggested. "Why don't we make the tree part, and then she can tell you the names to fill in. Do you know how many aunts and uncles you have?"

Buddy nodded uncertainly.

So I busied the girls with some toys, and then Buddy and I set to work. It took a lot of questioning and two phone calls to Mrs Pike, but we finally worked out where the Barrett relatives belonged on the tree. Then

I showed Buddy how to make boxes and lines and spaces. When he was finished, he had a beautiful blank tree. I just hoped it was accurate. If it wasn't, he'd have a lot of rubbing out to do.

A week later, Buddy showed up at my house after school. He'd never done that before. When I opened the door, he didn't say a word — just held out a large piece of paper. It was his completed family tree. A gold star was glued to the top.

"My teacher loved it," he told me. "Thanks for helping me, Dawn."

"You're welcome, Buddy," I replied, and gave him a hug. But all the while, I was thinking that Mrs Barrett should be hugging Buddy for his good work.

10th CHAPTER

Thursday, May 28th

This afternoon I baby-sat for David Michael. Poor kid. I bet it's hard being the youngest in a big family. Kristy, Sam, and Charlie were all off doing other things, and Mrs Thomas was at work, of course. So that left David Michael.

When I came over, he looked kind of sad. As soon as Kristy left the house, he said, "Stacey, let's have a snack and a talk." Little kids today have a lot to worry about.

You guys should know that David Michael is getting very worried about moving into Watson's house. That was why he wanted to talk to me. Because I moved recently. It turns out that he watched the men unloading our furniture from the van last August. He saw them drop a lamp and break it. And he saw something or other covered with a drop cloth that looked like a ghost to him. He's pretty scared, all right.

Apparently, David Michael was more interested in talking than in snacking. Stacey fixed him a plate of crackers and peanut butter and poured him a glass of juice, but he hardly looked at the food.

"Stacey," he said, "when you moved, did the men pack up *every*thing in the van?"

"Oh, yes," she said reassuringly. "Every last thing. Nothing was left behind."

"Are you sure?"

"Positive."

David Michael began to look tearful. "Do you have any pets?" he asked.

"No," Stacey replied, puzzled. Then suddenly she caught on. "Oh, David Michael," she cried. "They won't put *Louie* in the van. Dogs don't go in vans."

"I hope not. Louie doesn't like dark places."

"Anyway, you're only moving across town. Your mum will drive Louie to Watson's house in the car. Louie likes car rides, doesn't he?"

David Michael brightened. "He loves them!"

"Has he ever been to Watson's house?"

David Michael nodded. "A few times."

"See? He'll even know where he's going. No big deal."

A pause. Then, "Stacey, moving vans sometimes have accidents."

"They do?" Stacey said, wondering what David Michael was getting at now.

"Yesterday I saw on a TV show where this van was driving along a mountain road and suddenly it had an accident and it skidded and went *shwooo*" — David Michael demonstrated the van sailing over a cliff — "down the mountain and the doors flew open and things fell out and a man found the accident and saw a teddy bear on the ground all squashed and ripped. Also a tricycle with the wheels bent."

"But David Michael, there are no mountains here in Stoneybrook. It'll only take a few minutes to drive from Bradford Court to Watson's house. Anyway, our moving van travelled from New York City to Stoneybrook with no problems at all —"

"The lamp broke."

"— and Dawn Schafer's moving van travelled from California to Connecticut without any trouble. That's three thousand miles. . . . I *know* our lamp got broken. So did a vase. But moving men aren't perfect."

"Well, I don't want them moving my space station."

"I bet if you tell your mum that, she'll take it to Watson's in the car sometime. Or Charlie will. He'll be able to drive by then."

David Michael nodded. He bit a small corner off of one of the crackers. Stacey had the feeling that the moving van wasn't *really* what was worrying him. She waited patiently.

David Michael returned the rest of the

cracker to the plate, then let loose with a barrage of nervous questions. "When we move to Watson's, who will be my friends? Where will I go to school? Will I still see Patrick and Frankie?" (Current friends.) "Where will I sleep? Where will my mum sleep? Where will Louie sleep? What if Louie tries to come back to his old house?" The questions went on and on.

Stacey did her best to answer them, but she didn't think David Michael would stop worrying about the move until it was over.

She mentioned that to Kristy at the next meeting of the Babysitters Club. "That's a long time for a little kid to worry," Stacey pointed out. "It'll be three or four months before you move."

"Inobutthdobawt." Kristy had three pieces of nougat in her mouth. Claudia, the junk food junkie, had been sent a box of it by her aunt and uncle who were visiting Atlantic City in New Jersey. She had hidden it in her room, along with her Twix's and Crunchies and M&M's, and had handed around pieces at the beginning of the meeting. We all had gooey mouthfuls of the stuff, except for Stacey, who's diabetic and can't eat most sweets.

Stacey giggled. "What?" she asked Kristy.

Kristy swallowed several times. "I know," she said at last, "but there's nothing we can do about it. Mum and Watson aren't getting married until the end of September. Mum knows David Michael is scared, so they talk about the move sometimes. A little too often, in my opinion."

"What do you mean?" I asked.

"Well, I don't want to hear about the move day in and day out. I'm not thrilled with the idea, either — but for different reasons."

Mary Anne looked solemnly out the window. "I can't believe you won't be next door to me any more," she told Kristy. "All my life, when I've looked out my side bedroom window, I've looked into yours."

"Yeah," said Kristy huskily. "Me, too."

Before things got too sad, I said, "Well, when you look out your new bedroom window, Kristy, you'll look right into Morbidda Destiny's."

Everyone laughed.

"You know," said Kristy, "we've been saying that a move across town is really no big deal. I'll still go to Stoneybrook Middle School, and we'll still be friends and all that. But what are we going to do about the meetings of the Babysitters Club? And how am I supposed to sit for Jamie Newton and the Pikes and everyone? No one's going to want to drive all the way to Watson's to pick me up, when you guys are right here and can walk to our clients."

We chewed in thoughtful silence. We must have looked like we were at a funeral.

After a while Claudia spoke up. "Maybe it won't be so bad. You'll get new clients, Kristy. You'll have a whole new neighbourhood full of kids to yourself. When you can't handle the jobs, we'll go. Your move will expand our club. We'll be baby-sitting all over town!"

Claudia's excitement was contagious. She and Mary Anne and Kristy and I reached for more nougat. Stacey reached for a cracker.

"But the meetings," said Kristy, looking downcast again. "Who's going to drive me to Bradford Court three times a week?"

No one could answer her question. I began to have a funny feeling in the pit of my stomach.

"Can't you ride your bike over?" asked Stacey. "I know it's a few miles, but you don't mind a little exercise, do you?"

"Of course not," Kristy answered. "I love to ride my bike. But Mum won't let me ride from Watson's to Bradford Court."

"How come?" I asked. "She lets you ride to town and stuff."

"Only with a friend. Safety in numbers and all that," said Kristy.

"Oh."

"I mean, she's not strict, but she *is* careful. Even Mum has her limits. Besides, let's say Mum gave me permission to ride across town alone. Okay. It takes about a half an hour each way when you add in stopping at lights and running into rush-hour traffic. That means I'd have to leave Watson's at five o'clock for a five-thirty meeting, and I wouldn't get home until six-thirty. In the winter, it would be pitch-black by then."

The problem was looking bigger and bigger.

"Hey, you guys," said Claudia suddenly. "We're not thinking. We're assuming we have to go on holding the meetings in my room, but who says so? Just because we've held them here since the beginning doesn't mean it's the only place for them."

"But we need a phone," Mary Anne said.

"Well, there are phones all over town," said Claudia. "We could move the meeting around, hold them wherever it's convenient."

"Then our clients wouldn't know where to reach us," I said. "We have to stay at the same phone number."

"Oh, right." Kristy, who had just started to look hopeful, dropped her hands into her lap. "Stupid, stupid Watson," she muttered.

"Hey, Kristy, don't get down on Watson," I said gently. "It's not his fault. It's not anybody's fault."

"A lot *you* know." Kristy didn't even bother to look at me.

"I may know more than you think," I said quietly. "You're not the only one whose parents got divorced."

"No, but I'm the only one whose mother chose to get married to a jerk who's so rich he lives three and a half miles away on Millionaire's Lane, which is what they should call that gross street he can afford to live on. And I'm the only one who may have to drop out of the club. The club I started."

"Oh, Kristy!" I exclaimed, forgetting her jab at me. "You can't drop out of the club!"

"No. We won't let you," said Mary Anne staunchly. "We couldn't run your club without you. It wouldn't be right."

"Yeah," said Claudia. "No Kristy, no club."

Then we all looked at each other with the awful realization of what Claudia's words might mean.

11th CHAPTER

The next day was the beginning of Memorial Day weekend. The Stoneybrook schools were closed on Monday. In California, we usually spent most of the long weekend at the beach. There was no chance of that in Connecticut. Although we lived near the coast and the weather was beautiful, the temperature had dropped back to about seventy degrees. Mary Anne assured me that was normal. I didn't care. On Saturday morning, I shouted at my clock radio and called the weatherman a cheesebrain. (Several days earlier, I'd called him a magician and a saint.)

When I heard that the ocean temperature (the *Atlantic* Ocean temperature, that is) was fifty degrees, I called the weatherman a moron.

Nevertheless, my mother, who was giving a picnic on Saturday, decided to hold it outdoors. I told her it was probably going to be the first picnic ever attended by people wearing quilted jackets.

Mum just rolled her eyes heavenward and said, "For pity's sake, Dawn. It's perfectly pleasant outside."

No, it wasn't.

I tried to be enthusiastic about the picnic anyway. It had started off as just a small party for my parents and grandparents, but it had grown. First, Mum had invited Mr Spier and Mary Anne. Then I had asked if I could invite the Thomases, the Kishis, and the McGills. Then Jeff had asked if we could invite the Pikes, and finally I decided to ask the Barretts and (out of guilt) the Prezziosos.

Most of them couldn't come, since they already had plans. In fact, apart from my grandparents and the Spiers, the only people who were able to attend were the Barretts, and Kristy and David Michael. (Mrs Thomas was giving a party for her relatives and Watson and his kids on Saturday night, so she'd be busy getting ready for it during the day, but Kristy said she wanted to come to our picnic, anyway. I was flattered.)

On Saturday morning, shivering in a sweat shirt and blue jeans, I helped Mum set up a table and our lawn furniture in the garden. Then, while Jeff hosed everything down (the furniture was dusty from sitting in the barn) and decorated the yard with balloons, flags, crepe paper, and lanterns, Mum and I worked on the food.

"You know, Mum," I said, surveying the messy kitchen, "some people don't like tofu."

"Really?" she replied vaguely.

"And Mum, before the guests arrive this afternoon, could you find matching socks? Mr Spier would probably really appreciate it if your socks matched. And your earrings."

"My earrings? I know *they* match, honey. I just put them on . . . I wonder if I could substitute raw honey for sugar in this recipe."

"They don't match, Mum. They're both gold hoops, but they're different sizes. Here, let me look at the recipe." I was beginning to feel nervous.

"I've got a great idea," I said on impulse. "Instead of trying to make this fancy stuff, why don't we go to the grocery store, buy hamburger patties, hot dogs, buns, and potato salad, and serve that? Grandpa can barbecue. We won't have to cook at all."

"*Red meat?*" exclaimed my mother. "*Hot dogs?* Do you know what's in a hot dog?"

"Yes, and I don't even want to think about it. I'd rather eat tofu any day. But we're in *Connecticut*. In Connecticut, people barbecue things. Especially at picnics. Don't you think we should serve food our guests will like?" I tried to imagine Kristy looking at a table of dried fruit, tofu salads, and raw vegetables. She'd go hungry before she'd touch a thing.

"I suppose," said Mum. I could tell that the idea of not having to cook was very appealing to her. "Do you really think we can buy ready-made potato salad?"

"Sure. In the deli section at the grocery. I've seen it. Pots of it. We could probably buy ready-made green salad, too. It might be a little expensive, but we won't have to prepare anything."

Mum considered this for all of two seconds. "Let's go!" she cried. "What a relief!"

We made a dash for the car. On the way to the shopping centre I realized we didn't have a grill, so we had to buy one of those, too. It was a costly morning, but it was worth it.

As we were driving back home, the car loaded down with food and a big red grill, I said casually, "Hey, Mum, I thought when you were in high school your parents didn't approve of Mary Anne's father."

"That's right, sweetie."

"Well, what's going to happen when they see each other today?"

"Oh, nothing. That was years ago," Mum answered mildly.

But I thought she looked uncomfortable.

*

Our guests were invited for one o'clock. In California, one o'clock means two or two-thirty. Here in Connecticut, every last guest had arrived by 1.15. Luckily, since we didn't have much to do except start the barbeque, we were ready, anyway. The garden was decorated and the furniture was clean. All we had to do was carry out the food.

When that was done, I pulled Kristy and Mary Anne aside so we could survey the scene. Jeff, David Michael, Buddy, and Suzi were playing ball. Mrs Barrett was bouncing Marnie on her knees and talking to my grandmother. My grandfather was lighting the fire in the grill. And Mum and Mr Spier were sitting as close together as they could possibly sit, their heads bent in quiet laughter.

"Keep an eye on them," I said to my friends. "This is a good opportunity to see how they're acting with each other these days. And keep an eye on my grandparents and your father, Mary Anne. It could be interesting. We may have to — to avert a crisis," I said, remembering words Mrs Barrett had once used.

"Okay," whispered Mary Anne.

"Hey," Kristy exclaimed, looking awed. "Mary Anne, where are your father's glasses?"

"He got contacts," Mary Anne replied.

"Your *father*?"

Mary Anne nodded.

"Got *contacts*?"

"Yup."

I began to giggle.

"I don't believe it. I absolutely do not believe it," said Kristy. "It's amazing. Get me a chair, somebody. I may have to sit down."

Mary Anne made a great show of pulling up a lawn chair, and Kristy made a great show of collapsing into it with one hand pressed over her heart.

When she calmed down, I dragged a lounge chair next to Kristy's chair and Mary Anne and I both sat in it. Then the three of us watched the adults.

It didn't take me long to realize that my grandmother was only pretending to have a conversation with Mrs Barrett. All she did was ask questions that required long answers, and while Mrs Barrett was talking, Granny would keep shooting little glances over at Mum and Mr Spier.

Pop-Pop (my grandfather) was watching them, too. Once he got the fire started, there wasn't much for him to do until the coals were hot. Even so, he stood over the grill, occasionally poking a lump of charcoal, but mostly just gazing at the lovebirds.

Lovebirds. That's exactly what they looked like. If one of them had cooed — even Mr Spier — I wouldn't have been the least bit surprised.

I tried to read the expression on Pop-Pop's face. He didn't look angry. I nudged Mary Anne and then Kristy. "How would you say my grandfather looks?" I asked them.

"Well, he looks very nice," replied Kristy. "This is the first time I've ever met him, of course, but I'd say he looks good, although his shirt doesn't exactly match his trousers."

"No!" I exclaimed. "I mean, what does he look like he's thinking about as he watches my mum and Mary Anne's dad? Mary Anne, what do you think?"

"I don't know, I can't tell."

"Do you think he looks like he disapproves?"

"No," answered Mary Anne and Kristy.

"Do you think he looks deliriously happy?"

"No," they replied.

"Deliriously proud?"

"No."

We weren't getting anywhere.

"What about Granny?" I asked. "She's been watching them the whole time she's been talking to Mrs Barrett."

"It's hard to tell," said Mary Anne. "If you want my honest opinion, she has to pretend she's interested in what Mrs Barrett is saying, and there's no room on her face for any other expression."

Adults certainly are hard to understand.

Sometimes they seem to have several faces. It's as if they own masks, and you *know* they own masks, but you can't always tell their masks from their real expressions. Why do they make everything so complicated?

The picnic became more interesting when we started eating. Mum settled the little kids — Jeff, David Michael, Buddy, and Suzi — at a child-sized picnic table. Then she arranged Marnie and the adults — who were going to eat on their laps — in a semicircle of lawn chairs. She left Mary Anne and Kristy and me on our own, so we just inconspicuously tacked ourselves onto one end of the semicircle. From there we had a bird's-eye view of the adults.

The first interesting thing that happened was that Pop-Pop sat himself down next to Mr Spier and said, "So Richard, how are things at Thompson, Thompson, and Abrams?"

"Oh," replied Mary Anne's father, "I haven't been with them in quite some time."

"Oh?"

"No, I started my own firm about four years ago. I practice in Stamford."

"Oh?"

"Yes. It's doing very well, too. Leaving Thompson's was the best decision I ever made."

"Oh?"

(It's amazing how many meanings the

word *oh* seems to have. Mr Spier's *oh* had sounded surprised. Pop-Pop's first *oh* had sounded suspicious. His second *oh* had sounded impressed. His third *oh* had sounded sort of awed.)

Mary Anne and I glanced at each other. *That* conversation seemed to have gone all right.

A little while later, Granny leaned over and said, "Richard, are you still living on Taylor Street?" (Taylor Street is in the neighbourhood Mr Spier had grown up in.)

"Why, no," he replied. "We live on Bradford Court. Mary Anne's mother and I moved out of the house on Taylor Street several months before Mary Anne was born."

Again Mr Spier sounded surprised. He was probably wondering why my grandparents didn't know all this stuff. The truth is, Mum and her parents rarely discuss touchy subjects. And their three touchiest subjects at that time were the divorce, my father, and Mary Anne's father. I was beginning to think that Mum had brought Granny, Pop-Pop, and Mr Spier together just so that my grandparents could see how well Mary Anne's father had done for himself, not to mention the fact that he's a perfectly nice, normal guy.

Toward the end of the meal, Pop-Pop got into a discussion of banking laws with Mr Spier. (Pop-Pop is a banker.) The talk went on and on. Sometimes they seemed to be arguing, but at the same time enjoying themselves. The rest of the time they were agreeing with each other and talking earnestly.

Mum looked so happy about that that she relaxed and became involved in a conversation about the Phil Donahue show with Granny and Mrs Barrett.

Kristy and Mary Anne and I, satisfied that things were going well, sneaked over to the barn where Kristy and I took turns swinging through the loft on the rope, while Mary Anne sat outside on a bale of hay and daydreamed.

Later, as the guests were leaving, Mrs Barrett asked if I could baby-sit after school on Tuesday. I was busy, but Mary Anne was free, so she took the job.

I decided that it had been a good day all round, even if it had been chilly. I went to bed that night and had a lovely dream in which Mum and Mr Spier got married and Mary Anne and I were in the wedding. It was a beautiful ceremony, except that the bride and groom were wearing ski jackets and snow trousers.

12th CHAPTER

Tuesday, June 2

This afternoon I baby-sat for Buddy, Suzi, and Marnie Barrett. What a time I had! I don't know if it's the weather or problems with the divorce or what, but the kids were wild. Wild and cranky. I'm sure the sitter they really wanted was Dawn. I don't know how you handle them, Dawn. I hope they behave better for you than they do for me.

By the way, there was a really strange phone call from Mr Barrett today, wanting to know where Buddy was. I wouldn't give him any information. When I told Mrs Barrett about the call, she turned purple (not really) and said he shouldn't have called here when he knew darn well she'd be out. What's going on? I think we should all be careful of calls from Mr Barrett.

When Mary Anne got home from the Barretts' that afternoon, the first thing she did was call me. She was extremely miffed.

"Dawn," she exclaimed, "how can you possibly sit at the Barretts' so often?"

"What do you mean?" I asked.

"What do I *mean*! They're terrors, that's what I mean! If I were their mother, I'd have . . . I don't know what I'd have done, but I'd have done something by now. Something drastic."

"You've sat for them before," I pointed out.

Mary Anne calmed down somewhat. "I know, and they were a little wild then, but nothing like today."

"Maybe it was the weather." It had been raining for three days.

"Maybe. That must have been part of it, but you always get along so well with them. They really like you. It's almost as if you have — what do you call it? — some kind of chemistry with them. I don't think we have any chemistry at all."

"They do like me," I admitted. Lately Buddy had come over to our house more and more often, and since Suzi had learned how to use the phone, she had started calling me, although she never had much to say. "What did they do today?" I asked Mary Anne.

"What *didn't* they do?" she replied. She began to describe the afternoon. The first part of it sounded very familiar. When Mary Anne rang the bell, Buddy, Suzi, and Pow had answered the door. Buddy was wearing the cowboy hat and swimming flippers and was aiming his ray gun at Mary Anne.

He greeted her with a "Fshoo, fshoo! Bzzzzt," followed by a gleeful, "I got you! You're dead! You're completely dead!"

Although Mary Anne didn't mention anything about using guns, she did say, "Well, I'm not dead for long, because I'm coming into your house. Stand aside, Martian man."

"*Mar*tian man? I'm not a Martian man. I'm a cowboy from Venus. And this is my Venus weapon." Buddy jumped into a position of offence, legs spread, arms extended, holding the ray gun stiffly. He aimed it first at Mary Anne, then at Pow. But suddenly he dropped the gun and gave Suzi the Bizzer Sign instead.

Suzi burst into tears.

Marnie, sitting alone in her high chair in the kitchen (wearing only a nappy), burst into tears, too. (Sometimes tears are contagious.)

"Hi, Mary Anne!" called Mrs Barrett as she rushed downstairs. She ignored the crying children, frantically threw on her raincoat, and as usual, ran out the door without giving the baby-sitter any instructions. Mary Anne did, however, hear her call, "Don't forget that Marnie's allergic to chocolate!" as she got into her car.

"Great," muttered Mary Anne, closing the front door.

Mrs Barrett wasn't going on an interview that afternoon. She was just running errands and wanted to do them by herself. Mary Anne could see why.

In order to get the kids under control, Mary Anne sent Buddy outside to walk Pow. He asked if he could wear the flippers, and Mary Anne said yes, since she thought the walk would take longer that way.

Then she gave Suzi a cracker and told her to go try to find *Sesame Street* on TV. Suzi stopped crying right away. With Suzi and Buddy occupied, Mary Anne turned her attention to Marnie.

"Okay, Marnie-o," she said, lifting her out of the high chair. "First we'll get you cleaned up, and then we'll get you a fresh nappy, and then we'll get you dressed."

"No-no," said Marnie.

"Yes-yes," said Mary Anne.

Marnie screamed while Mary Anne wiped her face, changed her nappy, and dressed her. Then suddenly she stopped crying. Mary Anne held her up to a mirror and said, "Pretty!"

Marnie made the ham face. She was back to her usual sunny self.

Mary Anne was just carrying Marnie downstairs when Buddy returned with Pow.

He took Pow's lead off, hung it in the kitchen, patted the dog affectionately, ran into the playroom, and gave Suzi the Bizzer Sign.

Suzi burst into tears.

Marnie burst into tears.

Mary Anne was back where she started. "Buddy," she said, "you give one more Bizzer Sign to anyone today — *anyone* — and you'll have to stay in your room until your mother comes home."

"No, I won't."

"Yes, you will. I'm in charge here and what I say goes."

"Will you tell my mum if I'm bad?"

"I might."

"Telltale."

Mary Anne shrugged her shoulders. "That's the way it is." She turned to Suzi and Marnie. "Okay, you guys quiet down. You know what we're going to do today?"

"Not read," said Buddy.

"Not colour," said Suzi.

"Not watch TV," said Buddy.

"Not play Candy Land," said Suzi.

"Nope," replied Mary Anne. "I can tell you're tired of the same old rainy day stuff. Today we're going to go outdoors for a puddle walk, and then we're going to come back inside and go camping and have a picnic."

"*Really?*" cried Buddy.

"Yes," answered Mary Anne. "Now, to

take a puddle walk, the first thing you guys have to do is find your swimming costumes. Do you know where they are?"

"Yes, yes!" shouted Buddy and Suzi, jumping up and down.

Marnie tried to jump up and down, too, but all she could do was bend her knees and make the ham face.

"Okay, upstairs and into your suits."

"Even Marnie?" asked Suzi.

"What about you?" Buddy wanted to know. "Did you bring your costume?"

"No, but it doesn't matter. Marnie and I won't really need them. Go upstairs and change now."

Buddy and Suzi thundered upstairs and returned a few moments later with their swimming costumes on. Mary Anne couldn't help smiling. In his costume, Buddy turned out to be a skinny little boy wih a big, knobby knees, and Suzi was pudgy with a fat, round tummy.

"That was fast," said Mary Anne. "What did you do with your clothes?"

"Threw 'em on the floor," replied Buddy.

Mary Anne pointed up the stairs. "Back," she said. "Go back and pick them up. Put them on your bed — *neatly*." She turned to Suzi. "Where are your clothes?"

"In my doll bed."

Again Mary Anne pointed upstairs.

After much grumbling, Buddy and Suzi returned.

"Now what?" asked Buddy.

"Now," said Mary Anne, "Marnie and I take off our shoes, Marnie puts on her boots, we all put on our raincoats and rain hats, and then we go for a walk in the puddles."

"Barefoot?" asked Suzi incredulously.

"Almost," said Mary Anne. She had found a whole bunch of sandals — all sizes — in the cupboard, and she handed them around.

"Oh, boy!" cried Buddy.

So Mary Anne and the Barretts headed outside for a puddle walk. The day was wet but very warm. Mary Anne herded the kids down the driveway and onto the pavement. "Jump in as many puddles as you can," she told Buddy and Suzi. "Try to make big splashes."

"Eee-*ii*!" shrieked Buddy, running towards a wide puddle. "Bonsai!" he leaped into it, sending out a spray of warm puddle water.

"He splashed me!" accused Suzi.

"Good," said Mary Anne. "That's the idea. You're wearing your swimming costume and your raincoat. Those clothes are *supposed* to get wet."

"Oh," said Suzi. Then, "Blam!" She jumped into the puddle with Buddy. She and Buddy ran down the pavement.

Mary Anne followed slowly with Marnie, who liked to get into a puddle and stay in it, patting her boots in the water and laughing. Between puddles, she stooped down to examine every worm she saw. She would poke them, smile at them, and then look up at Mary Anne and give her the ham face.

The puddle walk ended when Suzi threw a worm at Buddy, and Buddy said, "The puddle walk rule is, if you throw a worm, you have to eat it. So, here. Take a bite." He held the worm out to Suzi.

"No, no, no!" Suzi began to cry again.

"All right," said Mary Anne. "The puddle walk is over. It's time to go camping."

Back at the Barretts' house, the raincoats and bathing suits were hung up to dry, and everyone got dressed again. Then Mary Anne helped the kids make a "tent" by throwing some old blankets over a card table in the playroom. They added "rooms" to the tent by overturning the kitchen chairs, placing them by the table, and covering them with more blankets.

"Kristy and I used to make tents all the time," Mary Anne told me over the phone, "but this one was the biggest I've ever seen."

The Barrett kids loved the tent. Suzi and Buddy crawled around inside it, playing an imaginary game about camping and bears and spacemen. Marnie invented a game of her own, which involved peeking at Buddy,

Suzi and Mary Anne from under the tent flaps.

When it was time for the picnic (orange juice and cheese crackers), the kids wanted to eat in the tent. Just as they were finishing, the phone rang.

"I'll get it!" shouted Buddy. "It's the space phone."

"Sorry," said Mary Anne, remembering that I'd said Mrs Barrett didn't want the kids to talk to their father. Besides, she had a feeling *I* might be calling.

Buddy scrambled out of the tent, anyway, but Mary Anne was hot on his heels. She reached the phone at the same time he did, and since she was taller, she answered it first.

Out of sheer frustration, Buddy gave her the Bizzer Sign.

"Hello," said Mary Anne. "Barrett residence. Can you hold on a sec?" She covered the receiver with her other hand. "Buddy, you are in trouble. Go to your room."

Buddy stuck his tongue out at Mary Anne and stomped upstairs.

"Hello?" Mary Ann said again.

"Hello," answered a man's voice. "Who's this?"

"This is Mary Anne Spier, the baby-sitter. Who's this?"

"This is Mr. Barrett. May I speak to Buddy please? Or Suzi?"

"I'm sorry, they're . . . they're at a friend's house," Mary Anne lied.

"Oh, *fine*," said Mr Barrett, and slammed down the phone.

Mary Anne felt afraid. What was wrong? Why didn't Mrs Barrett want Mr Barrett to talk to the children? Was Mr Barrett angry at Mary Anne now? Did he know she had lied?

Probably, Mary Anne decided.

There was a scene when Mrs Barrett came home. Buddy was mad because he'd been punished, and Mrs Barrett was mad both because Buddy had misbehaved and because Mr Barrett had phoned.

"He's only supposed to speak to the kids on alternate Tuesdays. That's part of the custody arrangement. This is the wrong Tuesday. He can't keep his own schedule straight," she said fuming.

"And Buddy, what is the *matter* with you? I get notes from your teacher; you give Mary Anne trouble. I don't have time for this, young man. I cannot be your mother and your father, run this household, look for a job, *and* straighten out the messes you get yourself into. It's too much to ask of anybody."

Buddy, standing at the top of the stairs, began to cry silently.

At the bottom of the stairs, Mrs Barrett did the same thing. Then she opened her arms and Buddy rushed into them. Mary

Anne, who had already been paid, tiptoed out the front door.

13th CHAPTER

The rain continued for several more days. Although it was dreary, I didn't mind it — much. It was kind of like the California rainy season. Meanwhile, my mum was in a great mood. She went around smiling and whistling. The house became organized. Three straight days went by in which I didn't once have to tell her to change her clothes.

She talked to Mr Spier on the phone almost every evening.

The Barrett kids, on the other hand, were being driven crazy by the rain. Four days after Mary Anne sat for them, I sat for them. There had not been a drop of sunshine since the puddle walk. It was Saturday. The weather forecast was for rain ending before twelve, followed by cloudy skies.

By the time Mrs Barrett had been gone

for an hour, I was as crazy as the Barretts were. They didn't want to do *any*thing, not even take a puddle walk or make a tent.

"How about putting on a play?" I suggested.

"No!" said Buddy.

"Making our own comic book?"

"Too hard," Suzi said grumpily. She was scrunched down in a corner of the couch, wearing a sundress, her mother's high heels, and a plastic mixing bowl as a hat.

"Well, what *do* you want to do?" I asked.

"I don't know. What do you want to do?" replied Buddy.

"Get a piece of paper and make a mural?"

"Nah," said Buddy.

"Pretend we're spacemen?"

"Nah," said Suzi, peering at me from under the bowl.

We were back where we had started.

I sighed and looked out the window. That was when I noticed that the rain had stopped — actually stopped. The sky was still heavy and grey, the ground was soaking wet, but it *wasn't raining*.

"Hey! Look at that!" I exclaimed. "The rain's stopped. Let's play outside."

"Yea!" cried Buddy and Suzi.

There was a mad scramble for the back door.

"Whoa! Just a sec," I said. "Buddy, you're dressed to go out — as soon as you put your boots on — but Suzi, you aren't.

And neither is Marnie. It's chilly out here today. You can go outdoors, Buddy, and we'll be there in a little while."

Suzi immediately began to whine. "I want to go *out*, Dawn. Not fair. *Buddy's* going out."

"You're going to go, too," I told her as I led her upstairs, Marnie in my arms. "But you need to put on trousers, a shirt, a sweater, and boots. Marnie, too. You guys'll freeze in those dresses."

I helped Suzi change first. From the window of the girls' bedroom, I could see Buddy in the front garden. He had put his boots on, as well as his Mets jacket, and was tossing a baseball around.

Then I sat Marnie on the changing table. It took a bit longer to dress her, because she needed a clean nappy, and as soon as I changed it, she wet it again, so we had to go through the whole process a second time.

At last the girls were ready. They struggled into their welly boots and we went out the door to the garage.

"Get the glove," I told Suzi. "Buddy's in the front garden with the baseball. Maybe he'll toss you a few."

"Okay!" She found the glove and she and Marnie and I ran into the garden. There was the ball, but no Buddy.

"He must have gone around the back," I said. I picked up the ball, and we looked in the yard behind the house.

No Buddy.

"Buddy?" I called. "Buddy? Bud-*dee*!"

I listened for his answer, but the only sounds were the rain dripping off the trees and, in the distance, a car horn.

"Bud-*deeee*!" Suzi yelled.

"Maybe he's hiding," I suggested. "Buddy! If you want to play hide-and-seek, come out so we can choose 'it'."

Nothing.

I began to get angry. "Buddy, if you don't come out right now, you're going to be in very big trouble. I'm not kidding."

"I bet he's over at the Pikes'," said Suzi. "I bet he wanted to play with Nicky."

"I hope so," I replied. "But even if he is, he's in trouble. He's always supposed to let me know where he's going to be."

I put Marnie in her pram and she and Suzi and I walked down the street to the Pikes'. Suzi rang their bell. Mrs Pike answered the door.

"Hi, Dawn," she said. "Hi, Suzi, Marnie. What a nice surprise." She reached out to tickle Marnie.

"Hi," I replied. "Listen, is Buddy here? I'm baby-sitting and he went outside a little while ago. Now I can't find him. I thought he might be playing with Nicky."

Mrs Pike frowned. "No, he's not here. At least I don't think so. Let me get Nicky, though. Maybe he knows where Buddy is." Mrs Pike leaned inside and called Nicky. A few moments later, he appeared in the doorway.

"Sweetie," said his mother, "Dawn's looking for Buddy. Do you know where he is? Did he come over today?"

"No," said Nicky. "I was hoping he would because I want to show him my new walkie-talkies."

"But he hasn't come by?" Mrs Pike asked again.

Nicky shook his head.

"Did he call you?" I asked.

"Nope."

"Well," I said, forcing a smile, "I'm sure he's around somewhere. I'll go back to the Barretts' and look some more."

"Try calling the Murphys. And the Spencers," suggested Mrs Pike. "And let me know if you don't find him in about half an hour."

"Okay," I replied.

I pushed Marnie to the Barretts' house so fast that Suzi had to run to keep up with me.

There's no reason to panic, I kept telling myself. This is a big neighbourhood with lots of kids. Buddy could be anywhere.

Even so, my heart was pounding and I was beginning to feel nervous. Buddy was my responsibility. I was supposed to know where he was.

At the Barretts', I plopped Marnie in her playpen, much to her dismay, and Suzi and I checked the house and the garden thoroughly. Unless he was in a very clever hiding place, Buddy was definitely not at his home.

I called the Murphys and the Spencers. No one had seen Buddy. But Mr Murphy gave me the names and numbers of four other neighbours. I called every one of them.

Not a trace of Buddy.

Feeling panicky, I phoned Mrs Pike. "I've looked everywhere and called all the neighbours!" I cried breathlessly. "I can't find Buddy."

"Keep calm," said Mrs Pike. "Call the Spencers and the Murphys again while I phone some other neighbours. We'll spread out and search for him. I'm sure he'll turn up."

Twenty minutes later, a big group of people, including Mr and Mrs Pike and seven little Pikes (Jordan was at his piano lesson), were gathered in front of the Barretts'. Mrs Pike took charge.

"Everyone spread out and look for Buddy," she instructed us. "Go in pairs or groups of three. Younger children go with an adult. Come back here if you have anything to report. I'll stay with Dawn by the phone in case Buddy calls."

The neighbours dispersed excitedly. Mrs Pike and I went inside and I put Marnie down for a nap. When she was settled, I ran into the kitchen, where Mrs

Pike was fixing Suzi a sandwich.

"Have you called Mrs Barrett?" Mrs Pike asked me.

"I can't," I replied. "She drove to Greenvale to shop. I don't know which stores she's going to."

Greenvale is a historic town about thirty miles from Stoneybrook. The main street has been fixed up to look the way it did two hundred years ago, and it's lined with quaint shops. The town is sort of a tourist trap, but it's a lot of fun.

"Oh, Greenvale," said Mrs Pike. "I suppose you can't reach her in that case. Unless — did she say anything about eating lunch there? We could try calling the restaurants."

I shook my head. "She just said she was going shopping."

"Oh, well, I don't suppose calling her would do much good, anyway. She'd just panic and come home."

I wandered anxiously to the front door and back into the kitchen. "Why hasn't someone found him by now?" I asked. "How far could he have gone?"

"I don't know, sweetie," said Mrs Pike, "but he'll turn up."

"What if he's hurt?" I cried suddenly. "What if he climbed a tree and fell out or got hit by a car or something? Maybe he's lying somewhere unconscious and that's why he hasn't come home."

"Try not to think that way," said Mrs Pike. She eased me into a kitchen chair across the table from Suzi and set a glass of milk in front of me.

I couldn't drink it. "Once I read about a little girl who fell in a septic tank," I said. "Buddy could have fallen down one. Or —"

At that moment the phone rang. I leaped for it.

"Hello. Barrett residence. Buddy, is that —"

"Hello?" said a woman's voice. "This is *The Stoneybrook News*. Would you be interested in a subscription? We offer a special discount to —"

"No, thanks," I interrupted her. "Sorry." I hung up the phone. "Newspaper subscription," I told Mrs Pike.

She looked disappointed.

"Dawn?" said Suzi. "Someone's at the front door."

Mrs Pike and I dashed to the front door, where we found Mr Murphy, Mr Prezzioso, and Mallory Pike.

"Just checking in," said Mr Murphy. "No luck. The three of us walked all up and down High Street. Then we looked in the back gardens along Slate Street."

A few minutes later Vanessa Pike, Mrs Prezzioso, and Jenny checked in. They hadn't had any luck, either.

Just as they were leaving, Jordan Pike turned up. "Hi, Dawn," he said. "Hi,

Mum. I got your note and I came over like you said to. What's going on? There are all these people outside."

"Honey, Buddy's missing. Everyone's out looking for him. You haven't seen him by any chance, have you?"

"Sure I have. And he's not missing," replied Jordan.

I could have jumped for joy. "Where is he? Where is he?" I cried.

"He's at his lesson."

"Lesson? What lesson?" I asked. Mrs Barrett was disorganized, but she wouldn't forget to tell me if one of the kids was supposed to go for a lesson — would she? "Suzi, come here for a sec," I called.

Suzi ran out of the kitchen and joined Jordan and Mrs Pike and me on the front porch. "Suzi, does Buddy take any kind of lessons — like piano lessons or art lessons?" I asked her.

She frowned. "No . . ."

"Are you sure?"

"No . . ."

"Honey, what makes you think Buddy is at a lesson?" Mrs Pike asked Jordan.

"Because at the same time Mrs Katz and Sandy picked me up for my piano lesson, I saw someone pick Buddy up. So I just thought —"

"You saw Buddy get in a car with someone this morning?" Mrs Pike exclaimed.

Jordan nodded.

Mrs Pike turned to me. She looked stricken. "I'm going to call the police," she said.

I followed her inside the house, feeling dazed.

14th CHAPTER

After Mrs Pike called the police, everything started happening so quickly that the afternoon went by in a blur.

First Suzi began to cry — hard. So when Mallory came by the Barretts' again, her mother told her to take Suzi, Claire, and Margo back to the Pikes' house for a nap. It would be quieter there and they didn't need to be around when the police arrived.

Shortly after Mallory left, Mrs Spencer arrived, carrying a small red sneaker. It was rain-soaked and muddy. "I found this near the sewer on High Street," she reported. "It's not Buddy's is it?"

I breathed a sigh of relief. "No, thank goodness. It's too small for him, and he was wearing boots."

The police arrived next. There were five of them. Two left as soon as they had a recent photo of Buddy. (I grabbed it off the coffee table in the Barretts' living room, frame and all.) Another one asked me questions, while the last two asked Jordan questions. They were more interested in Jordan than in me.

Over and over, they asked him the same questions: What did the car look like? Did you see the licence plate? Can you describe the driver? Was it a man or a woman?

Jordan became frustrated, then frightened, and finally burst out tearfully, "I don't *know*, okay? We live three houses away, and besides, I wasn't paying attention. I didn't think there was any reason to. Mrs Katz was backing down our driveway and as we returned onto the street I saw the car pull up next to the kerb in front of the Barretts' house and I saw Buddy get in. That's *all*."

"It was a blue car?" asked one of the policemen.

"Yes."

"And you didn't notice the driver?"

"No."

"Did Buddy look scared as he got in the car? Did he look like he didn't want to go?"

"No, he was just opening the door and getting in."

"Did you recognize the car? Have you seen it around here before?"

"I don't know. It was just a car." A tear slipped down Jordan's cheek. He wiped it away with the back of his arm and glanced around, looking ashamed. Most of the neighbours had gathered, and Jordan was embarrassed to be seen crying.

Mr Pike put his arm across Jordan's shoulders. "Any more questions?" he asked the police.

"Just a couple," replied one. "Jordan, I know we've asked you this before, but are you positive you didn't see the driver? You can't even tell us whether it was a man or a woman?"

Jordan took a deep breath and let it out slowly. He was trying to control his temper. "I didn't see," he said after a moment. "I was looking at Buddy, not at the car or the driver."

"One last thing," said the policeman. "About what time was it that you saw Buddy get into the car?"

(I thought this was a silly question because I'd already told him that Buddy had disappeared sometime between eleven and eleven-fifteen, but I suppose they had to follow certain procedures.)

Jordan turned to Mrs Pike. "Mum, what time did Mrs Katz pick me up?"

"At eleven-fifteen, honey."

"Eleven-fifteen," Jordan told the policeman. "My piano lesson was at eleven-thirty."

The cop nodded his head and made a note on a pad of paper.

Meanwhile, I had finished answering the

questions the third policeman was asking. He wanted to know what Buddy was wearing, how old he was, where his mother was, whether anything unusual had happened during the morning — and a lot of stuff about his father. He especially wanted to know where Mr Barrett lived and what I knew about the divorce. He looked disappointed when I said I didn't know where Buddy's father lived, or anything about the divorce, but he was quite interested when I said that Mrs Barrett didn't like Mr Barrett to call the kids.

When he had finished talking to me, I sat down on the ground right where I'd been standing, bent my head down so that my hair fell around me, hiding me, and let the tears begin to fall. I cried and cried.

After a while I felt a hand on my back.

"Dawn?" said a gentle voice.

It was Mum. Someone must have called her. Probably Mrs Pike. I could tell she had sat down next to me. Without a word, I leaned over to her. She put her arms around me and held me for a long time.

When I felt better, I sat up. "I guess I ought to get back to work," I said, sniffling. "Marnie will be awake soon, and the police are trying to find out where Mr Barrett lives."

Mum patted my back. "You're a brave girl. I'm proud of you."

"I wouldn't mind if you stuck around

though," I told her.

She smiled. "I plan to. The police have decided to organize a search of the neighbourhood, even though Jordan saw Buddy get in the car. Jeff and I are going to help out. We'll stay right around here."

"Thanks," I said. "Thanks a lot."

For the next hour, the police came and went. They searched the house for an address book or any clue to Mr Barrett, but didn't find much. Mrs Barrett seemed to have hidden away all information about her ex-husband. I even called Suzi to see if she knew where her daddy lived, but all she said was, "In his 'partment."

I took care of Marnie, who was up from her nap and hungry. Sometimes the police asked questions, sometimes they needed to use the phone. Under the direction of the cops, the searchers combed the neighbourhood. Six alsatian dogs joined in.

I fed Marnie, then brought her out on the front porch and let her toddle around the garden. I recited nursery rhymes to her. I sang songs. Marnie made the ham face.

"Silly girl," I said.

The phone rang.

I picked Marnie up and ran into the kitchen.

"Hello?" I said urgently.

"Hello?" said a small voice. "Dawn?"

"Buddy, is that *you*?" I cried.

"Yes, I —"

"Buddy, where are you? We're worried to death. Where *are* you?"

"In a petrol station."

"A petrol station? What — Where —" I didn't know what to ask next. "How did you get there? Whose car did you get into?"

"Dad's."

"Your father's?"

"Yeah, but I don't think I'm supposed to be with him. I knew you'd be worried, though, D —" Click, click. The connection went bad. Buddy's voice faded away.

"BUDDY? BUDDY?" I shouted.

Very faintly, I could hear him saying, "Dawn? Hey, how does this thing work?" He must have been in a pay phone.

Just before the line went dead, he yelled, "We're on our way home, Dawn. Okay? Dawn? We're on our w—"

"Buddy!" I shouted.

At that moment, the phone was grabbed out of my hand.

I screamed and whirled around.

It was one of the policemen. "It's Buddy, it's Buddy!" I babbled. "He's with his dad. He's at a petrol station somewhere. He said they're on their way home."

The cop, whose name was Detective Norton, looked puzzled. "There's no one on the line," he said. He hung up and got on the phone with the police station.

I began to indulge in a fantasy. The fantasy was that Mr Barrett would return, the police would see that Buddy was okay and would leave, the neighbours would do the same thing, and Mrs Barrett would come home and never know anything had gone wrong.

Unfortunately, Mrs Barrett showed up about fifteen minutes later. She came home to find the neighbourhood swarming with searchers (they hadn't been called off, despite the phone call), and two policemen having coffee in her kitchen.

She turned pale and dropped her shopping bags on the floor. "Dawn, what's going on?" she exclaimed.

I cleared my throat. "Well, Buddy disappeared this morning, and Jordan Pike saw him get into some car. So Mrs Pike called the police and everyone's searching."

"Oh, no." She sank into a chair.

"But Buddy called a little while ago. He's with his father. I don't know what's going on, but, anyway, he said he was on his way home. Oh, and Suzi's at the Pikes'. She's fine."

Mrs. Barrett looked dazed.

"Are you all right, ma'am?" asked Detective Norton.

"Yes, fine, thanks," she said briskly. She put her hand to her forehead. "I'm just trying to think . . . I'm sure this isn't Ham's — that's Hamilton, my husband — I'm sure this isn't his weekend to see the kids. At least I don't think . . ." She got up and crossed the kitchen. By the phone was her engagement calendar. She flipped a few pages. "Oops," she said. "It *is* his weekend. I was mixed up. But I wonder why he only has Buddy, and why . . ." She trailed off in confusion.

Twenty minutes later, Mr Barrett still had not arrived.

"Ma'am, I don't mean to alarm you," Detective Norton began, "but has your divorce been a friendly one?"

"No, it hasn't," Mrs Barrett answered. "Why?"

"Because," replied the detective, "many of the children missing today in this country are children of divorced parents. They've been taken by parents who want custody of them, but have not been granted custody."

"Oh, *no*," exclaimed Mrs Barrett firmly. "Ham and I have problems, and I know he feels he doesn't get to see the kids enough, but he'd never kidnap them."

"Are you sure? A parent will do desperate things for his children."

Mrs Barrett poured herself a cup of coffee. She stirred it thoughtfully. But before she said a word, we heard car doors slam, and the next thing we knew, Buddy burst into the kitchen, followed by a tall, sheepish-looking man.

Buddy ran to his mother and gave her a hug. Then he ran to me and gave me a hug. "I'm sorry I made you worry, Dawn," he said. "I'm starving. Do we have any cookies?"

I found cookies for Buddy while the police sat Mr Barrett down and began asking him questions furiously. Apparently, earlier in the week Mr Barrett had become angry when he'd realized that once again, Mrs Barrett had confused the dates and had forgotten that today was to be Mr Barrett's day with Buddy, Suzi, and Marnie. He had decided to teach her a lesson. His plan was to come by on Saturday, simply take the children, and wait for Mrs Barrett to figure out her mistake. So he drove over to the Barretts' house. There he found Buddy by himself in the front garden. At that moment, he decided that the easiest course of action would be just to take Buddy without bothering to look for the girls. So he did. He drove Buddy to an amusement park and took him out to lunch, but Buddy didn't seem to be enjoying himself. When he asked him what was wrong, Buddy said he was worried about me. He didn't think I knew where he was. That was when Mr Barrett realized that Mrs Barrett wasn't even home. Concerned about what a baby-sitter might do when she discovered that one of her charges was missing, he headed home immediately, stopping briefly at the petrol station on the way. He'd tried to call before that, but had got only busy signals, and didn't even know Buddy had phoned until they were on the highway again. (Buddy had called while his father was in the men's room.)

The police gave Mr Barrett a warning, but that was all. However, they did strongly suggest that the Barretts talk to their lawyers about the custody arrangements. Just before I finally left, I told Mrs Barrett I would be back the next day.

I had something to tell her.

15th CHAPTER

Mrs Barrett and I were sitting on the Barretts' back porch. It wasn't Mr Barrett's day to spend time with Buddy, Suzi, and Marnie, but Mrs Barrett had suggested that he take them — considering the mess she had caused the day before.

The house was so quiet. I had never heard it so quiet. No running feet or yelling voices or crashing toys. Mrs Barrett had served us glasses of iced tea and had brought out a plate of cookies.

We both added sugar to our tea, stirred it, and took a sip.

"So, Dawn," said Mrs Barrett, "what is it you wanted to talk about?"

I put my iced tea down and drew in a deep breath. "Mrs Barrett," I said, "I really like Buddy and Suzi and Marnie, but I can't baby-sit for them any more."

Mrs Barrett looked at me in dismay.

"You *can't*? Why not?"

"Because of what happened yesterday."

"Mr Barrett? But we're going to straighten our problems out. We're going to talk to our lawyers just like the police suggested, and maybe a counsellor, too. You won't have any more problems with my ex-husband."

"That's not really what I meant," I replied. "The problem is . . ." How did I tell Mrs Barrett the problem was *her*? "The problem is that I've had a lot of trouble because of mistakes that . . . mistakes-you've-made," I said in a rush.

Mrs. Barrett knitted her eyebrows. I couldn't blame her. After all, I was just a twelve-year-old kid, and I was telling her she was careless.

"I'm really sorry," I said, "but I can't be a good baby-sitter unless the parents give me a little help. I don't know your children as well as you do. I need you to tell me things about them — like whether they have allergies. And I have to know where you are while I'm in charge. If you're doing errands, that's one thing, but when you go somewhere in particular, I need to have the phone number."

"The right phone number," Mrs Barrett added thoughtfully, and I knew she was thinking about Hurley's Garage.

"Yes," I said. "But it's even more than that. I need . . . I need some organization.

And I can't do all your housework any more. And yesterday was very scary. And you know what else? Buddy and Suzi are starting to depend on me — a lot. Buddy comes to me with school problems now. Suzi calls me on the phone. Sometimes she doesn't really know what to say, but other times she's telling on Buddy or telling me about something that's gone wrong. I love Buddy and Suzi, Mrs Barrett. Marnie, too. But I think they should be going to you more. I mean, *you're* their mother. Not me."

Mrs Barrett didn't say anything. She just stared at me. She was looking as beautiful as usual — all cool and fresh, with her long, slim legs crossed in front of her. Mrs Barrett was gorgeous. She always looked so together. But her house didn't and her kids didn't. And I had decided that not only was baby-sitting for them too risky and too much work, it wasn't even good for the Barretts. I wasn't helping them. I was just allowing Mrs Barrett to go on being rushed and disorganized. As long as I was around to take care of things, then Mrs Barrett didn't have to take care of them herself.

Since Mrs Barrett wasn't saying anything, I stood up. "I'm sorry," I said. "That's why I can't sit for you any more. Your kids need *you*, not a baby-sitter. I talked this over with the Babysitters Club, and they agree with me. The other members think I'm doing the right thing."

Mrs Barrett suddenly found her voice. "Oh, Dawn, please. Just a minute. Don't go. You're the best sitter I've ever found. The children *adore* you. They talk about you all the time. I think they'd be very hurt if you stopped sitting for them."

"Well, I'll still come and visit them sometimes. And I'll see them in the neighbourhood when I'm baby-sitting at the Pikes' or the Prezziosos'."

"Couldn't we work something out?" Mrs Barrett asked.

"Like what?"

"How about if I asked you to come by ten or fifteen minutes earlier than I actually need you? That way we'd have time to talk before I leave. I could give you phone numbers and information. You could ask questions."

"Well . . ."

"And I'll try to keep the house in better shape."

"You know, Buddy and Suzi can help you with that," I told her. "They help me all the time. They're getting good at it."

"Maybe," Mrs Barrett went on, "if you did decide to sit for us, I could leave you specific chores to do sometimes and pay you extra for them. That seems fairer."

"Well . . ."

"Would you reconsider, Dawn?"

I thought for a moment. At last I said, "How about a trial? I'll baby-sit for you three more times and we'll see how things go."

"It's a deal," said Mrs Barrett. She stuck out her hand and we shook on it. Then we finished our iced tea and had a very nice time talking about Buddy and Suzi and Marnie.

At the next meeting of the Babysitters Club, I told my friends what had happened when I talked to Mrs Barrett. They thought I'd been very brave to have the talk in the first place.

"And so," I said as I finished up the story, "I think it was all right to agree to sit for them again. After all, it's just for a trial period."

"I think it was okay, too," said Kristy. "It was reasonable. And we don't want to give the Babysitters Club a bad name by being unfair. It was good that you compromised."

Lately Kristy almost always agreed with me. Not when she didn't really mean it, of course. But she *used* to disagree with me on everything, just so she could pick a fight.

"How are the Barrett kids doing, anyway?" asked Mary Anne. "I mean since Saturday."

"They're fine," I said. "Marnie never really knew anything was wrong, of course. And Suzi spent most of that afternoon with Mallory Pike. Mallory is really good with little kids."

"I suppose because of all her brothers and sisters," said Stacey.

"She'll make a good babysitter," added Claudia.

"Maybe one day the Babysitters Club will be a huge organization," I said dreamily, "and Mallory will be part of it." I smiled at the thought. "Anyway, Buddy's okay, too. A little confused, I guess, but his parents have explained to him that although they do have some problems, they're trying to work them out."

"The thought of parents kidnapping their own children is scary," said Claudia.

"Yeah," said Kristy. "I wonder if my dad would ever do that to my brothers and me. Or what if he just took David Michael — and we never saw him again? How awful." Kristy shivered.

I did, too. If my father kidnapped me, would I want to go back to California now? I wasn't sure. Although if he did kidnap me, I suppose we couldn't go back to California. We would have to go somewhere that no one would think to look for us. Like Alaska. I definitely did not want to do that. Anyway, Connecticut isn't so bad when you get used to it.

I looked at the members of the Babysitters Club — my friends. We were sprawled all over Claudia's room. Mary Anne and I were lying side by side across her bed on our stomachs. Kristy was slumped thoughtfully in the director's chair, and Stacey and Claudia were sitting on the floor. All of us, except for Stacey, were eating liquorice that Claudia had stashed in a pencil case in her desk drawer.

The phone rang.

I picked it up while Mary Anne poised her pen over the appointment book.

"Hello, Babysitters Club," I said.

"Hi, Dawn. It's me, Buddy."

"Hi, Buddy," I replied. I raised my eyebrows at the girls as if to say, "What now?"

"You know what happened in school today? All I did was drop my pencil on Steve's desk and my teacher goes, 'Okay, Buddy, no break for you.'"

A thousand questions popped into my mind like, Did you *throw* your pencil on Steve's desk or did you really just drop it? How many times had you already dropped your pencil on Steve's desk? But instead I asked, "Buddy, is your mum home?"

"Yes."

"I think you should tell *her* about this. She'll help you decide what to do. She's good at that."

"Not as good as you."

"Give her a try, Buddy," I said. "But you know what you can tell me? You can tell me if anything funny happened at school today."

"Well," said Buddy slowly. "Ashley

Vaughn's lunch fell out of the window."

"That's pretty funny," I told him, laughing. "Okay, I've got to get off the phone now." (Kristy was shooting looks at me because we're not supposed to have personal phone conversations during the meetings.) "Talk to your mother tonight, Buddy, and tomorrow when I baby-sit you can tell me what she said."

"All right," he agreed.

We hung up.

The members of the Babysitters Club discussed business for a few minutes. Then Kristy cleared her throat and got to her feet.

Something was about to happen. I could tell. Mary Anne and I sat up, and Stacey and Claudia stopped fooling around with the liquorice and looked at Kristy.

"You guys," Kristy began, "I've been thinking over this problem of what to do about the club after I move. I know we have all the summer before that happens, but I can't help worrying about it. And I've come to a decision."

I turned to Mary Anne in horror. Suddenly I was sure — *sure* — that Kristy was going to break up the club. I could feel tears pricking at my eyes. I looked down so that no one would see me cry.

"My decision is to raise our club subs."

My head snapped up in surprise. "Raise our subs? Why?" I asked.

"Because the only solution I can think of

is to pay someone to drive me to and from the club meetings. Not a cab driver — that's much too expensive — but someone who'd like to earn a little money. It would be an easy job, and for someone young who's just learnt to drive —"

"Charlie!" cried Mary Anne suddenly. Charlie is Kristy's older brother. "Charlie will be able to drive then, won't he? Oh, Kristy, that's a wonderful idea! He'll be dying for excuses to use the car."

"But do you mind paying for it out of our subs?" she asked us. "It seems like a club expense to me, since I *am* the chairman and I have to be at the meetings, but —"

"No, it's the perfect solution!" I agreed.

"Perfect!" echoed Stacey and Claudia.

Whew. What a load off everybody's minds.

Two days later, a "surprise" visitor came to one of our club meetings. It was my brother, Jeff, and the only person he was a real surprise to was Mary Anne. The rest of us had asked him to come over with the new camera my dad had sent him. Kristy and I had an idea. Mary Anne was almost finished redecorating her room. (She even had a new rug, a new bedspread, and newly painted walls, courtesy of her father, who was becoming less and less tight with pennies and dollars.) But she didn't have the one thing she'd been talking about ever since she started the project — a framed photo of the members of the club.

The day Jeff came over, Kristy, Claudia, Stacey, and I went to the meeting very carefully dressed. (We knew Mary Anne would look nice, because she always does.) When we told Mary Anne why Jeff was there, she burst into tears. But she dried them quickly.

"Okay, everybody, why don't you pose on the bed?" suggested Jeff.

So we did. Claudia, Stacey, and I kneeled against the wall and Kristy and Mary Anne sat in front of us.

"Smile!" said Jeff.

We grinned. Mary Anne grinned the hardest.

Click, click went the camera.

And five members of the Babysitters Club were captured for ever.

The Babysitters Club

KRISTY'S BIG DAY

1st CHAPTER

"Old Ben Brewer was crazy. As crazy as anything. He ate fried dandelions, and after he turned fifty, he never left his house . . . except to go out in the yard to get dandelions. When he died, his ghost stayed behind. I'm telling you, he haunts our attic."

Karen Brewer looked at me with wide eyes. "Honest, Kristy. *He haunts our attic,*" she repeated. Karen loves to talk about witches and ghosts. She thinks her next-door neighbour, old Mrs Porter, is a witch named Morbidda Destiny.

Karen's four-year-old brother Andrew turned to me with eyes as round as an owl's. He didn't say a word.

"I think you're scaring your brother," I told Karen.

"No, she's not," whispered Andrew.

I leaned over to him. "Are you sure?" I whispered back.

"No." I could barely hear him.

"I think that's enough talk about ghosts," I said.

"Okay," replied Karen. Her tone of voice implied that it was foolish of me not to arm myself with information about old Ben. "But when you move into our house, you'll wish you knew more about my great-grandfather. Especially if you get a bedroom on *the third floor*." Karen made "the third floor" sound like Frankenstein's castle.

I couldn't help giving a little shiver. Why was I letting a six-year-old get away with this?

Karen looked at me knowingly.

Karen and Andrew are the children of Watson Brewer, who is engaged to my mother, the divorced Elizabeth Thomas. This means that when they get married, Karen and Andrew will become my little stepsister and stepbrother. It also means that my brothers and I will be moving out of our house on Bradford Court, where we grew up, and into Watson's house.

There are pros and cons to this situation. The pros are that Watson is rich. In fact, he's a millionaire. And his house isn't just a house, it's a mansion. Charlie and Sam, my older brothers, who have shared a room for years, will each have his own bedroom at Watson's. They could probably each have a suite of rooms if they asked nicely. And

David Michael, my little brother (he just turned seven), will finally have a room bigger than a cupboard.

I don't benefit at all where bedrooms are concerned, since I already have my own and I think the size is fine. The main drawback to moving to Watson's is that he lives across town. I have never lived anywhere but right here on Bradford Court. All my friends are here. Mary Anne Spier lives next door, Claudia Kishi lives across the street, and Stacey McGill and Dawn Schafer live nearby. The five of us make up the Baby-sitters Club (I'm the chairman), and it won't be nearly as easy to run the club when I live clear on the other side of Stoneybrook, Connecticut.

The other "con" is that Watson is mostly okay, but sometimes he can be a jerk.

"Kristy? Karen? Andrew?"

"Yes, Mum?" It was a Saturday evening, and my mother had invited Watson and his kids over for dinner.

Karen and Andrew and I were crowded into a lawn chair in our back garden. They're good kids. I like them a lot. And I know them well since I've been sitting for them off and on for about nine months, since the time the Babysitters Club began. Watson and their mother are divorced, and while they live with their mother, they do spend every other weekend and certain holidays with Watson, and some in-between time, too, if they want. The arrangement is pretty loose.

"Dinner's ready!" called Mum.

"Come on, you guys," I said. "You know what we're having?"

"What?" asked Andrew cautiously. He's a very picky eater.

"We are having spaghetti."

"Oh, yum!" cried Karen.

"Pasketti?" Andrew repeated. "Jody Jones said pasketti is dead worms."

"Ew, ew, ew!" exclaimed Karen.

"Well, Jody Jones is wrong," I told them. "Spaghetti is . . . noodles. That's all."

We entered through the back door of our house and went into the dining room. The table was set for eight. Candles were burning and the lights had been dimmed. A bottle of red wine stood next to Watson's place. The dining room had been transformed into an Italian restaurant.

"This looks great, Mum," I said, "but it's June. We should be eating outside. We're wasting the nice weather."

"Oh, honey," my mother replied. "Eat spaghetti on our laps? That sounds like the start of a Persil commercial. We'll be much better off in here."

I laughed. Ever since Mum got engaged to Watson, she's been in a great mood.

My brothers crowded around the table. (They're never too far off when food is about to be served.)

Karen and Andrew approached them shyly. (Yes, even Karen gets shy sometimes.) I think she's shy around Charlie, Sam, and David Michael because she knows they're going to become her stepbrothers and she wants to make a good impression on them. She knows me a lot better than she knows them because of all the baby-sitting I've done for her and for Andrew.

"Hi, Charlie. Hi, Sam. Hi, David Michael," Karen addressed each one solemnly.

"Hi, kid," replied Charlie. (Charlie is my seventeen-year-old brother. He just got his driver's licence.)

Sam, who's fifteen, couldn't answer Karen because he was busy scooping up olives from a little dish my mother had set on the table next to the pepper grinder.

"Hey, Mum!" I called into the kitchen. "We need an olive refill."

Sam gave me a dirty look.

While we kids stood around waiting for Mum and Watson, who were doing last-minute spaghetti things in the ktichen, Karen and David Michael eyed each other. Mum is afraid there's going to be some trouble between the two of them after the wedding. David Michael is used to being the baby of the family. He's not just the youngest, he's the *much*-youngest. There's a ten-year difference between Charlie and him. There's even a five-and-a-half-year difference between him and me. (I'll be thirteen in August.) But suddenly he's going to acquire a part-time six-year-old sister and four-year-old brother.

Meanwhile, Karen is used to being the oldest. And she's going to acquire *three* part-time older brothers plus me.

Furthermore, Karen and David Michael are so close in age that Mum is sure they're going to be competing for things — toys and privileges and stuff. She wonders whether David Michael will feel cheated because he'll be in state school, while Karen goes to private school. On the other hand, she thinks David Michael would feel resentful if she switched him *out* of the school he's used to.

Things could get pretty messy.

Karen broke the silence in the dining room by gazing around and saying, "Yikes, after Dad and Elizabeth get married, I'm going to have *four* brothers."

"And me," I reminded her. "You'll be my very first sister."

"We better stick together," said Karen. "We're the only girls."

"Oh, yuk, yuk, yuk," said David Michael. "Pew, pew pew. One sister's enough. Now I'll have two." He made a horrible Halloween face.

"Hey!" exclaimed Karen. "You said a poem, David Michael!"

"I did?"

"Yeah. Say it again."

David Michael tried to repeat his nasty remark, but couldn't remember it.

"Serves you right," I said. "What'd I ever do to you?"

David Michael looked puzzled. Then he smiled. "Nothing!"

I shook my head.

Through all of this, Andrew did not say a word.

Mum and Watson came into the dining room then, Mum carrying a pot of tomato sauce, Watson following with the spaghetti. When everyone had been served, Watson poured wine for Mum and himself.

"Can I have some?" asked Charlie.

Watson looked at Mum. We all knew what the answer would be, but I liked the fact that Watson let Mum say it. For the time being, she was still our boss. The Thomas boss. And Watson knew it.

"When you reach the drinking age," replied Mum pleasantly, "then you may drink."

"But Mum, a year from now I'll be going to college. All the kids —" Charlie stopped. Mum isn't too partial to any sentence that begins with "all the kids".

Charlie gave up. He looked like he might sulk for a while, though.

"Well," Mum said cheerily, "we've set the date."

"What date?" I asked. I twirled a huge

mound of spaghetti onto my fork, raised it, and watched the spaghetti slide off.

"The date of the wedding."

"Oh, yeah?" said Sam. He sucked a mouthful of spaghetti in through pursed lips. Andrew watched with interest. Sam never looked up from his plate. "When's the big day?" he asked.

"The third Saturday in September," Mum answered proudly. She was about to make goo-goo eyes at Watson. It's got so I can tell when this is going to happen.

"What's a wedding?" asked Andrew suddenly. He had not touched his pasketti.

Mum's goo-goo eyes changed to surprised eyes. She looked from Andrew to Watson and back to Andrew.

"*You* know," Karen told Andrew. "I showed you a whole wedding. Remember when I put on the long white dress and kissed Boo-Boo?" (Boo-Boo is the Brewers' cat.)

Andrew nodded.

"We've talked about the wedding, Andrew," Watson added. "And everyone here is going to be a part of it."

It was my turn to act surprised. "We *are*? I mean, *I* am? *I'm* going to be in the *wedding*?"

"If you want to be," said Mum. "I'd like you to be my bridesmaid."

"Your bridesmaid?" I whispered. "Really? Like in a long, fancy dress with flowers in my hair?" I was awed.

"Since when do you like long, fancy dresses and flowers?" asked Sam.

"Since right now," I replied. "Oh, *Mum*!"

"Is that a yes? You'll be my bridesmaid?"

"It's a YES-YES-YES!" I jumped up and ran around the table to hug my mother.

When I was sitting down again, she went on. "And Charlie, I'd be honoured if you'd give me away."

"*Sure*," said Charlie eagerly. (He must have forgotten about the wine.)

"Sam," Watson spoke up, "I'd like you to be my best man."

"And David Michael to be the ring-bearer," said Mum.

"What about *me*?" cried Karen.

"How would you like to be the flower girl?" asked Watson. "You'd walk up the aisle in front of Elizabeth and me, carrying a basket of rose petals."

"Oooh," breathed Karen.

"And Andrew can escort you," said Mum. "That means he'll walk beside you."

"What does that make him?" asked Sam. "The flower boy?"

Everyone laughed. Everyone except Andrew. When we calmed down, he said softly, "I don't want to be in the wedding. And I mean it." (I wasn't too surprised. Andrew is terribly shy.)

Watson and Mum looked at each other.

"When he means it, he means it — usually," said Watson. He turned to Andrew. "Well, think it over. We'd like you to be in the wedding, but it's up to you, okay?"

"Okay."

I didn't give another thought to Andrew all evening. The only thing I could think about was the wedding. I, Kristin Amanda Thomas, was going to be a bridesmaid.

2nd CHAPTER

I have usually found that, in life, good things are followed by bad things. One day you get an A-plus on a spelling test, the next time around you get a C (or worse). A run of good luck is followed by a run of bad luck. Good news is followed by bad news.

It was that way with the wedding.

On Saturday we had all that good wedding news. Mum and Watson had settled on the September date. They'd asked us kids to be part of the ceremony. Mum had even told me later that my wedding shoes could be my first pair of shoes with heels. I couldn't believe it.

That was Saturday.

On Wednesday, just four days later, came the bad stuff. The whole wedding fell apart. In one glump.

My first clue that something was wrong was that Mum was at home when I got there after school. She's almost never home before six o'clock. She has this important job with a big company in Stamford and she works very hard. My brothers and I are used to looking after ourselves after school.

Needless to say, I was surprised to find Mum sitting at the table in our kitchen at three-thirty in the afternoon. She wasn't doing anything — just sitting there.

"Mum?" I said, as I set my bag on the table. "Are you sick?"

"No, honey, I'm fine," she replied.

"How come you're home? Is David Michael sick?"

"No, no. Everyone's fine. But, well, I just can't believe what happened today."

"Uh-oh," I said, "What?"

"For starters, the company wants to send me on a two-week business trip to Europe."

"Europe!" I shrieked. "Europe? What's wrong with that? London! Paris! Rome! Oh, Mum, can I come? Please? Are you going over the summer? I promise I'll be good. I'll stay out of your way. I won't ask you to buy souvenirs or anything. Just food. *Please*?"

Mum gave me a wry smile. "I'd like nothing better than to take you to Europe, sweetie," she said, "but unfortunately the trip is scheduled during the school year."

It was June. There wasn't much left to the school year. "You mean you're going *now*?" I cried. "Who'll stay with us?"

Mum shook her head. "I'm not going now. The trip is scheduled for September." She let that sink in. "I'm supposed to be in Vienna on the day of the wedding."

"Oops," I said.

"Oops is right."

"So have an October wedding," I suggested. "Think of it — a fall wedding with the leaves turning. It would be really pretty."

"I did think of it, actually," said Mum. "I was sitting at my desk, mentally adding sleeves to our gowns and changing the flowers from roses to chrysanthemums, when the phone rang. Guess who it was."

I'm got good at guessing games. "I'll never guess, Mum. Who was it?"

"The estate agent. And guess — wait, I won't make you guess again. Believe it or not, she's already got a buyer for our house."

"Already! You only put put the house on the market two days ago. You thought it would take months to sell it. That's great news, Mum!"

"Sort of great. The buyer is desperate. He's in a rush. He's willing to pay what we asked for, which is more than we thought we'd actually get for the house. Here's the catch: He's in such a big hurry that he wants to move his family in by July fifteenth."

"Mum, no! That's next month. It's impossible. Sell the house to someone else."

"I don't think anyone else will pay us this much money."

"Well, what do we need money for? You're marrying Watson."

"Honey, Watson and I and Watson's ex-wife and your father all have various ideas about how to spend our money. It's quite complicated, but for the time being, let's just say that I don't want Watson to feel obliged to finance four extra college educations. The money from the house, half of which, first of all, is your father's, goes towards college for you and your brothers. So the more we make, the better."

"Mum. I'm trying as hard as I can to follow all of this, but what exactly are you saying?"

"I'm saying that Watson and I are going to have to get married at the end of the month so we can move into the Brewers' house two weeks later."

I was stunned. I stared at Mum with my mouth hanging open. David Michael came home, let Louie (our collie) in, sat down in Mum's lap, and still I was open-mouthed and speechless.

The phone rang. Mum answered it. It was a friend of hers. They had a long, chatty conversation which ended with Mum saying, "So the upshot is that the wedding will be in two and a half weeks."

"Two and a half weeks," I moaned.

"What's going on?" asked David Michael.

"It's a long story," I told him.

Mum hung up the phone. She seemed awfully calm — too calm.

The next thing I knew, she was going crazy. She leapt to her feet (David Michael jumped out of her lap just in time), held her hands to her head, and cried, "Oh, my lord! How can I plan a whole wedding in two and a half weeks? Two and a half *weeks*! Planning a wedding is like having a baby. You need time to pre*pare* things! You have to talk to the florist, the minister, the dressmaker, the caterer. You have to tell the relatives. You have to *rent chairs*! I can just picture the caterer when I order crab crepes for three hundred. He'll say, 'And what month is the wedding? December?' and I'll say, 'No, it's this month,' and he'll *laugh* at me!"

"Mum —" I started to say.

David Michael tiptoed across the kitchen and held my hand. He stared at Mum, fascinated.

Louie hid under the table.

"A tent! We have to rent a tent!" she cried.

"Rent-a-tent, rent-a-tent," chanted David Michael, giggling.

"Mum —"

"We'll hold the wedding in Watson's garden. We'll never be able to rent a hall somewhere for the reception. What if it *rains*?!"

"Mum —"

"Oh, lord — decorations!"

"Mum, why don't you call Watson?" I managed to say.

"I'd better call Watson," said Mum. (She hadn't heard me.)

Good. I hoped he could calm her down.

Mum went into the bedroom and called Watson privately. When she returned, she looked saner. Sort of. But then she opened up a cupboard and began pulling pots and pans and things out of it. She seemed to be sorting them into piles.

"What are you doing?" I asked her.

"Not only do I have to plan a wedding, I have to get ready to move. This whole house needs to be packed up. We can take the opportunity to clean things out. I bet we haven't cleaned the house out in five years. We can make a big donation to Goodwill."

David Michael began to whine. And even though I'm too old to whine, I joined in.

David Michael started with, "But I don't *wanna* move. I wanna stay *he-ere*." (David Michael is a champion whiner. Anybody who can turn a one-syllable word into a two-syllable word is good — very good.)

I added, "I want one more summer here. I don't *wanna* leave yet."

Mum pulled her head out of the cupboard.

Very slowly she turned around to face us. She didn't say one word, just looked at David Michael and me.

"Uh-oh," said David Michael under his breath. He apologized quickly. "Sorry, Mum." Then he hustled out of the kitchen with Louie at his heels.

Mum was still looking at me. But I wasn't about to apologize. I was sorry I'd whined at her, but I was still upset about the move. "You said we weren't moving until the autumn," I told her. "You said we'd still be here this summer."

"Those weren't promises, Kristy," replied Mum. "That's simply what I thought was going to happen."

"But Mum, it's not fair. I don't want to spend this summer at Watson's."

"You'll be spending next summer at Watson's," she pointed out. "And the one after that and the one after that."

"I know. That's why I want this summer *here*, with my friends. One last summer with Mary Anne and the Babysitters Club and Jamie Newton and the Pikes and — and in my own room . . ." I trailed off.

"I'm sorry, honey," said Mum. "This is the way things are, fair or otherwise."

"*Boy*," I exclaimed. I stomped upstairs.

When I got to my room I closed my door. I considered slamming it, but I wasn't really angry. I was sad.

I sat down at my desk and looked out the

window. There are two windows in my room. One faces the front garden. The other faces the side. Mary Anne Spier's house is next door, and I can look right into her bedroom from that side window.

She wasn't there that day. She was baby-sitting for Jenny Prezzioso. I was kind of glad, because I just wanted to be able to stare and think. If Mary Anne had seen me at the window, she would have wanted to talk.

A lot of things, both good and bad, have happened at those windows. For years, every night after Mary Anne's strict father had made her go to bed, we used to stand at the windows with flashlights and signal each other with a secret flashing code Mary Anne had made up. (We don't have to do that any more, though, because Mr Spier has changed. Now he lets Mary Anne talk on the phone at night like a normal person.)

When Mary Anne and I had fights, I knew I could always get to her by pulling my window shade down. It was like not speaking to her. When we weren't fighting, which was most of the time, we would string a paper-cup telephone between our rooms, or sail paper aeroplanes with messages on them through the windows. What was I ever going to do without Mary Anne next door?

And what was I going to do in a new bedroom? The room I was in had been my bedroom since the day my parents brought me home from the hospital. It was fixed up just the way I wanted it. Over at Watson's, I could have my pick of bedrooms. I could be on the second or third floor. I could be near my brothers or away from them. I could have a big room or a not-so-big room, but it didn't matter. It wouldn't be the same. No matter what my room was like, I wouldn't be able to look out the window and into Mary Anne's room. "My" room would never feel like *my* room.

I tried to picture all the bedrooms I had ever seen at the Brewers'. Maybe there was one like mine — with a window facing front, another window facing the side, the cupboard opposite the front window, the door opposite the side window. Maybe I would take that room and arrange my furniture in it just the way it's arranged now. It wouldn't be the same, but it would help.

"Kristy?" I heard Mum call.

I opened my door. "What?" I shouted back.

"I need you here."

"All right." I went slowly downstairs.

Mum was sitting at the kitchen table with papers spread out all around her. Before I asked her what she wanted, I peeked in the cupboard she'd started to clear out. Everything had been thrown back in. I guessed the packing was going to wait until later.

"Can you help me make some lists,

sweetie?" said Mum. "We've got to start listing *everything* if we're going to pull off this wedding: things to do, things to buy, people to call . . ."

"Okay," I said.

"First we'll list people to invite to the wedding. I'll go through our address book and you write down the names I call out."

When we had finished, Mum looked at the list I had made. "Hmm. An awful lot of these people are from out of state, and a lot of them have a lot of children. It's a good thing they'll only be in town a night or two."

We started some other lists. Weddings sure are complicated. I didn't know they take so much work. By five-thirty, when it was time for a meeting of the Babysitters Club, I was overwhelmed. I realized why Mum had gone crazy earlier.

I began to feel sort of sorry for her.

3rd CHAPTER

Mum had kept me so busy with the wedding lists that by the time I dashed across the street to Claudia's house, it was five-thirty-six and I was the last to arrive. As club chairman, that was not an ideal situation. However, since the others were all there already, I took advantage of the situation to get a good, long look at them. Since I knew I'd be moving soon, I felt I wanted to do that, even though I'd still see them at our meetings and in school.

Claudia Kishi, our vice-chairman and a junkfood addict, was prowling around her room, trying to remember where she'd hidden a large bag of M&M's. She was wearing one of her usual outrageous outfits: a black leotard and skintight red pants under a white shirt that was so big it looked like a lab coat. Claudia's a wonderful artist and she had decorated the shirt herself, covering it with designs painted in acrylic. She had pinned her long, black hair back at the sides with red clips.

Mary Anne Spier, secretary of the club and my best friend, was sitting on the floor, leaning agianst Claudia's bed. Her wavy brown hair had recently been brushed and looked shiny and full. Until a few months ago, she had always worn it in two plaits. I still wasn't used to seeing it loose. As secretary, Mary Anne was in charge of the Babysitters Club Record Book, where we write down appointments and keep track of our clients' addresses and things.

Stacey, our treasurer, was sitting cross-legged on the bed with the envelope containing the club subs in front of her. Like Claudia, Stacey enjoys looking good. She enjoys putting together outfits and she enjoys shopping. So does her mother, who has time for such things. (I'm happy in jeans and a T-shirt.) But Stacey is from New York City, where shopping is the official city sport. Stacey's blonde hair was permed, and what with that, her purple nail polish, and her Swatch accessories, she looked, well, kind of like a thirteen-year-old Madonna. (If Claudia wasn't Japanese, she'd look a little like Madonna, too.)

Seated on the floor next to Mary Anne was the newest member of the Babysitters Club and Mary Anne's other best friend (I'm the first one). Dawn Schafer had been named our official alternate officer, which means that she's familiar with the job of every club officer and can substitute for anyone who can't make a meeting. Dawn has the most amazing hair I've ever seen. It's straight and fine and hangs down past her waist, and it's so light I couldn't even call it blonde. It's almost white, it's the colour of sunlight or bleached straw. I hope she never cuts it or changes it.

"Hi, everybody," I said.

"Hi!" replied the members of the Baby-sitters Club.

"Want some?" asked Claudia. She'd just found the M&M's in a box under her bed labelled ARTWORK: STILL LIFS AND PORTRITS. (Claudia is a terrible speller.) She tore a corner off the bag and motioned for me to hold my hands out. I did, and took a few.

"Sorry I'm late," I said, settling myself in Claudia's director's chair. "Any calls yet?"

"One," Stacey answered. "I have a feeling it was Sam. The person said, 'Hello, this is Marmee March. I need a sitter for Amy tonight, someone who has experience with little women.' "

I scowled. "Sam, all right. He never takes this club seriously."

"Oh, well," said Mary Anne, holding out her hands as Claudia went by her with the M&M's. "Who cares?"

"Yeah," I said. "Well, we better get

down to business. Have you all been reading the notebook?" (We also keep a notebook in which we write up each baby-sitting job we go on. Everyone is supposed to read the book a couple of times a week so we know what's going on with the kids we sit for.)

The others nodded.

"How much money is in the treasury, Stacey?" I asked next.

"Seventeen dollars and twenty-five cents."

"Oh, that's good! Can you guys think of anything we need?"

The money in the treasury doesn't come from what we earn baby-sitting (at least not directly), but from our club subs, and we use it to buy things we need for the club as well as to give ourselves a little treat every now and then, such as a slumber party.

"I don't think we need anything," replied Claudia. "Maybe we should have a party — an end-of-school party or something."

"Maybe," I murmured.

"Kristy?" asked Mary Anne. "Anything wrong? You seem sort of quiet."

I might as well get it over with. "I've got good news and bad news," I replied.

"Uh-oh," said Dawn.

"The good news is that I'm going to be a bridesmaid in Mum's wedding."

"Oooh," the other members of the club sighed happily.

"The bad news is that the wedding's in

two and a half weeks and we're moving in July."

"*What*?" cried Mary Anne, jumping up. "You can't move in July!"

"I tried to tell Mum the same thing," I said, "but she wouldn't listen. She has all sorts of reasons for selling the house right now. They're too complicated to explain."

Mary Anne looked like she might cry, but Dawn couldn't get past the wedding part. "You're going to be a bridesmaid, Kristy? Oh, you're so lucky!"

At that moment, Claudia's phone rang. Usually we all lunge for it, but we were so caught up with the news of the wedding that it rang twice before Stacey reached lazily for the receiver and said, "Hello. Babysitters Club."

As soon as she said that, though, we went into action. Mary Anne opened up our club record book and turned to the appointment pages so she could see our baby-sitting schedules; the rest of us paid attention.

When Stacey hung up she said, "That was Dr Johanssen. She needs a sitter for Charlotte after school on Friday, from three-thirty to five-thirty."

"Well," said Mary Anne, "Dawn and I are the only ones who don't have jobs then."

"But Jeff and I are going over to our grandparents' house that afternoon," Dawn spoke up, "so you can sit for Charlotte,

Mary Anne." (Jeff is Dawn's younger brother.)

Mary Anne pencilled the job into our calendar.

Then Stacey called Dr Johanssen back to let her know she had a sitter. When she hung up the phone, she said, "Tell us about the good news first, Kristy. Tell us about being a bridesmaid."

"Well," I said, "actually, I've known about that since Saturday, but I didn't say anything because . . . because . . ." How could I explain that the reason I hardly ever talked about the wedding was that, deep down, I still wasn't sure I wanted Mum and Watson to get married? The girls would never understand. They'd all met Watson and they liked him. They'd all baby-sat for Karen and Andrew, and they thought they were adorable and wonderful. They'd all have swapped their own houses for Watson's mansion in a second. And Mary Anne, whose widowed father has been going out with Dawn's divorced mother, would have died with pleasure if *those two* had decided to get married.

Finally I said, "I didn't say anything because we still thought the wedding was going to be in September and it seemed so far off."

Mary Anne looked at me sceptically.

"But *tell* us about it," Stacey persisted. "Like, what are you going to wear?"

Even I had to admit that what I was going to wear was glamorous and exciting. "Well," I said . . .

And just then the phone rang again.

Business first.

"Hello. Babysitters Club," said Dawn. "Oh, hi . . . Yes . . . Yes . . . Just Claire and Margo? Okay, I'll call you right back." She hung up. "That was Mrs Pike. She needs a sitter next Tuesday afternoon, but only for the two little ones" (Claire and Margo Pike have six older brothers and sisters) "from three-thirty until six."

Mary Anne looked in the book. "Let's see. Kristy, you'll be watching David Michael then. Claudia, you have an art class. And I'm sitting for Jenny Prezzioso. Dawn or Stacey?"

"I've got to see the doctor in New York on Tuesday," said Stacey. "We'll be gone the whole day."

"Everything all right?" asked Claudia.

"Yup," replied Stacey. "Just a checkup." (Stacey has diabetes. She's on a strict diet — none of Claudia's junk food allowed — and the doctors and her parents keep a sharp eye on her.)

Dawn called Mrs Pike back to say that she'd be sitting.

"Bridesmaid gown," said Stacey the second Dawn had taken her hand off the receiver.

"Okay," I said with a smile. Mum and I

had finally decided on exactly what we'd all be wearing. "It's going to be a long gown —"

"Oooh."

"— With short sleeves and a ribbon sash above my waist. Mum says that'll make me look taller — and older."

"What colour?" asked Mary Anne.

"Whatever colour I want, as long as Karen agrees to it. She's going to be the flower girl, and her dress is supposed to look like a younger version of mine. I mean, it won't be long, and the sash will be at her waist, but it has to be the same material."

"I think you should choose pink," said Dawn.

I wrinkled up my nose. "Too cutesy."

"Green," said Claudia.

"For a wedding?"

"How about yellow?" suggested Mary Anne.

"Pale yellow. That would be pretty for the summer. And you and Karen both look good in yellow."

Everyone agreed that yellow was the best choice for my dress.

"What about your shoes?" said Claudia.

"Hey!" I said. "Get this. Mum said I can wear heels —"

"Oooh."

"— and we're going to buy these special shoes that you can dye to match your dress."

"Oooh."

In spite of myself, I was beginning to feel excited again. "Did I tell you that all us kids are going to be in the wedding?"

"Really?" squealed the others.

"Well, everyone except Andrew. He's shy about things like that. Karen's going to be the flower girl, like I said. Charlie's going to give Mum away, Sam's going to be the best man, and David Michael's going to be the ringbearer."

Everyone began talking at once: "Oh, you're kidding!" "I wish *I* could be in a wedding."

"When did you say it will be?" asked Claudia.

"In just two and a half weeks. On a Saturday. A week after school is over."

Claudia sighed with joy. "I can't stand it! Only a week and a half of school left and then . . . *summer*!" (As you can probably tell, Claudia does not like school.)

"A week and a half!" Stacey exclaimed. "Gosh, it crept up on me. In New York, I went to a private school. The summer holiday began right after Memorial Day. I thought I'd never last until June the nineteenth. But now it's almost here. What happens at the end of school? Anything special?"

"The Final Fling," Claudia replied.

"The Final Fling?"

"It's the last dance of the year," I told her.

"And the usual stuff," added Mary Anne.

"Room and teacher assignments for eighth grade."

"Report cards," said Claudia, making a face that looked as if she'd accidentally taken a swallow of sour milk.

"Let's decide what we're going to wear to the dance," suggested Stacey.

"I'm not going," Mary Anne said immediately.

"But you don't have to be asked to the Final Fling," I pointed out. "You can just go."

"I'm still not going. I don't like dances."

"Well, I'm going," said Claudia.

"With Trevor?" I asked. Trevor Sandbourne was the love of Claudia's life last fall.

Claudia looked at me as if I'd asked if she was going to the dance with Winnie-the-Pooh. "*Trevor*? No. Trevor's probably dating his own poetry at this point. That's all he cares about."

We giggled.

"If Alan Gray asks me, I'll go," I said. "I still think he's a pest, but he can be a lot of fun."

"I'll go," said Stacey, "with or without Pete." (Pete Black was part of Stacey and Claudia's crowd. He and Stacey had gone to several dances together.) "I think he likes

Dorianne now. Are you going, Dawn?"

Dawn frowned. "I have to decide."

We began to discuss what we'd wear. The phone rang with several more calls. By the time our meeting was over, I was more excited about the Final Fling than the wedding.

4th CHAPTER

The Final Fling came and went. I did go with Alan Gray. He was himself — fifty percent pesty and fifty percent fun. Claudia went with Austin Bentley, a new boy in school, and Stacey went with Pete after all. (Dorianne made wicked faces at them during the dance.) Dawn decided not to go. Mr Spier had offered to take Mary Anne and the Schafers out for pizza, and Dawn and Mary Anne never turned down a chance to see their parents together.

The last day of school came and went, too, and before I knew it, I was home that afternoon, hugging a rubbish bag full of junk I'd cleaned out of my locker.

It was one week and one day before the wedding. Mum decided to take the following week off from work to get ready for the big day. To make up for it, she'd said she would have to work extra hard ahead of time.

So when I came home to find Mum sitting at our kitchen table looking hysterical, I was surprised.

"Mum!" I exclaimed. "Today was your last day at the office before the wedding. I thought you'd be there forever. How come you're home already?" I began checking the contents of the fridge.

Sam appeared in the kitchen doorway. "That's a touchy question, Kristy. I just asked her the same thing, and you know what she said?"

"What?" I asked. I took an orange out of the fridge.

"I can't repeat it in mixed company."

I stuck my tongue out at Sam. But his comment rated a smile from my mother.

"Oh, Sam, it wasn't that bad," said Mum.

"Don't tell me," I said, suddenly inspired. "Let me make a guess. The wedding's in five days and we're moving in two weeks."

"No," said Mum with another smile.

"The wedding's tomorrow and we're moving on Wednesday?"

"No."

"The wedding's in five minutes and we're moving tonight?"

"No. But how about this? Sheila and Kendall" (they're Watson's ex-wife and her new husband) "called Watson to say that they're going to England for most of next week, and leaving Karen and Andrew with Watson."

"So?" said Sam and I.

"And Aunt Colleen and Uncle Wallace decided to come down on Sunday to help me with the wedding next week."

"Goody," I said. Colleen and Wallace are my favourite aunt and uncle.

"They're bringing Ashley, Berk, Grace, and Peter with them."

"Oh." (They're my cousins.)

"And Aunt Theo and Uncle Neal also called to let me know they're arriving on Sunday to help with the wedding. They're bringing Emma, Beth, and Luke."

"Oh." (More cousins.)

"*And* —" Mum went on.

"Uh-oh," said Sam and I at the same time.

"Tom Fielding, Watson's best friend — they haven't seen each other for a couple of years — is coming on Saturday evening. With his wife, and Katherine, Patrick, Maura, and Tony. I think."

"More kids?" I asked.

Mum nodded.

"Where," I said cautiously, "are all these people going to stay?"

"Our relatives are staying at the Ramada Inn in Shelbyville, and Watson's friends are staying with him." Mum paused. "However," she continued, "the adults are all going to be helping at the Brewers' during the day next week. That means that thirteen children are going to be running around, too. Fourteen, if I have to bring David Michael with me."

I raised my eyebrows.

"Holy . . ." Sam started to say, and then trailed off. "Fourteen? Are you sure?"

I counted them off. "Ashley, Berk, Grace, Peter, Emma, Beth, Luke, Andrew, Karen, David Michael, and — who are Watson's friend's kids?"

"Katherine, Patrick, Maura, and Tony," said Mum.

"Yup. That's fourteen."

Sam let out a low whistle.

"Next week," said my mother, "I need adults to help me cook, arrange flowers, set up chairs, shop, and do about a hundred other things, I do not need fourteen children underfoot."

Mum buried her head in her hands. "I will never pull this wedding off. Never. We're not going to get a thing done. We'll spend all next week breaking up fights over Tinker Toys and deciding who gets the last cookie."

In a flash, a brilliant idea came to me. (My best ideas come in flashes.)

"Hey, Mum, today was the last day of school," I pointed out.

"Oh, I know, honey. I'm sorry. How was it? How was your report card?"

"I got straight A's again, but that's not what I mean. I mean that school's *over*. Starting right now, I have nothing to do — except baby-sit."

"Kristy, you're a good, responsible babysitter, but even you can't take care of fourteen children."

"No, but the Babysitters Club can. There are five of us. The kids could come over here during the day."

"Oh, brother," exclaimed Sam. It was his turn to sit down and bury his head in his hands.

"That way," I said, "the adults could work at the Brewers' without any interruptions."

"Well, Kristy," said Mum, "that might be the solution."

"I have to check with the other club members, of course, and we might have to cancel some appointments, but I think we could do it. Would you really hire the whole Babysitters Club for the whole week?"

"I really would. And if the girls would really sit from nine to five Monday through Friday, Watson and I would really pay the club, let's see . . ." (Mum did some fast mental arithmetic) ". . . six hundred dollars."

"*What*!" exploded Sam.

"That's three dollars an hour apiece,

which comes to a hundred and twenty dollars for each of you for the week."

My jaw almost fell off. A hundred and twenty dollars in just one week!

'Mum, I'll give you a bargain," said Sam. "For just five hundred dollars, *I'll* take care of the kids."

"All fourteen of them? No way. Besides, I believe you already have a summer job."

"I know, I know." Sam was going to deliver groceries for the supermarket. He had done it the summer before. It didn't pay too badly, but five or six hundred dollars *was* an awful lot of money, even divided five ways. No wonder Sam was jealous.

"Don't you think you're overpaying them?" he asked.

"It's only three dollars an hour," replied Mum. "That's slightly more than what they usually charge, but there are fourteen children involved. How much do *you* make?"

"A little more than that per hour — but I get tips," said Sam.

"Kristy! Kristy!"

David Michael came crashing through the front door and into the kitchen. He was loaded down with rolled-up artwork, his lunch box, a shopping bag, and an envelope holding old papers and worksheets. "Oh, Mum, you're home already. Hey, guess what, everybody!" He dropped all his stuff on the floor, jumped over it, and thrust a piece of paper across the table at us.

Mum took it. I peered at it. A large gold star was glued to the top.

"'Citizenship Award'," Mum read. "'This certifies that David Michael Thomas has been chosen best citizen of the year in Mr Bowman's room, by his peers.'"

"That means the other kids," David Michael explained.

"Duh," said Sam. (Mum hushed him with one look.)

She turned to David Michael. "Honey, congratulations!" she said. "We'll have to frame this."

"They voted me," David Michael told us breathlessly, "and Mr Bowman wrote my name on the blank and gave it to me and said I should be proud. Can we put this with the other awards?"

(There's a wall in the study that's covered with awards Charlie and Sam and I have won. There's also a table filled with trophies. Until today, David Michael didn't have any awards or trophies, so this was a big deal for him.)

"Of course," said Mum. "As soon as it's framed."

Mum began helping David Michael to put away all the junk he'd brought home from school. Sam and I drifted onto the back porch.

"You know," I said, stretching out in a wicker chair and putting my feet up on the table, "in about two weeks, there isn't going to be an awards wall any more. Everything will be packed away for the move."

"Yeah, I thought of that," said Sam. He eased himself into a lawn chair and ran his fingers through his curly hair. "Poor kid." (I guessed he meant David Michael.)

"Do you think Mum'll put up our awards wall and the trophy table at Watson's?" I asked.

Sam shrugged.

"Hey, Sam, um . . . what do you think about going to the Brewers'? I mean, I know you like Watson, but . . . it's just . . . everything's going to be so different."

"I don't mind. I don't have to change schools. That's really important. None of us has to change schools. Did you know that Mum and Watson have to pay to let you stay at Stoneybrook Middle School instead of switching to Kelsey Middle School?"

"You're kidding. How come?"

"Because Kelsey is closer to Watson's, so technically you should go there when you change school districts. But the officials make an exception if you pay a fee. Mum has to pay for David Michael to stay at Stoneybrook Elementary School, too. It doesn't make any difference to Charlie and me, though, since there's only one high school."

"I didn't know all this," I said.

"Mum and Watson are trying to make the

move as easy on us as possible."

"I suppose so. But Sam, we still aren't Watson's kids, you and Charlie and David Michael and I. Even though we'll be living over there, we won't be his kids. Just his stepkids."

"What are you getting at, Kristy?"

"Well, for instance, if Watson was my real father, and he was still a millionaire, I could ask him for big things, like a video for my bedroom. But since he'll only be my step, can I ask him for *any*thing? I mean, say I need to borrow a couple of dollars and Mum's not around. Could I ask Watson? Mum said something about Watson not having to be responsible for our college educations."

"There's a big difference between four college tuitions and two dollars," said Sam.

"I know. But there's a big difference between four tuitions and a video, too, and I wouldn't ask him for a video. Where do you draw the line? In what ways is he our father?"

"Those are heavy questions," said another voice.

Charlie had come home. He joined Sam and me on the porch.

"I've been doing a lot of thinking," I told them. "You know how I don't like guessing games. Well, I don't like surprises, either. I like to know what's going to happen."

"But no one knows what's going to

happen, Kristy," said Charlie, the voice of reason. "Even Mum and Watson don't really know what to expect."

"I feel like we're in a movie," I said.

"*The Bride of Frankenstein*?" asked Sam.

"No, not *The Bride of Frankenstein*." I stuck my tongue out at Sam. Fifteen-year-old brothers are a real drag. It's too bad boys can't skip from fourteen right to sixteen or seventeen.

"*I Married a Witch*?" Sam guessed.

"*No*! It's just . . . well . . . think about it. Mum and Dad get divorced, Mum meets new guy, new guy has two kids, new guy turns out to be millionaire, Mum and new guy get married, we move to mansion. But that doesn't mean it has a happy ending."

"Yeah, stay tuned for Part Two," said Charlie. "I know what you mean. It's hard to believe."

"And scary."

"But," said Sam, turning serious, "we can make it work."

"You think so?" I asked hopefully. I looked at my brothers.

They nodded.

"Then stay tuned for Part Two!" I said.

5th CHAPTER

The next day, I called the first emergency meeting of the Babysitters Club that we'd had in a long time. It wasn't easy keeping my news a secret, but I managed not to say a word about the fourteen children or the six hundred dollars until Mary Anne, Claudia, Stacey, Dawn, and I had gathered in Claudia's room.

"What's this all about?" asked Stacey. She was lying on her back across Claudia's bed with her head hanging over the side, brushing her hair.

"Yeah, an emergency on the first day of summer holiday?" said Claudia from the end of her bed where she was leafing through a fashion magazine.

"Well, maybe it's not a true emergency," I said, "but it's very important and we have to take care of it right away."

"Did something happen?" asked Dawn.

"Just this," I said. "You all know that the wedding is a week from today."

"Oh, and I can't wait!" exclaimed Mary Anne. "I know exactly what I'm going to wear."

"I'm dying to see your bridesmaid gown," added Stacey.

The wedding was going to be on the big side. Mum and Watson had each asked a lot of guests, and they had let my brothers and me invite some people, too. Of course, my guests were the Spiers, the Kishis, the McGills, and the Schafers. They were all going to be there.

"Well, anyway, it's in a week," I said again. "And since Mum has so much to do and so little time to do it in, my relatives and some friends of Watson's decided to give her a hand."

"That's nice," said Stacey.

"It is," I agreed, "except that they all live out of town and they're all arriving by Monday — with their kids. Mum realized that while the adults are working on the wedding this week, there are going to be fourteen children who need looking after."

"Fourteen!" exclaimed Claudia.

"Yup. Seven of my cousins, four kids who belong to Watson's friend, plus Karen, Andrew, and David Michael. At first Mum thought the kids would just have to hang around Watson's while the adults are working, but she knows they're going to be in the way. So I sort of made a suggestion."

"What?" asked Dawn suspiciously.

"I suggested that the kids come over to my house every day this week and we'll baby-sit for them. That way the grown-ups will be able to get their work done."

"Us? Take care of fourteen children?" squeaked Mary Anne.

"Mum said that if we baby-sit for them from nine to five every day, she and Watson will pay us each . . . *One hundred and twenty dollars.*"

I looked around the room, expecting something to happen. I thought for sure someone would screech or gasp or fall off the bed.

Nothing.

I gave them a few moments to recover. Then I broke the stunned silence by saying, "That's six hundred dollars all together."

Finally I got a reaction.

In a teeny-tiny voice, Claudia said, "One hundred and twenty *dollars*? With one hundred and twenty dollars, I could buy one hundred and twenty bags of peppermints. That's about a year's supply."

Everyone began to laugh.

"You could buy three hundred packets of crisps," said Stacey.

"Or one thousand two hundred gob stoppers," I said with a giggle.

"Four hundred packets of gum," suggested Dawn.

"Sixty cartons of ice cream," said Mary Anne.

"Ice cream," said Claudia, "is one thing I've never been able to hide in my room."

There was another pause.

"You're serious about this, right?" Dawn asked me.

"Of course I'm serious," I replied. "Mum's in a real bind. We didn't figure on this happening. And with everyone coming from out of town . . ." I shrugged. "We have to do something."

"And your mum thinks we can handle it?" Mary Anne ventured timidly.

"Yes. So do I," I said. "It works out to two or three kids for each of us. We can do that easily."

"But fourteen at once," said Mary Anne.

"A hundred and twenty dollars each," Claudia reminded her.

"What do you say?" I asked the members of the group.

I looked at Claudia. She nodded emphatically. I looked at Dawn and Stacey. They nodded, too.

"Mary Anne?" I asked.

She hesitated. Then she nodded as well.

"All *right*!" I cried. "Now look, you guys, we have some work to do. Nine to five means all day, every day next week. A couple of times I'm going to have to leave for dress fittings and wedding things, but otherwise we'll have to stay at my house with the kids. We'd better see if we have any jobs lined up next week. Mary Anne, can you check our calendar?"

Mary Anne opened the record book to the appointment section. "Let's see," she said. "This isn't too bad. Kristy, you're supposed to sit for Jamie Newton on Tuesday. I'm supposed to sit for Jenny Prezzioso on Wednesday evening. I can still do that, I suppose. Stacey, you're supposed to sit for Charlotte on Thursday, and we have several things lined up for David Michael and for Karen and Andrew, but those aren't a problem because we're going to be sitting for them, anyway."

"Hmm," I said. "It isn't very good business, but we'll have to call the Newtons and the Johanssens and cancel. Unless . . ." I went on thoughtfully.

"What?" asked Dawn.

"Maybe the kids could just come over to my house. What difference will one more make when we're already watching fourteen?"

"That's true," said Stacey.

I picked up the phone. "I'll call Mrs Newton," I said, "then you call Dr Johanssen, Stace."

I explained the situation to Mrs Newton, who was not only understanding, but enthusiastic. She said she thought the experience would be good for Jamie. He was starting nursery school in the autumn and needed to get used to other children.

Then Stacey called Charlotte's mother. "Dr Johanssen?" she said. "Hi, it's Stacey. Listen, I'm calling about next Thursday. I — what? . . . Oh . . . Oh, sure . . . No, it's no problem. Not at all, I'll see you some other time. Say hi to Charlotte. Okay . . . Okay . . . 'Bye." She turned to us with a smile. "Well, I got out of that one. Dr Johanssen was just about to call us to cancel. Her schedule at the hospital got switched around, so she doesn't need me on Thursday."

"Great!" I said. "Does anyone have anything else to cancel? Dentist appointments? Claudia, art classes?"

They shook their heads.

"All right," I went on, "now we'd better do some planning for next week. First, let me tell you about the kids — their ages and stuff."

"I'm going to take notes while you talk," Mary Anne spoke up.

'Good idea. Okay, we'll start with my cousins. First, there are the Millers — Ashley, Berk, Grace, and Peter. Ashley is . . . I think she just turned nine. Berk's about six."

"Boy or girl?" Mary Anne interrupted.

"Boy," I answered. "Grace is five, and Peter's three."

"Okay," said Mary Anne.

"Then there are the Meiners. Luke is ten,

Emma is eight, I think, and Beth is about a year old."

"Okay."

"And then there are those kids of Watson's friend. I don't know anything about them. Maybe I'd better call Watson," I said.

I dialled Watson's number.

"Hello?" a small voice answered.

"Hi, Karen," I said. "It's Kristy."

"Hi, Kristy! Oh, guess what! Daddy took me shopping today. I got shoes for the wedding and they're very, very beautiful. They're black and shiny and they have a strap that buckles around my ankle."

"Oh, lucky girl! I can't wait to see them. I don't have shoes yet. Listen, Karen, is your daddy there?"

"Yes, he is. But Kristy, Ben Brewer's ghost broke a vase in the living room today. It was really scary."

Karen went on about the ghost for a while, then finally I was able to talk to Watson. When I got off the phone, I said, "All right. Watson's friends are the Fieldings, and the kids are young. Katherine's the oldest. She's five. Patrick is three and Maura's two. Tony is the baby. He's only eight months old."

"Hmm," said Mary Anne. "Let me just add David Michael, Karen, and Andrew to my list." She scribbled away. Then she looked up. "Well, I count seven girls and seven boys, one ten-year-old, two six-year-olds, one nine-year-old, one eight-year-old, a four-year-old, one seven-year-old, two five-year-olds, two three-year-olds, a one-year-old, a two-year-old, and a baby — Tony."

"Gosh, it sounds like kind of a handful when you put it that way," said Dawn. She and the others began to look worried.

"But we'll manage," I said. "You know, maybe we should divide the kids into age groups, organize your list according to age, oldest to youngest."

Mary Anne began writing busily. "Okay," she said after a minute.

Mary Anne's list looked like this:

Luke — 10	Katherine — 5
Ashley — 9	Andrew — 4
Emma — 8	Peter — 3
David Michael — 7	Patrick —3
Berk — 6	Maura — 2
Karen — 6	Beth — 1
Grace — 5	Tony — 8 months

"All right," I said. I borrowed Mary Anne's pen and drew four lines, one under Emma, one under Karen, one under Andrew, and one under Maura. "Look at this, everybody. Now we have five groups of kids, one group for each of us. The top group is the oldest kids, and the bottom is the babies. There are three kids in each group except the last. I think whoever has the babies will have her hands full with just two. Nappies and everything."

"We'd better decide right now who will be in charge of which group," said Dawn.

"Okay," I agreed. "Does anybody especially want the oldest kids?"

Stacey's hand shot up.

I wrote her name next to the top group. Then I asked, "Does anybody especially want the babies?"

Mary Anne raised her hand.

I wrote her name by the babies. Before I could ask who wanted David Michael's group, Claudia said, "I don't really care which kids I have, I like any age."

"Me, too," said Dawn.

"Me, too," I said. So I assigned Dawn to the six and seven-year-olds, Claudia to the two and three-year-olds, and gave myself Grace, Katherine, and Andrew. "Andrew feels most comfortable with me," I said. "And also on Tuesday, Jamie Newton will fit right into that age group, and I think he should be my responsibility."

"Hey!" said Mary Anne. "You know what we should do to help keep the groups straight? We should call them the red group, the blue group, or whatever we want, and make red nametags for Stacey's kids, blue tags for Dawn's kids, or something. That way the children will know what group they're in, and we'll be able to spot our kids easily. It'll help us learn their names, too. Kristy, you know most of them, but the rest of us only know Karen, Andrew, and David Michael. And nobody knows the Fieldings."

"Terrific!" cried Claudia enthusiastically, and the rest of us agreed with her.

So Claudia rummaged through her art supplies and found scissors, card, and string. We made red star nametags for Luke, Ashley, and Emma; bluebird tags for David Michael, Berk, and Karen; yellow suns for Grace, Katherine, and Andrew; green dinosaurs for Peter, Patrick, and Maura; and pink hearts for Beth and Tony, the babies.

"Now we should make tags for ourselves," Stacey pointed out. "The group leaders should have tags like their kids'. Then the older children will be able to read our names, and the younger ones at least will be able to figure out who their leader is by matching the tags."

So we made five more nametags. When we were done, we attached all the tags to string, except for Beth's and Tony's, which we decided to safety-pin to them.

Claudia then announced that it was time for a high-energy snack, so she rustled up a Mars bar (from the drawer of her jewellery box), a packet of Smarties (from the STILL LIFE AND PORTRAITS box), and a Crunchie (from her pocket). For Dawn, who often prefers healthier food, and for Stacey, she went to the kitchen and got a box of crackers and some fruit. When she returned, she was with her grandmother, Mimi, who was carrying a tray of drinks for us.

"Hello, girls," said Mimi in her gentle voice. "You seem to be working very hard."

Claudia told her what we were doing.

"Oh, my," said Mimi softly. "Fourteen children! Next week, while your mother is busy, Kristy, and your parents are at work," Mimi nodded to Claudia and Mary Anne, "you must be sure to call on me if you need anything. I will be here at home. You must let me know if you have any problems. I will be happy to help out."

"Thanks, Mimi," I said. "That's really good to know."

"It sure is," said Mary Anne, jumping up to kiss Mimi's cheek.

I could tell Mary Anne was still a little nervous about what we were going to be doing. But she loves Mimi, and if anybody could make her feel better, Mimi could.

Mimi is special to all of us.

When Mimi was gone, I said, "You know, you guys, taking care of fourteen children is kind of like teaching school or running a play group. Maybe we should think of some activities for our kids."

"Yeah, different groups can do different things," said Dawn.

"We could take them to the infant school

playground," suggested Stacey.

"Do art projects," said Claudia.

"I can even take the babies on walks," said Mary Anne.

We were all starting to get excited. We talked and planned and made lists. We couldn't wait for Monday.

6th CHAPTER

Wedding Countdown:
Sunday – Six days to go

Sunday is my favourite day of the week, summer or winter, for one reason: I get to sleep late.

That's why, when Mum came into my room the next morning, I was not at all pleased.

She opened my door and began pulling up my shades and straightening the things on my dresser, humming all the while.

"Come on, Miss Sleepyhead," she said finally. "Rise and shine."

I scrunched my pillow over my face to block out the light. "Mu-um," I complained. "Why are you doing this to me? What time is it?"

"Eight o'clock."

"Eight o'clock!" I figured she wouldn't

be bothering me unless it was at least ten.

"All your brothers are up already."

"But I won't have another chance to sleep late until next Sunday. That's *after* the wedding." I tried to make "after the wedding" sound farther away than it really was, like when you say, "See you next year" on December 31st.

"Honey, I need you today. This is the countdown to the wedding. Only six days left. Aunt Colleen and Uncle Wallace, and Aunt Theo and Uncle Neal are arriving today. They're going to the motel first, but then they're coming over here. They'll probably stay for dinner. And Nannie is going to come over. She wants to measure you again."

Nannie is Mum's mother. She lives in an apartment about forty-five minutes away from us. Nannie is really great. She's in her seventies, but she does all sorts of things. She goes bowling, she gardens, she volunteers at the hospital, she's a terrific cook — and she sews.

Nannie had offered to make my bridesmaid gown and Karen's flower girl dress. She had already taken Karen and me shopping, and we had chosen the patterns and material. Every so often, she needed to measure us.

"Is Nannie going to stay for dinner?" I asked.

"I think so," said Mum. "I'm sure she'll

want to see your cousins."

Ashley, Berk, Grace, Peter, Emma, Beth, and Luke are Nannie's grandchildren, too, of course, and since they live so far away, she doesn't get to spend nearly as much time with them as she does with my brothers and me.

"Good," I said. I found the courage to remove the pillow from my face. "Aughh, the sun is *bright*!"

"That's because it's a beautiful day out," Mum said cheerfully. "Now get a move on."

Nannie was supposed to arrive early in the afternoon. After I'd eaten lunch, I decided to sit on the front steps and wait for her. Louie waited with me. He took a nap with his head resting on my knees while I watched the street.

I spotted Nannie's car when it was still a couple of blocks away. Nannie's car is easy to pick out. It's a secondhand car that's about a hundred years old, and when she bought it last year, she had it painted pink.

"Pink!" my mother exclaimed when she heard the news. "For heaven's sake, why pink?"

"Why not?" Nannie had answered gaily. And then she had fastened a pink plastic flower to the aerial and hung a little stuffed koala bear from the rearview mirror. She named her car the Pink Clinker. (It's not in very good condition.)

As the Pink Clinker pulled into our drive, I woke Louie up, moved his head off my lap, and ran out to meet Nannie.

"Hi!" I called.

"Hi, there!" Nannie replied. She waved to me with one hand, and turned off the ignition with the other. The Pink Clinker shuddered into silence.

I helped Nannie into the house. She never comes over empty-handed. She carried a casserole, and I carried her handbag, a shopping bag full of presents, and her recipe box. (Mum and Nannie were going to discuss hors d'oeuvres or something.)

When Nannie had had a chance to sit down with a cup of tea on the back porch, I asked her an urgent question. "How's my dress coming along?"

"Now, Kristy, don't pester Nannie," said Mum as she and David Michael joined us on the porch.

"Oh, she's not pestering me," said Nannie with a smile. "She's just excited. Kristy, your dress is coming along nicely. But I think the sleeves are going to be a bit long, so I want to measure your arms again."

"How much is done?"

"Well, it's almost all tacked together," Nannie answered. "Karen's dress, too. But they're both a long way from being finished."

"Oh." My face fell.

"But don't worry. They'll be ready by Saturday. I promise."

"Okay," I said uncertainly, even though Nannie has never broken her promise.

"Kristy, relax," said Mum. "Have a cup of tea with us. Then I want you to round up your brothers so you kids can give me a hand with some things."

"Some things" turned out to be cleaning the entire house. Mum handed Charlie the floor waxer, Sam the vacuum cleaner, me a roll of paper towels and a bottle of window cleaner, and David Michael a rag and a can of furniture polish. Then she and Nannie sat in the kitchen and talked about wedding food.

It was not as if wedding food hadn't already been discussed endlessly, but Mum and Nannie had to work out how to instruct seven adults to prepare hundreds of hors d'oeuvres (appetizers) and canapés (crackers with stuff on them), not to mention salads and desserts, during the week. Mum had been very lucky in finding a caterer who, at short notice, could prepare the main dish for the buffet at the reception, but she and Watson were on their own for everything else.

By late afternoon, the house was shiny and clean, Mum and Nannie had finished with recipes for the time being, and the relatives were arriving. The first were Aunt

Theo (Mum's younger sister), and Uncle Neal, with Emma, Beth, and Luke.

They drove up, hooting.

"They're here! They're here!" David Michael called, and all of us, including Nannie, dashed outside.

Uncle Neal was just getting out of the car. He is not my favourite relative. His trousers and shirt never match, he smokes cigars, and he talks too loudly. But he's really okay. At least he never says to me, "My, Kristy, how you've grown. What grade are you in now?"

That's Aunt Theo's department. She stepped lightly out of the car and began hugging everyone. The second she got to me, she said, "My, Kristy, how you've grown. What grade are you in?"

"I'll be in eighth," I replied, and thought, And I have *not* grown. I'm the shortest person in my class.

She moved on to David Michael. "My, how you've grown," she told him. "What grade are you in?"

I stood behind Aunt Theo and crossed my eyes at David Michael. He tried not to laugh as he replied, "Second."

During all this, Luke and Emma had scrambled out of the car. I took a good look at them, since I hadn't seen them in almost two years.

Luke was the oldest, the oldest of all the kids we'd be sitting for, in fact. He seemed kind of skinny and little for ten (I should talk) and stood back shyly while his mother hugged everyone, his father told loud jokes, Mum and Nannie laughed, and Louie jumped up and down with doggie joy. Luke had a thatch of thick, dark-blond hair that quite possibly hadn't been brushed since December, and serious brown eyes.

Emma seemed to be the opposite of Luke. Although she looked like him — a little peanut of a thing, with messy blonde pony-tails and sparkling brown eyes — she raced around the yard excitedly.

"Hi, Nannie!" she cried. "Guess what, I won a second-place ribbon in the gymnastics competition! Did you bring me a present?"

Before Nannie had a chance to answer, Emma had rushed over to David Michael. "You're David Michael, right? I'm a year older than you are." She ran on to Louie, leaving my brother looking bewildered.

Uh-oh, I thought. Luke will probably be easy to baby-sit for, but Emma looks like a bundle of energy. I was glad she and Karen weren't going to be in the same group.

Suddenly I realized that little Beth was still sitting patiently in her car seat. I leaned into the car and said quietly, "Hi, there, Beth."

She regarded me solemnly. Didn't laugh, didn't cry. I figured she was sizing me up, so I decided not to push things. I sat down next to her. She was barefoot, and after a while I tickled her toes. Very slowly, a smile spread across her face until she was grinning.

"Want to get out of the car?" I asked her.

I unfastened about a million straps and buckles. Then Beth raised her arms and I picked her up. "Ooof, you're heavy!" I exclaimed.

"Mm-po-po?" she asked me.

"Whatever." Mary Anne would have to learn Beth's baby talk. I handed Beth to Aunt Theo. She looked surprised. "Goodness," she said, "I'm amazed that she let you pick her up. Ordinarily, she screams when a stranger comes too near her. We have the most awful time with babysitters."

At that moment, Sam caught my eye. He gave me a look that clearly said, "The Babysitters Club is really going to *earn* the six hundred dollars."

I stuck my tongue out at him.

"*Beep-beep! Beep-beep!*"

Another hooting car was pulling into our driveway.

"Aunt Colleen! Uncle Wallace!" I shouted.

As soon as my aunt had opened her door and straightened up, I practically threw myself at her.

Colleen is my Mum's youngest sister of all, the baby of the family. And I love her. She's sort of a younger version of Nannie —

busy and active with a wild streak in her. She understands me so well, it's almost scary.

"Hi, punkin. How are you doing?" she asked. She held me tight for a few seconds.

"Fine," I answered. I drew away and she cupped my chin in her hand and looked at me critically.

Meanwhile, cousins were spilling out of the car. First came Berk, the six-year-old. He made a beeline for David Michael. We see the Millers more often than the Meiners, and David Michael and Berk are good pals. I was glad that I remembered to assign them to the same baby-sitting group.

David Michael and Berk, followed by Louie, ran off towards the back of the house.

Next out of the car was Peter, who's three. He climbed out slowly, with tears in his eyes.

"Hey, Peter," I said. "What's wrong?'

Peter snuffled miserably.

"He's a little carsick," Aunt Colleen answered for him.

"Yeah," said Grace, the five-year-old, jumping to the ground, "He just puked. All over his colouring book!" She looked gleeful.

"Grace, that's enough," said her mother.

"How do you feel now, Peter?" I asked nervously. He looked awfully green.

"Not too good," he replied.

"I'd better get him in the house," said Aunt Colleen.

I watched them run inside, then turned back to the car and realized that Ashley was still sitting in it and Uncle Wallace was leaning a pair of crutches next to her door.

"Ashley!" I cried. "What happened to you?"

"I broke my leg roller-skating."

"We didn't say anything," my uncle added, "because we didn't want anyone to think we shouldn't come. Old Ash here is actually in pretty good shape. You should see her zip around on her crutches."

"I'm almost as fast as I was on my skates!" she exclaimed.

I helped Uncle Wallace get Ashley out of the car, and she swung herself up our driveway and into the house. (She *was* fast.)

Nannie made a big fuss over Ashley, then gathered her grandchildren around her and handed out gifts. She even had presents for my brothers and me, although she sees us often and has plenty of opportunities to give us things. I suppose she didn't want us to feel left out.

All of Nannie's presents were handmade. Mine was a beautiful sweater, bright red with little black Scottie dogs trotting across the front. I hugged Nannie and thanked her eight times.

After the presents, we ate supper on picnic tables in the back garden.

Here's what happened during the meal:

Beth stored up a cheekful of carrots as her father fed her, then spat them all over his shirt.

Peter and Grace got into a fight and began to cry.

Berk and David Michael got into a fight and began to cry.

Emma teased Ashley. Ashley whacked Emma with her crutch. Emma cried. Ashley was sent to the Millers' car and Emma was sent to the Meiners' car until they were ready to apologize to each other.

Luke did not say one word from the beginning of the meal to the end.

A horrible, stuffy feeling began to build up in my stomach. It might have been due to the big dinner I'd eaten. Or it might have been due to seeing the trouble caused by eight children with ten adults present.

What would the next day be like — with just five baby-sitters in charge of *fourteen* children?

7th CHAPTER

Wedding Countdown:
Monday – Five days to go

Stacey, Mary Anne, Dawn, and Claudia showed up at my house at eight-thirty sharp. Stacey brought her Kid-Kit, a box of games and toys she sometimes takes on baby-sitting jobs (we each have one); Dawn brought a big book of rhymes, songs, games, and activities for children; Mary Anne brought the club record book and notebook; and Claudia brought the nametags and some art supplies.

"Let's put on our own tags before we forget them," I said. "Then we'd better get organized."

"It's such a beautiful day," said Stacey as she slipped the red star over her head. "Maybe we should try to stay out in your back garden as much as possible, Kristy.

The picnic tables would be good for reading stories and colouring and stuff. And the kids can play ball, run after Louie, play games, anything — all in one place where we can easily keep an eye on them."

"Okay," I agreed. "We'll see how it goes. If it gets crazy, we can start splitting the groups up. Oh, Mary Anne, Mum got out our old playpen. You might need it."

"Thanks. That's perfect. I'll set it up outside so Tony and Beth can be with the big kids."

We set to work in the back garden.

Just before nine o'clock, the Millers arrived. While Mum talked to Aunt Colleen and Uncle Wallace, the members of the Babysitters Club showed Ashley, Berk, Grace, and Peter to the garden. We gave them their nametags, and I tried to introduce the kids to my friends and explain about the groups and leaders. But before I had got very far, Aunt Colleen called me from the back porch.

"Just a few instructions," she said, as I ran to her. "I know you and your friends will have your hands full today, but I need to tell you a couple of things. Peter goes down for a nap sometime after lunch — around two. Grace generally doesn't take a nap, but if she's tired, she'll sometimes go down with Peter."

"Wait, I'd better write this down," I said.

I got a pencil and a pad of paper from the

kitchen. "Okay, Peter — nap at two," I said to Aunt Colleen, trying to sound professional. "Grace — maybe a nap at two."

"Right," said my aunt.

Then she handed me two bottles of pills. "These are prescriptions," she told me. "Put them somewhere safe, out of reach of Peter and Beth and all the small children. I hope you won't need them but you might. This bottle, the one with the pink cap, is Berk's. It's for his allergies. He's been in good shape lately, but if you're outdoors a lot and he starts wheezing, give him one of these and make sure he lies down inside for a while. He's used to this and knows what to do."

I scribbled away frantically. I was beginning to panic. What if Berk (or any of the children) got sick? One of us would have to care for the sick child, and the others would have to take over the rest of the kids from that group. Another thing: We hadn't thought to "childproof" my house. We were inviting little kids into a home where electric sockets, medicine, and poisonous cleaning supplies were all over the place. We didn't have to keep those things out of the way any more. David Michael was seven years old and knew better. But when Aunt Colleen said to put the pills away in a safe place — where the little kids couldn't reach them — I began to worry.

However, my aunt didn't know what I

was thinking. She was still talking. "These other pills," she was saying, "are pain-killers. They're for Ashley. The doctor at the hospital gave them to us after he set her leg. Ashley hasn't taken one in a week, but every now and then her leg will swell under her cast, and it's quite painful. Give her *half* a pill with food if she complains of pain."

"Ashley — one half pill with food for pain," I repeated.

"I suppose that's everything," said Aunt Colleen. "I don't think you'll have any problems."

"Great," I said. I took my notes outdoors so I could share them with the other members of the Babysitters Club.

So far, things in the back garden looked peaceful. Everyone was wearing a nametag (although Ashley was complaining that hers looked babyish), and the kids were exploring the garden and the toys in the Kid-Kit.

"Yoo-hoo! Kristy! We're he-ere!" It was Aunt Theo. (Who else would say, "Yoo-hoo"?)

"Hi!" I shouted.

Emma burst outside, followed, at a much slower pace, by Luke. Aunt Theo came last with Beth — and a lot of equipment.

"Hi, girls," said my aunt.

"Aunt Theo, this is Mary Anne, Stacey —"

"Fine, fine," my aunt interrupted. "Now I've brought Beth's Walk-a-Tot chair so she can scoot around safely. She loves the chair. And here's her pram in case you want to take a walk. If she cries when we leave — and she probably will — just put her in the pram and walk her around. She'll calm down after a while."

I looked at Mary Anne, who was taking notes this time. My head was swimming. Naptime, pills, strollers, Walk-a-Tots . . . What had we got ourselves into?

Aunt Theo wasn't finished yet. "Beth usually takes two naps, one around eleven and another around two."

Well, that was something, I thought. At least the afternoon nappers would be asleep at the same time.

"And she usually takes a bottle to bed with her. Make sure you only give her the prepared bottles I brought. She's allergic to cow's milk, so the bottles are filled with a soy formula."

"Beth — allergic to milk," Mary Anne murmured.

I nudged Stacey. "Where are all these kids going to sleep?" I whispered.

Stacey widened her eyes. I guess she hadn't thought about naps and bottles and pills, either.

Aunt Theo stopped talking.

And just in time. Mary Anne, Stacey, Dawn, Claudia and I were about to get our first glimpse of the Fielding kids. Mum was leading a whole group of people into the back garden — all six Fieldings, plus Watson, Andrew, and Karen.

Courage, I told myself. Make like you're the Cowardly Lion. If you *think* you're courageous, then you'll *be* courageous.

"Honey," Mum said to me, "I want you to meet Mr and Mrs Fielding."

I shook their hands, Then I said, "And these are the other members of the Baby-sitters Club — Stacey, Dawn, Mary Anne, and Claudia."

Everyone exchanged hellos.

Karen took Andrew's hand and led him to the table where Claudia's art stuff was set out.

"I'm going to draw a big, ugly picture of Morbidda Destiny," I could hear her say.

But the Fieldings hadn't moved an inch. A baby was huddled in his mother's arms with his face buried in her neck. A girl about Grace's age was holding Mr Fielding's hand solemnly. And a little boy and girl were clutching their father around his legs, their faces also buried.

Watson leaned over and whispered to me, "They're all very shy."

Now this is the sort of thing that kills me about Watson. Duh. Of course they were shy. Any fool could see that.

Mrs Fielding spoke quietly to her children. "This is where you're going to play today. Andrew and Karen are here. See?" She pointed to the table where Andrew and Karen were colouring and giggling.

I knelt down to child level. "I'm Kristy. We're going to have lots of fun," I said. "There are swings and games and friends to play with."

The oldest child (Katherine?) bit her lip and gripped her mother's hand more tightly.

"Do you like dogs?" I tried. "We've got old Louie —"

"A dog, Daddy?" whimpered the little boy.

Oops, bad idea, I thought.

Mrs Fielding tried to untwine the baby from around her neck. "This is Tony," she said. "I think I'll just put him in the playpen."

She did so, with Katherine trailing behind, holding onto her mother's skirt.

Tony's face slowly crumbled. He sat on his bottom with his arms in the air and his lower lip trembling. His eyes filled with tears. Then, very slowly, he opened his mouth and let out a shrill, "Wahh!"

Mary Anne turned pale.

Mrs Fielding looked flustered. "I think — well, we'll just leave him there. He'll stop crying after a while. Now, this is Katherine."

"And this," said Mr Fielding, indicating the little boy attached to his left leg, "is Patrick. And this is Maura." (Little girl attached to right leg.)

Katherine, Patrick, and Maura made no moves to leave their parents.

I glanced at Mum. Mum glanced at Watson. They talked to each other with their eyes. Finally Watson clapped his hands together and said heartily, "Are the adults ready to go?"

"We have a lot to do today," added my mother.

Mr Fielding pulled Patrick and Maura off his legs.

Mrs Fielding got herself out of Katherine's grip. "We'll see you this afternoon," she said to her children. I could tell that Mr and Mrs Fielding were having as much trouble leaving as their children were having letting them go.

The adults walked around to the front of the house and piled into their cars.

Katherine, Patrick, Maura, Tony, Beth, and Peter all began to cry. Andrew took stock of the situation and began to cry, too.

Something else us baby-sitters didn't count on: seven crying children.

"Quick, put on the rest of the nametags and divide into groups," I said.

We did. Stacey and Dawn had no criers, Mary Anne and I had two criers each, and every kid in Claudia's group was crying.

But nobody panicked. Mary Anne put Tony in Beth's Walk-a-Tot and Beth in her pram, and walked Beth around the garden as Aunt Theo had suggested.

I talked quietly to Andrew and he stopped crying right away. After all, he knew where he was. Then I took my group off to a corner of the garden, pulled Katherine onto my lap, and began to read *Green Eggs and Ham*.

Claudia had a tougher job, but she did what I did, and led her three criers to a different corner, sat down and began reading *Where the Sidewalk Ends*. Soon every one of our criers had become a giggler. And Mary Anne's criers were quiet.

When I finished reading *Green Eggs and Ham*, I looked around the yard and took a fast head count. Stacey was sitting at one of the picnic tables with Luke, Ashley, and Emma. They were making woven placemats out of paper.

Nearby, Dawn was playing piggy-in-the-middle with David Michael, Berk, and Karen.

Claudia and I were reading to our groups, and Mary Anne had successfully put both babies in the play-pen and was tickling their feet.

Good. Fourteen happy chldren. The first crisis was over.

The rest of the morning went fairly

smoothly. There were a few arguments and tears but nothing to complain about. At lunchtime, we seated the twelve older children around the picnic tables, and put Tony in the Walk-a-Tot and Beth in her pram. Then Stacey and Dawn went into the kitchen to get the children's lunches. Mum had asked the parents to pack a separate lunch for each kid. This was a little hard on my aunts and uncles since they were staying in a motel, but it worked well because my friends and I didn't have to spend time making lunch. Also, we knew the parents would send food their kids would eat. This was important: We had a lot of picky eaters and a few kids with food allergies.

After lunch Tony, Beth, Maura, Patrick, and Peter went down for naps. We simply lined them up on a blanket in the living room, and after a while they all fell asleep.

Good timing. At two-thirty a hooter beeped in our drive.

"That's Nannie," I told Mary Anne. "She's here for Karen and me."

Nannie was helping out at Watson's that week, too, and she was supposed to take Karen and me to the florist to look at wedding flowers. Mary Anne was watching the nappers while Claudia took over my group. Claudia was reading to Grace, Katherine, and Andrew on a blanket under a tree, and the three of them looked pretty drowsy.

"Come on, Karen!" I called.

Karen raced across the yard and we scrambled into the Pink Clinker.

"How come we're going to see the flower lady, Nannie?" Karen asked. (Nannie isn't any relation to Karen, of course, but Karen loves my grandmother and started calling her Nannie that first time they met.)

"We have to see about flowers for your hair," Nannie told her.

"Flowers for my hair?" Karen squealed with delight.

"And for Kristy's," said Nannie. "You two will have matching flowers."

"What about the flowers for my basket?" Karen wanted to know.

"Rose petals. We'll talk to the florist about them, too. And Kristy, we'll see about your bouquet."

Who would have thought that choosing a few flowers could be so difficult? You would have thought we were choosing flowers for a royal wedding in London instead of just Mum and Watson's garden wedding.

First, Nannie showed the woman in the store swatches of the material from Karen's dress and my gown, which were going to be yellow. The woman said, "How about white flowers?" and Karen said, "Yuck," and Nannie said, "Salmon," and I said, "Yuck." And Karen said, "What's salmon?" and I said, "It's a fish," and Karen said, "Yuck" again.

After about fifteen minutes of that, we finally settled on yellow and white, with yellow petals for Karen's basket.

But the job was only half done. We still had to decide how Karen and I would wear our hair so the florist would know whether to make up wreaths or rosettes or what.

An hour later, we left. I was exhausted.

And a herd of children would be waiting for me when I got home.

However, coming home turned out to be the nicest part of the day. The little kids were rested from their naps and stories, and the older kids were excited because Stacey and Dawn had helped them put together a play, which they performed with great delight for Claudia, Mary Anne, me, and the younger children.

At five o'clock, the parents came home to fourteen happy children.

The members of the Babysitters Club decided that the first day had been success.

8th CHAPTER

Wedding Countdown:
Tuesday – four days to go

Tuesday, June 23rd

Today was another bright, sunny day, thank goodness, and almost as warm as a nice September day in California. Yesterday was fine with all the kids in Kristy's back yard, but we decided to do different things this morning. The kids would get tired of the Thomases' yard pretty quickly. So after the parents left, Mary Anne took the babies for a walk, Stacey took the red group to the brook to catch minnows, Kristy and Claudia walked their groups to the public library for story hour, and I took David Michael, Berk, and Karen to the school playground.

What a morning my group had— all thanks to Karen's imagination.

Tuesday morning started off a lot like Monday morning, except that the mothers didn't have any more instructions, us babysitters were a lot more confident and a lot less worried, and Mr Fielding had a much easier time prying Maura and Patrick off his legs.

When the parents left, there were only six criers (Andrew barely noticed that Watson was gone), and they were just crying token cries, except for the babies, who kept Mary Anne's hands full for quite a while.

We had agreed the evening before that we would take the kids on the trips that Dawn described in the Babysitters Club Notebook, and we decided to get started right away.

We must have looked pretty funny.

First of all, once the pink group had calmed down, Mary Anne had to fit both babies into Beth's pram. It wasn't easy, but finally she sort of smushed Tony into Beth's lap.

Claudia and I had to get seven small children (our two groups, plus Jamie Newton) all the way to the library. We worked out it would take about half an hour to walk them there.

"Wagons!" said Claudia suddenly.

"Oh, great idea!" I breathed a sigh of relief. Then I loaded Maura, Patrick, and Peter into David Michael's old wagon, and Claudia loaded Grace, Katherine, and

Andrew into Mary Anne's old wagon. After each packed a bag containing crackers, cans of juice, toys and extra nappies, and we were ready to pick up Jamie and go.

Despite the fact that David Michael hadn't used his wagon in at least two years, he yelled after me as I pulled my load down the driveway, "And those kids better not hurt my wagon while you're gone, Kristy!"

It must be a little hard for him practically to have a day-care centre in his house.

Anyway, everyone left for wherever they were going. Stacey set off for the brook with Luke, Ashley, and Emma. They reached it pretty quickly, even with Ashley gallumping along on her crutches, and settled in for a morning of fun, which Stacey told me about later.

Stacey had taken along a rubbish bag to wrap around Ashley's cast so it wouldn't get wet. Even so, Ashley wasn't able to do much at first.

"I can't get into a good fishing position!" she exclaimed. "My leg just won't go that way."

It was true. Luke and Emma were crouching along the bank with buckets and nets, but Ashley could only stand up or sit with her leg straight in front of her.

"I could help you wade," Stacey said uncertainly. "You could take off your sneaker, and I could help you stand in the brook on your good leg."

Ashley looked from her cast to the water tumbling over the rocks and then at Stacey. "I'd better not," she said, sounding disappointed.

"It's probably just as well," replied Stacey. But she was afraid Ashley would be bored.

It turned out that she didn't have to worry. Ashley sat down a safe distance from the bank and assigned herself all sorts of jobs, like minnow-counter and storyteller. Later she moved to a patch of clover and made clover jewellery for the whole group.

Meanwhile, Mary Anne was walking the babies. The arrangement in the pram had lasted about two minutes. Then Beth wanted to get out and walk. At first that seemed like a good solution, but Beth wasn't very steady on her feet yet, and toddled along slowly, often losing her balance and sitting down on the pavement. After ten minutes, they had travelled about six feet.

Thanks to the wagons, Claudia and I were having somewhat better luck, even though every few seconds one of us would have to turn around and call out, "Keep your hands in the wagon!" or, "Don't dangle your feet over the side!"

On the way to the library, we stopped at the Newtons' house.

"Hi-hi!" Jamie shouted when he saw us.

We introduced him to the other kids — and then realized there was no room for him to sit down. Three kids in a wagon was already a tight squeeze.

"Hey," Claudia, "you know what we need? We need a wagon watcher. The wagon watcher walks beside the wagons. When he sees anybody sticking their hands and feet outside of the wagon, he gets to trade places with that person, and that person is the new wagon watcher."

Claudia's idea was great. None of the kids wanted to be caught by the wagon watcher, yet they all wanted a chance to *be* the wagon watcher (except for Maura, who was really too little to understand the game). So we rolled cheerfully to the library, stopping eight times to switch kids, and arrived exactly one minute before the start of story hour.

Now, while we were on our way to the library, and Mary Anne was inching along with the pink group, and Stacey was taking Luke, Ashley, and Emma to the brook, Dawn was walking the three bluebirds to the infant school playground. This might seem like an easy job, and in fact it started out that way, but Karen Brewer always seems to make things more interesting than usual.

Tuesday was no exception.

"You know what?" she said, as she, Dawn, David Michael, and Berk reached the end of our street.

"What?" asked David Michael warily.

He had heard enough stories about witches and ghosts from Karen to be suspicious whenever she said, "You know what?"

"Yesterday when I got home, this big kid on my street said that at seven o'clock tonight, an army of Martians is going to attack the earth."

"Martians?" yelped David Michael.

"Tonight?" cried Berk.

"That's just a story, a joke," Dawn told them.

"No, it's true," Karen insisted. "This was a *big* kid. He's in *eighth grade*. He told me that a lot of people know about this, but they just don't want to believe it. Only the ones who believe will be safe, because they'll be able to hide in time."

"Hide where?" asked Berk.

"Underground," said Karen.

"In a hole?" said David Michael.

"I'm not sure," replied Karen slowly. "The kid didn't say."

"Karen, you know this is all just silly stuff, don't you?" asked Dawn.

"*No*," said Karen firmly. "No way. This is not silly stuff."

"There are no such things as Martians," Dawn told Berk and David Michael.

David Michael looked like he wanted to believe her, but he said, "I've seen Martians on TV."

Dawn noticed then that all three kids kept glancing up at the sky.

"Do you believe everything you see on TV?" asked Dawn. "Do you believe that Bugs Bunny and Mickey Mouse are real?"

"No," said David Michael, "but there might be Martians."

"Yeah," agreed Berk. "There might be Martians."

"There are no Martians," Dawn repeated, exasperated.

"Are, too," said David Michael, Karen, and Berk at the same time.

"I wonder what will happen," my brother went on quietly.

"You wonder what will happen when?' Dawn asked him.

"When they land."

Dawn threw her hands in the air. There was no point in arguing.

"They're going to fight us," Karen said fiercely.

"Martians have ray guns," Berk added. "Ray guns and spray guns."

"Spray guns?" repeated David Michael, alarmed.

"Yeah. They spray stuff on you so you can't move. Then they just pick you up and put you in their flying saucer and speed you away to Mars."

"Are they coming in flying saucers tonight, Karen?" asked David Michael.

"Hundreds of 'em," Karen answered. "All shiny and silvery."

David Michael searched the sky so long

that he tripped and fell on his knees. "I thought I saw one!" he said breathlessly as he stood up.

"Now it's gone."

They had almost reached the playground. Dawn tried to distract her group. "Hey, look at this!" she said, pointing to a poster that was tacked to the fence surrounding the schoolyard." 'Arts and crafts today. Puppet-making contest.' A contest, you guys! Wouldn't you like to enter? I wonder what the prize is . . . You guys?"

"Huh?" The three bluebirds were looking at the sky.

"I wonder if you could hide in your basement," David Michael whispered. "That's underground."

"Can I stay at your house tonight?" Berk asked my brother. "I don't know if the motel has a basement."

"*Berk*!" Dawn cried. "David Michael! Karen! *Enough*!" She thought about telling them they weren't allowed to discuss Martians any more, but decided that was too mean.

She led them through the gate and into the playground.

A handful of children were playing on the swings and seesaws and climbing frame. A big group was seated around a table that was covered with paints, scraps of felt, glue, scissors, buttons and all sorts of trimmings.

"How about making puppets?" Dawn

suggested desperately. "Let's at least find out what the prize is."

The three kids looked at each other. Karen leaned over and whispered something to David Michael and Berk.

"Hey, no secrets!" said Dawn. Karen finished whispering and the boys nodded their heads.

"We'd rather swing," said Karen.

"All right," Dawn agreed uncertainly. "You go ahead. I'm going to see about the contest."

Dawn found the playground counsellor at the arts and crafts table. She asked her about the contest and about what other activities were coming up. She thought Stacey might want to bring Emma, Luke, and Ashley to the playground later in the week.

Their conversation was interrupted by an ear-piercing shriek. Dawn whirled around, afraid one of the bluebirds was hurt. Instead, a little girl came tearing across the playground and threw herself at the counsellor.

"Fran! Fran!" she cried.

"Tina, what's wrong?" The counsellor picked Tina up and gave her a hug.

"Martians!" Tina managed to sob.

Uh-oh, thought Dawn.

"Martians!" exclaimed Fran. "What do you mean, honey?"

"They're coming! Tonight! They're

going to take us away!"

That was all Dawn needed to hear. She turned around and marched across the schoolyard. Karen and my brother and cousin were at the swings, all right, but they weren't swinging. They were surrounded by an awed bunch of kids.

Dawn reached them in time to hear Karen saying, ". . . hide underground."

"Like in your basement," David Michael added.

The other children were looking at them with fear in their eyes. One boy was wiping tears away. Suddenly, he turned and ran.

"Where are you going?" another boy shouted after him.

"Home!"

"I'm coming with you!"

"Me, too!" chorused the others. The entire group fled towards the gate to the playground.

"Karen Brewer . . ." Dawn warned.

Karen looked up guiltily. "Yeah?"

"I do *not* want you scaring the other kids with that story."

"But we have to *warn* them. They have to be ready for the attack." Karen was quite serious about that.

"Right," Berk and David Michael.

"Wrong," said Dawn. "Now come over to the arts and crafts table and forget about the Martians."

Dawn settled her charges with Fran and

the other kids. They began to work busily. She was helping Berk put a nose on his puppet when she heard a crashing noise behind her. She looked around and saw a branch falling from a tree nearby.

"Martians!" Karen screamed.

"Aughh!" shrieked David Michael and Berk.

"I want my mummy!" cried Tina.

"Martians?" asked several children.

"Coming to get us!" Karen told them. "They're going to attack! They're here already! We have to hide!"

Every single child at the art table scrambled out of his or her seat and rushed for cover.

Fran turned to Dawn, looking slightly cross.

"I'm sorry," Dawn said quickly. "I don't know what got into her. I'll take her home as soon as I help you find the kids."

"That's all right," said Fran. "Another counsellor will be here in about ten minutes. He can help me. Please take her home now, okay?"

"Okay." Dawn paused, then added, "I really am sorry."

Fran nodded.

"Karen Brewer!" Dawn called. "Berk! David Michael. I want you three to come out right this minute. Do you hear me?"

Nothing.

"There are *no Martians*," Dawn added.

"Just me. And I'm getting mad."

The blue group crawled sheepishly out of a storage shed.

"Come on," said Dawn. "We have to leave." She wondered if she should tell Karen to apologize to Fran, but Fran looked busy and annoyed. Dawn hustled the three kids away.

As they walked home, she gave them a talk about telling stories and scaring children, and Karen became grave and concerned. She promised not to mention the Martians again. David Michael and Berk promised, too.

The bluebirds were the first group to return to my house that day, even beating Mary Anne and the babies. They were on their best behaviour all afternoon, and Tuesday passed quickly.

Late that night, after my lights were out and I was in bed, something occurred to me. Wedding presents were starting to arrive at our house. The wedding was then just about three days away. I would have to get a present for Mum and Watson, but what? What do you get for your mother and a millionaire? They already had everything they needed and could buy anything they wanted.

I lay awake thinking. My present had to be just right.

9th CHAPTER

Wedding Countdown:
Wednesday – three days to go

Wednesday, June 24th

This is a confession, you guys. I know you think I'm so sophisticated, since I'm from New York and my hair is permed and everything, but no kidding, my favourite movie is "Mary Poppins." I've seen it 65 times. (That's because we bought the movie so that I could watch it on the VCR whenever I want, and I watch it at least once a week.) I know it by heart. Anyway, when I saw that it was going to be at the Embassy Theater for a "special engagement", I decided I had to have another chance to see it on a big screen. That's one reason I was so determined to take the red group to it. Besides, since it's my favourite movie, I was sure Luke, Emma, and Ashley would love it, too. Believe me, if I'd had a crystal ball to see into the future, I would never have taken them.

Stacey didn't mention it in her notebook entry, but one o'clock on Wednesday marked the halfway point of the Babysitters Club's adventure taking care of fourteen children. Two and half days were behind us. Two and a half days were ahead of us.

Of course, we'd had our share of problems.

There was Dawn's experience at the playground, for instance. "I keep thinking of all those scared children," she said. "Especially the ones who ran home. I hope they found mummies or daddies or big brothers or sister who told them not to worry. And Karen can't ever show up at that playground again, at least not as long as Fran is the counsellor."

Then there was the problem with toilets. We have three: one downstairs and two upstairs. One of the upstairs ones is Mum's and off limits, which left two toilets for nineteen people, two of whom were in nappies and needed to be changed a lot, and one of whom (Maura) had only recently been potty-trained.

It seemed as if somebody always had to use the toilet. Since the little kids were more urgent about it ("Kristy, Kristy! I have to go *now*!"), we decided that the yellow group, green group, and pink group would use the downstairs toilet, which was nearer; and the five baby-sitters, the red group, and the blue group would use the upstairs toilet. We stuck a yellow sun, a green dinosaur, and a pink heart on the door of the first-floor toilet, and a red star and a bluebird on the door of the second-floor toilet as reminders. But there were always mix-ups.

"Kristy, which toilet do I use?" David Michael asked me as I was rummaging through the fridge, getting the lunches out on Wednesday.

"What group are you in?"

"I don't know."

"Well, look at your nametag" I told him.

"I lost it."

"You're a bluebird. Go upstairs."

"I was just up there. Somebody's in it."

"Then wait."

"I can't."

"Then go downstairs."

"Someone's in there, too."

"David Michael, you're going to have to wait, or else go across the street and ask Mimi to let you use the Kishi's toilet."

"No way!"

At that moment, Luke and Andrew walked out of the house and into the garden.

"I think the toilets are free," I said.

"*Which* one do I use?"

I groaned. "It doesn't matter. Just go."

The kids had almost as much trouble keeping their groups straight. The baby-sitters knew who their charges were, but even with the nametags, the kids were never sure. If Stacey, for instance, called for the red group, eight children would run to her.

But none of that mattered much. As long as we could be outside, we were fine. The kids were having fun.

Wednesday afternoon was the special showing of *Mary Poppins*. Stacey had known about it for several days, and on Tuesday she asked my aunts and uncles for permission to take the red group to the Embassy and for money to buy tickets.

The Embassy was all the way downtown, but Nannie was going to take me shoe shopping that afternoon (while Mary Anne watched the nappers again), so she planned to drop Stacey and the red group at the cinema on our way back.

The Pink Clinker was loaded down as Nannie pulled out of the drive. "I'll drive very slowly," she told Ashley, who was sitting next to her in the front seat. "I don't want to jar your leg."

"I hope she doesn't drive *too* slowly," Stacey whispered to me. "I don't want to miss the beginning."

Nannie did creep along, but we reached the cinema in plenty of time for the show.

Luke and Emma hopped out of the car, while Stacey helped Ashley out.

"Good-bye!" Nannie called as the Pink

Clinker roared to life. "Have fun! I'll be back in two hours."

Stacey led the three kids to the ticket window. "Now, do you all have your money?" she asked.

"Yup," said Luke.

"Yup," said Ashley.

"Nope," said Emma.

"*Nope?*" Stacey repeated. "Emma, where is it? I told you three kids to make sure you brought your money."

"I *did* bring it," Emma whined.

"Mine's in my pocket," said Luke.

"Mine's in my knapsack," said Ashley.

Emma looked blank. "I don't *know* where mine is."

"I'd pay for you," Stacey told her, "but I've only got about a dollar extra. Emma, think. What did you do with your money?"

"I don't *kno-ow*." (She was a good whiner. Very good.)

"Do you want me to call Kristy's house and see if you left it there by mistake? Maybe Claudia's grandmother could drive it over here," she said uncertainly.

"All right," agreed Emma, scuffing the toe of her shoe along the pavement.

"Stacey, I'm going to sit down on that bench," said Ashley.

"Okay. This'll only take a sec. I hope." Stacey fished a quarter out of the pocket of her overalls and called my house.

Mary Anne answered the phone.

Stacey could hear crying in the background.

"What's going on?" she asked.

"The phone woke the babies."

"Oops."

"What's up? I thought you were at the movies."

"We're almost there. Emma can't find her money. She thinks she might have left it at Kristy's . . . Would you mind looking?"

"Well, no. Let me just quiet Tony and Beth down. Then I'll look around. Hold on."

Mary Ann looked so long that Stacey's quarter ran out and the pay phone clicked off.

"Darn!" exclaimed Stacey. She didn't have much change left. She put a dime and three nickels in the slot and called back.

The line was busy. It was still off the hook.

Stacey was growing impatient. The movie would start in five minutes. She tried again.

"Stacey?" said Mary Anne. "Where were you?"

"We got cut off. Did you find the money?"

"No, and I looked everywhere. Dawn and Claudia looked, too."

"Oh, brother. This is great, just great."

Emma was tugging on Stacey's sleeve. "Stacey?" she asked.

"Just a minute," Stacey told her.

"Stacey, it's important."

"Not now, Emma."

"But Stacey, I found my money."

Stacey looked at Emma, who was holding her money out triumphantly. "Mary Anne?" she said. "Never mind. We found it."

Stacey thanked Mary Anne and hung up. "Where was it?" she asked Emma.

"In my shoe."

Stacey shook her head. "Well, hurry up, you guys. The movie's starting."

She helped Ashley over to the ticket window. Then, to save time, she collected the money from her group, gave it all to the man in the booth, and said, "One adult and three children, please."

The man handed four tickets to Stacey, who in turn handed them to a young woman at the entrance to the lobby, while Emma, Luke, and Ashley filed in ahead of her.

"Go right into the cinema. Hurry, you guys," said Stacey. "The lights are about to . . ."

But the kids weren't listening to her. They were standing at the sweets counter, looking like they hadn't eaten in weeks.

"I want mints," said Emma.

"I want M&M's" said Luke.

"I want popcorn," said Ashley.

"We don't have enough time — or money," Stacey said. She glanced into the cinema. The lights were dimming. "Besides, you just ate lunch."

"But we have room for a snack," said Emma, who was on the verge of whining again. And our mums gave us extra money for a movie treat."

It took five minutes to buy the sweets and popcorn. When the children were ready, they tiptoed into the dark cinema.

"We need four seats together, with one on the aisle for Ashley," Stacey whispered loudly to them.

"*Shh!*" said a woman nearby.

They walked up and down the aisles. Finally an usher with a flashlight found seats for them in the balcony.

Towards the end of the movie, Emma spilled the last of her sticky mints over the railing. Below her, someone shrieked. Emma began to giggle and couldn't stop. Ashley began to giggle, too, and after a while even Luke joined in.

The usher ushered them outside.

Stacey stood on the pavement, her cheeks flaming, and was never so relieved as when she saw the Pink Clinker cruising down the street.

She climbed into the car, her eyes blazing.

"What happened?" I asked, not sure I really wanted to know.

"Ask *her*," Stacey said, glaring at Emma.

Emma tried to tell me, but she began

giggling again. Before I knew it, Ashley and Luke were giggling, too.

Their laughter was contagious. Nannie and I caught it. When I dared to look at Stacey, I found that even she was laughing.

"Oh, well," she said as Nannie pulled into our drive, "I can always see *Mary Poppins* on TV."

That was Wednesday. I now had my wedding shoes — low with a little heel — but no idea about a gift for Mum and Watson.

10th CHAPTER

Wedding Countdown:
Thursday – two days to go

Thursday, June 25th

Until today, I didn't know that "barber" is a dirty word. But it is— to little boys. Here's how I found out: When the mothers and fathers dropped their children off at Kristy's house this morning, they all looked guilty. It turned out that they'd decided the boys, except for Tony, needed their hair cut before the wedding. Since the barber is only open from 9:00 until 5:00, guess what they asked us poor, defenseless, unprepared baby-sitters to do? They asked us to take Luke, David Michael, Beck, Andrew, Peter, and Patrick to poor, defenseless, unprepared Mr. Gates, whose barbershop is just around the corner from the infant school. When we told the boys about their field trip, all six of them turned pale, then red, and began throwing tantrums...

Well, Mary Anne may not have been prepared for the trip to the barbershop, but I've gone there with David Michael many times. So I had a dim idea of what could happen. You just take David Michael's tears and whining and complaining and multiply them by six. That's what I thought. But there must have been something wrong with my calculations, because the boys definitely caused more than six times the trouble my brother causes by himself.

After the adults left that morning, the members of the Babysitters Club turned the children loose in the garden and held a quick meeting on the porch while we kept an eye on things.

"Six boys will be going to Mr Gates'," I said, "and the seven girls plus Tony will stay behind. How should we divide ourselves up? Should three of us go to the barber?"

"That sounds like too many," said Dawn. "Doesn't Mr Gates have an assistant? Two boys can get their hair cut at once. Then there'll only be four to watch."

"That's true," I said. "Okay, two of us will go and three will stay here. I'd better be one of the ones to go, since I'm related to most of those boys."

Mary Anne giggled.

"Who else wants to go?" I could tell that the other baby-sitters wanted the easy job of staying at my house with the girls and Tony.

At last Mary Anne spoke up. "I'll go with you, Kristy," she said. "I've been stuck here with Beth and Tony all week."

"Are you sure you want to do this?" I asked her.

"Positive," she replied, sounding entirely unsure of herself.

"All right," I said just as uncertainly.

You've probably never taken a ten-year-old, a seven-year-old, a six-year-old, a four-year-old, and two three-year-olds to the barber. I certainly never had. Mary Anne and I waited until the kids had eaten lunch before we rounded the boys up. After lunch, the kids were full and the younger ones tended to be sleepy.

When the rubbish had been cleared away and the picnic tables wiped off, I stood bravely in the garden and announced, "Okay, barbertime."

"No-no-no-no-no!" shrieked Andrew.

Peter and Patrick joined in. "No-no-no-no-no!"

Luke, David Michael, and Berk were too old for no-no's. They climbed a tree instead.

"We're not coming down!" David Michael shouted.

"Fine," I said. "Mary Anne, will you get Nannie on the phone, please, and tell her to bring the Pink Clinker over here? Tell her the boys are —"

"Wait! Wait! Here we come!" cried Berk. The boys jumped out of the tree.

Nannie is a terrific grandmother, but she expects kids to do what they're told, and when it's time for discipline, she is very firm about things.

"Thanks," I said to the older boys.

They didn't answer. David Michael scowled at me. At last he said, "You want me to look like an owl, don't you? That's what I looked like after I went to Mr Gates the last time. An owl. A horned owl. My hair just got normal, and now you and Mum are going to make me look like an owl again."

"David Michael, for heaven's sake, calm down. After all, it's Mum's wedding. She wants you to look good. If she thought Mr Gates was going to make you look like a horned owl, I'm sure she wouldn't send you to him."

"No barber," Peter spoke up piteously.

"Sorry, guys," I said. "Haircuts all round. Let's get going."

"I'll find a wagon," Mary Anne offered. "Peter and Patrick and Andrew can ride in it."

As the boys filed out of the garden, the girls watched them.

Nobody said a word for the longest time. Finally, Emma couldn't stand it any longer.

"Ha, ha. Ha, ha. You guys —"

Ashley hobbled forward and clapped her

hand over Emma's mouth.

Emma tried to bite her.

"*Ow*! Quit it!"

"Well, leave me alone!" exclaimed Emma.

Mary Anne whispered to me, "The girls may be harder to handle than the boys!"

We loaded the little guys into the wagon, and in no time were ushering the boys into Mr Gates' place.

Now, if I'd been Mr Gates and had seen six unhappy boys come in for haircuts, I might have had a nervous breakdown. But not Mr Gates. He simply finished up the customer he was working on, then turned to Mary Anne and me. "Well, what have we here?" he asked pleasantly.

"Isn't it obvious?" murmmured Luke.

Mary Anne shot Luke a hideous look and he quieted down.

I stepped forward. "Hi, Mr Gates," I said. "My mum's getting married on Saturday —"

"Well congratulations!"

"Thanks. And my brother's going to be *in* the wedding, and the rest of these guys are going to be *at* the weddding, and they all need their hair cut."

"But not too short," said David Michael.

"Not over my ears," said Luke.

"Not too long at the sides," said Berk.

"Leave my parting alone," said Andrew.

"I don't *want* a parting," said Peter.

"Do you have lollipops?" asked Patrick.

"One at a time, one at a time," said Mr Gates calmly. "Do you know Mr Pratt? He's the other barber here."

A skinny, jumpy-looking man stepped in from the back room and right away I sensed trouble. He must have been new. I didn't remember seeing him before. He laughed nervously.

"Mr Pratt," said Mr Gates, "these young men need haircuts."

"All of them? Heh-heh."

"That's right." Mr Gates turned back to the boys. "Okay, which two will be first?"

"Not me!" said six voices.

Mary Anne made a quick decision. "Luke and David Michael," she said. It was a good idea. They were the two oldest.

"No," said both boys.

I took them aside. "There's a phone in the corner," I told them, pointing to it. "And I've got change in my pocket. I can get hold of Nannie easily."

"Okay, okay," said Luke.

"David Michael, you go with Mr Pratt. And be *good*."

Meanwhile, Mary Anne had taken the four younger boys to some chairs by the front door. She was trying to get them to sit down, but they were climbing over everything like monkeys.

"Come *on*," Mary Anne urged them.

"I'm Rocket Man!" cried Peter.

"Not in here you aren't." Mary Anne picked Peter up and sat him in her lap.

I didn't know whether to help her or to watch Luke and David Michael. I decided I'd better keep an eye on the boys, and especially on my brother and Mr Pratt.

David Michael climbed into the barber's chair as if he were on his way to a funeral.

"Well, heh-heh," said Mr Pratt.

"Don't make me look like a horned owl," said David Michael rudely. He caught sight of me glaring at him in the mirror and stuck his tongue out.

Mr Pratt thought it was meant for him.

"Oh, goodness, heh-heh." He patted his pockets, searching for something, then walked into the back room.

Luke leaned over from the next chair and whispered to David Michael, "He probably forgot his brain."

"Now, now," said Mr Gates. "Hmm. It seems to me I've got a box of lollipops over by the cash register. But I only give them to my well-behaved customers."

"I'm too old for lollipops," said Luke.

"Me, too," said David Michael, who had asked for two the last time he'd had his hair cut.

That did it.

"Excuse me a sec, Mr Gates," I said. I stepped between the chairs and said to the boys, "You two are being plain rude. Who taught you to speak this way to adults? I can't believe it. I want you to know that I am now walking over to that phone and calling Nannie. I guess I just can't take care of you guys after all. My friends and I tried to make things fun for you, but you're too much to handle. I'll have to turn the job over to Nannie."

"No, Kristy! Please don't!" David Michael cried. "We'll be good. All of us. I promise." He turned to his cousin. "She means it, Luke. She's my sister. I know her."

"All right," said Luke sulkily.

Luke and David Michael's haircuts went fine after that. They even seemed reasonably satisfied with the results. David Michael made no references to owls.

Then came Berk and Andrew's turns. They protested as they climbed into the chairs, but behaved nicely after Mr Gates promised them lollipops.

Pete and Patrick were last. Pete tried to kick Mr Pratt in the shin, and Patrick cried the entire time. I sang seventeen verses of "Old MacDonald" to him, but it didn't help much, and Mr Gates looked pained.

However, by the time we left, the barber shop and both barbers were still pretty much in one piece.

"We did it!" Mary Anne exclaimed as we were putting the littler boys in the wagon. "Somehow we did it!"

"I know! Now if I could just think of a

wedding present to give Mum and Watson, this would be a perfect day."

"How about a toaster oven?" asked Mary Anne.

"Too expensive. Besides, Watson's got three.

"A tray," Luke suggested.

"We've got dozens."

"A picnic basket," said Berk.

"We've got one and Watson's got one."

"A fire engine," said Pete.

"A robot," said Patrick.

"Do I have to give them a present, too?" asked David Michael.

"It would be nice," I replied.

"Help me think of one, Kristy."

Oh, brother. *Two* presents?

11th CHAPTER

Wedding Countdown:
Friday – one day to go!

Firday, June 26

Unfiar! Today it rained! all day!

I guess we baby sitters shouldnt complain to much since this was the first rainy day all weak. But still it was a yucky day. wether wise. The kids were not to bad though.

Hey Kristy how come we have to write in the diary this weak? Were all sitting so we all know whats going on right? I guess its just the rules right? Anyway it cant hurt.

Anyway the morning went okay but by the time lunch was over we were running out of things to do then I got this really fun idea . . .

I have to admit, Claudia's idea was one of her better ones. As she mentioned, we used up all our usual ideas in the morning. The little kids watched *Sesame Street* and *Mister Rogers' Neighbourhood*. The older kids played board games. Claudia set up some art activities, Dawn read aloud, and Mary Anne even plopped the babies in the play-pen and helped Stacey's group bake cookies.

But by the time lunch was over, our ears were ringing with the sounds of:

"What can I do *now*, Kristy Dawn Stacey Mary Anne what's-your-name-again?"

"I don't *wanna* read another book."

"There's nothing *good* on TV."

"We *played* that already."

"Hey, let's give the babies a bath!" (That was Emma.)

"No!" cried Mary Anne.

Things were on the verge of getting out of hand. Ten of the fourteen children were crowded into our playroom. (The babies, Patrick, and Maura were asleep on a blanket in the living room.) Ashley was lying on the couch, moaning that her leg hurt and her head ached. Emma was tearing through the room after Katherine, who clearly did not enjoy being chased. Andrew and Grace were jumping up and down around Claudia, complaining that they didn't know what to do. In one corner was Karen with Berk and David Michael. She was talking to them earnestly and furtively (she kept glancing at

Dawn), and from time to time I could hear the word *Martian*. Peter was using the couch as a trampoline. And Luke was lining up coffee tins on the floor. When I saw him bring a skateboard in from the garage and head for his obstacle course, I knew we were in trouble.

Stacey saw Luke at the same time, and talked him out of his activity.

At that point, I pulled the baby-sitters aside. "We've got to do something — *fast*!" I said. I looked outside. It was pouring.

"We need to separate them, first of all," said Dawn. "We should divide them, into their groups and go off in different rooms. This is too much."

"Go off and do what, though? That's the problem," said Stacey. They've done everything, already. They've been through every Kid-Kit, played every game, read every book, sung every song —"

"Okay, okay," said Dawn. "I still think we need to separate them."

"What would be fun," said Mary Anne thoughtfully, "would be a project for the whole group that the smaller groups could work on separately."

"You mean like putting on a show?" asked Claudia.

"Exactly," said Mary Anne.

"How about a talent show?' Dawn suggested. "Even the littlest kids could be in it."

"That would be fun," I said. "You know, we only have to occupy them until about four o'clock. Then we should start getting them dressed."

"Oh, yeah! I almost forgot," said Mary Anne.

The rehearsal dinner was to be held that night, and everyone, including the kids and us baby-sitters, had been invited. Actually, the Babysitters club had been asked more to watch the kids than to be guests (although I would have gone anyway, of course), but it was still a good opportunity to get dressed in our very best clothes.

When Mum first told me about the special evening, I had to ask her what a rehearsal dinner was. It turns out that on the day before a wedding, the minister (or rabbi or priest) and the bride and groom and anyone who's going to be in the wedding get together to rehearse the ceremony, just as if it were a play. Afterwards, the families, the people in the wedding, and a few special friends are invited to a big dinner, which is usually given by the groom's family.

In our case, what with the fourteen children and the crazy, last-minute preparations for the wedding, the schedule for the evening was wild. Finally, the adults had decided that things would go much more smoothly if my relatives didn't have to drive the kids all the way to their motels to dress for the dinner and then drive all the way back to Stoneybrook. So guess what? They asked the Babysitters Club to dress the children and have them ready for the evening when they were picked up at five o'clock.

After that, the members of the club (except for me) would go home, change quickly, and somehow get themselves to Watson's house. Meanwhile, the rest of us would go either to the rehearsal or to Watson's to help get ready for the dinner.

The children had shown up at my house that morning each carrying two bags. One bag was lunch, the other was clothes — a complete outfit. I had peeked in Maura's bag and seen a dress, a slip, a pair of tights, a change of underwear, party shoes, and hair-clips. I hoped the other bags were as complete. Dressing fourteen kids for a fancy party had all the makings of a disaster.

But I couldn't worry about that then.

"You know," Claudia spoke up, grinning, "I just had a really funny idea. The rehearsal dinner made me think of it. Instead of putting on an ordinary show or play, how about putting on a wedding?"

"A wedding?" I exclaimed.

"Yeah. The kids can play all the different parts. Someone can be the bride, someone can be the groom. You know."

"You mean marry off a couple of the children?" said Stacey, laughing.

"Sure," replied Claudia. "The wedding

is all these poor kids have heard about for the entire week. We might as well prepare them for the real thing. What do you think?"

We were all laughing by then.

"It's a great idea," I said.

"Do you still have those old clothes you used to play make-believe with?" asked Claudia.

"I can do better than that," I said. "Last year, out of the clear blue, Grandma — my other grandmother — sent us all these funny dress-up clothes. Some of the clothes would be perfect for our wedding. I'll go and get them."

"We'll talk to the children," said Dawn.

By the time I returned to the playroom with my load of clothes, the kids were sittting on the floor talking excitedly to Mary Anne, Stacey, Dawn, and Claudia.

"Well, we've chosen the bride and groom," said Claudia.

Karen couldn't contain herself. "It's me! Me and David Michael!" she cried. "Because we're the same height."

The rest of the children volunteered for other parts in the ceremony. Luke was going to be the minister. Ashley reluctantly agreed to be the bride's mother (so she could sit down most of the time). Emma and Grace were to be the maids-of-honour, and Katherine wanted to be the flower girl. Berk decided to play the bride's father and give her away. Andrew and Peter decided to be ushers, and Patrick (who was awake and eager to participate) volunteered to be the ringbearer.

We divided into our groups and went off to rehearse the various parts and find costumes. Mary Anne watched the babies and helped with costumes. (Ashley had made a miraculous recovery from her various aches and pains.)

Half an hour later, we gathered in the playroom again to rehearse. The kids were dressed up to the nines. David Michael had put on his best suit. (If he didn't wrinkle it, he could leave it on and wear it to the rehearsal dinner.) Mary Anne had found a top hat for him among the antique clothes. It was too big, but my brother liked it.

Karen, who loved to dress up, had put together the most amazing costume of all. She showed it off proudly.

"Here's my veil," she said, brushing aside a garish pink piece of netting, "and my lovely, lovely hat." (On top of the lovely, lovely hat was a lovely, lovely fake bird's nest with two fake bluebirds inside.) "And I put on my best bracelets. I guess my shoes are a little big" (they were a pair of Mum's) "but that's okay. Now, my dress is the most beautiful part of all. See the jewels?"

The dress was wilder than the veil. For starters, it wasn't white; it was bright blue, with shimmery sequins sewn all over it. The waistline fell around Karen's knees.

"That's a *wedding* dress?" cried Ashley. "Wedding dresses are supposed to be white. Or maybe they could be yellow or something, but not *that*!"

Karen looked crushed. "Kristy?" she asked in a small voice.

"Well, technically," I said, " a wedding dress can be any colour."

Karen stuck her tongue out at Ashley, "*See*?"

"*See*?" Ashley mimicked her.

"Okay, okay, you guys," said Claudia. "Let's not spoil the wedding."

"But I'm her mother," Ashley protested. "Aren't mothers supposed to complain?"

I giggled. "Maybe," I replied, "but let's just go on, okay?"

The kids ran through their parts. When they knew them pretty well, they looked at us expectantly.

"Let me get the camera!" I said suddenly. "I'll be the wedding photographer." I found Mum's Polaroid, hoping she wouldn't mind if I borrowed it. "Into the living room, you guys. We'll have the wedding in there, if you promise to be careful."

"Oh, we will! We will!" the kids chorused.

"All right, then. Places, everyone."

Luke stood importantly in front of the fireplace. David Michael and Patrick (the ringbearer) were next to him.

Andrew and Peter (the ushers) led Ashley and the baby-sitters with the three little children to seats on the couches and arm-chairs. Then they joined Luke, David Michael, and Patrick at the front of the room.

"Okay, bridesmaids," I whispered to Emma and Grace, who were peeping into the living room.

The girls walked slowly through the room, Grace tripping over the hem of her long dress with every step.

They positioned themselves on the other side of Luke.

Katherine came next, wearing what looked like a ballerina's tutu, and tossing confetti out of an old Easter basket. Karen, the beautiful bride, followed with Berk at her side.

She joined David Michael, they turned to face Luke, and Berk sat down next to Ashley.

Click, click. Click, click. I was trying to record every important moment.

"Ladies and gentlemen," said Luke solemnly, beginning a speech he had made up, and which seemed to change every time he recited it, "we are gathered here today to join these two guys in . . . in . . ." He looked helplessly at Stacey. "What did you say it was called?"

"Holy matrimony," Stacey whispered.

"In . . . in holy moly."(The baby-sitters

managed not to laugh.) "Weddings are very important," Luke continued. "You have to know what you're getting into. If you think you're ready, then you can take the oath. Are you ready?"

"We're ready," said Karen and David Michael.

"Okay, then, Karen, do you promise to love your husband and help him out and not hog the television?"

"I guess so," said Karen.

"Okay. And David Michael, do you promise to love your wife and help her out and show her how to ride a bicycle?"

"I guess."

"Okay. By the way, are you two going to have any kids?"

"Yes," said Karen.

"No," said David Michael.

"Well, if you do, be nice to them, all right?"

"Yeah," spoke up Berk. "Don't give them any bedtimes."

"And don't yell at them when they forget to feed the dog," added Luke.

"And once in a while," said Emma, "let them go into a toy shop and when they say, 'Can I have this?' you say, 'Yes,' even if it costs forty dollars."

"All right," said the bride and groom.

"Great." Luke nodded to Patrick.

Patrick handed David Michael a ring, and my brother slipped it on Karen's finger.

"You may now kiss the bride!" Luke announced triumphantly.

"*What*?!" shrieked David Michael, and his hat fell down over his eyes. "You never said *that* before!"

"Ew, ew!" cried Karen.

My last photo of the wedding showed Karen and David Michael running, horror-stricken, from the living room.

It was time to get ready for the (real) rehearsal dinner.

12th CHAPTER

Wedding Countdown:
Friday evening – half a day to go

As soon as we got Karen and David Michael calmed down, it was time to begin dressing the children for the dinner at Watson's. I handed the bags containing the clothing to the baby-sitters and they went off to various parts of the house with their groups. I took Grace, Katherine, and Andrew (who were not modest) into the playroom to change.

My first clue that anything was wrong was when I opened Andrew's bag and pulled out a yellow dress.

"Oops," I said. "Wrong bag. Katherine, this must be yours. Or yours, Grace."

"Not mine," said Katherine.

"Not mine," said Grace.

I checked the bag again. Sure enough, it was labelled ANDREW.

"Hmm," I said.

"Hey, Kristy!" Mary Anne called from the kitchen. "Come here."

"You guys stay right there," I told the yellow group. "What is it, Mary Anne?'

"Look at this," she said as I entered the kitchen. She held up a bow tie and a pair of grey flannel trousers. "I found these in Beth's bag. And this slip in Tony's bag," she added, showing me a lacy, white undergarment. "It's got to be Ashley's. It's too big for any of the other girls."

Just as Claudia, sounding exasperated, called to me from the living room, Stacey marched into the kitchen, pushing Emma along in front of her. "Okay, Emma Meiner, tell your cousin what you told me."

Emma looked as if she couldn't decide whether to giggle or cry.

"Emma . . ." Stacey said, nudging her.

"I switched the clothes," Emma whispered.

"*What*?" I squawked.

"I switched the clothes," she repeated, more loudly. "Not all of them. Just one or two things from each bag. I did it while you were getting lunch."

"Emma!" I shouted. I was angry. I don't usually get angry when I'm baby-sitting, but Emma had made me *really* angry. The Babysitters Club had been anxious to prove that it could be responsible for a large group of children, and it had done a good job right up until now — four o'clock on Friday afternoon. I couldn't believe Emma was going to make us look bad in the final hour of our biggest job ever.

"Emma . . ." I said again, trying to control my temper.

"Yes?" she answered, and a tear slipped down her cheek.

"Emma, what you did was really naughty. It's four o'clock. There's only one hour until our parents are going to come and get us for the rehearsal dinner. They expect us — *all* of us — to be dressed and ready then. Thanks to you, we might not be ready after all. Now, while we sort out the clothes, I want you to sit by yourself in the study and think about what you did."

I led her into our study and sat her on the couch. "Sit there and don't move. Don't touch anything. Just sit and think." I closed the door.

Then I gathered all the baby-sitters, all the children (except Emma), and all the bags of clothing in the living room. It took half an hour, but finally we were pretty sure we had the right clothes in the right bags. Some of the clothes were labelled with name-tags, the older children recognized their clothes and most of the things belonging to their little brothers and sisters, and my friends and I used common sense to figure out what was left over.

At four-thirty we divided up again, and I

let Emma out of the study.

"I'm sorry, Kristy," she said, and I felt sort of mean. I could tell she'd been crying.

"And I'm sorry I got mad. But promise me you won't do anything else naughty today. Or tomorrow," I added, thinking of what could happen while the wedding was in progress. "We all have to be on our best behaviour."

"I promise," said Emma in a small voice.

"Okay," I replied. I gave her a hug. Then I sent her off with Stacey.

Half an hour later, fourteen very dressy children were milling around our living room. Their parents had not shown up yet.

"Hey, how about a picture?" I asked. There were two shots left on the roll of film in the Polaroid.

"Yes! Yes!" cried the kids.

Claudia, the artistic one, began to pose them. "You big kids sit on the couch . . . No, not on the *back* of the couch, Berk. Just *on* the couch, like a normal person. Okay, good. And you shorter kids sit on the floor in front of them. Katherine, hold your little brother, okay? No, *hold* him. He's sliding over. Grace, give Beth a hand. She's escaping. Put her in your lap, okay?"

Claudia turned to me. "Hurry, Kristy! Before they move!"

I snapped the picture. When the film was developed, we saw that Tony was slumped over so you couldn't see his face, Beth was pulling Grace's hair, two kids had their eyes closed, and Berk was poking David Michael in the side.

"Let's try it again," I said. "We have one more picture left. Now this time, open your eyes, look at the camera, smile, and don't poke anybody!"

Click!

The second picture was perfect.

And the kids were still posed at the couch when the adults walked in.

There was much oohing and aahing.

"Aren't they adorable?"

"Oh, who's this handsome crowd?!"

"Wouldn't this make a cute Christmas card?"

"Isn't Patrick wearing somebody's else's tie?"

"What's Beth doing wearing tights?"

The members of the Babysitters Club glanced at each other, then at Emma. Nobody said a word. We weren't about to tell.

Luckily, there wasn't time to worry about the clothes. The kids looked gorgeous, anyway. So the aunts and uncles and the Fieldings drove their kids, plus Karen and Andrew, back to Watson's. The other members of the Babysitters Club left to get dressed.

When they were gone, I turned to Mum. "Gosh, the house feels *empty*," I said. "I'm really going to miss those kids."

"We won't," spoke up Sam and Charlie. They had been pretty scarce all week. That evening, they had managed not to come home until precisely five minutes after everyone had left.

"I might miss them," said David Michael, "and I might not." He ran upstairs to his room.

"He won't miss sharing," I informed my mother, "but he'll miss having kids his own age around."

"Maybe," said Mum thoughtfully, "he and Karen will get along better than I think."

I beamed with pleasure, but as I passed Sam on my way into the kitchen, I heard him mutter, "Don't lay any bets on it."

I won't bother you with the details of the rehearsal itself. All you need to know is that it went reasonably well, considering we were rehearsing an outdoor wedding in the all-purpose room of a church, and that Karen, upon hearing that the florist shop was not going to be able to provide her with yellow rose petals and that she'd have to make do with white ones instead, turned pale and widened her eyes until I thought they'd spring out of their sockets.

"What's wrong?" her father asked, alarmed.

"*White* petals," moaned Karen. "They

mean white magic. Morbidda Destiny will be right next door with her black magic. The two magics will crash into each other — BA-ROOM — and then . . ." Karen made a slashing motion across her throat.

David Michael screamed.

"What?" said the confused minister.

"Nothing, nothing," Watson replied hurriedly. "Karen, not another word about that nonsense. Not *one*."

But Karen didn't say anything, and I knew that meant she wasn't agreeing to keep her mouth shut.

Everyone but me forgot about Karen and the magics.

The dinner at Watson's was really fun. All us baby-sitters were as dressed up as if we were going to an important school dance. Claudia had helped me choose a new dress the week before. It was a gigantic white sweater with silver designs woven into it. It was a very un-Kristy-type dress — and I felt glamorous.

During the dinner, which was eaten at two long tables in Watson's dining room, the baby-sitters had to help the kids and keep them quiet. But afterwards, we were more like guests. I showed my friends the room that I had recently decided I'd like for my bedroom.

"It's . . . it's *big*," said Dawn, awed.

"Think of the slumber parties we can

have here," added Stacey.

"Think what you can do with the room," said Claudia. "A mural on the wall . . . Maybe you'll get a canopy bed or something."

"Yeah," I said slowly. "More important, it doesn't look into Morbidda Destiny's house, after all. It doesn't look into yours, either Mary Anne, but the garden is better than Mrs Porter's."

"I suppose so," answered Mary Anne sadly.

The highlight of the evening came as the dinner was drawing to an end. Watson and Mum took the members of the Babysitters Club aside and handed us each an envelope containing a cheque for one hundred and thirty dollars.

"That's one hundred and twenty for a job *very* well done," Mum told us.

"And a ten-dollar bonus," added Watson.

I gawked at my friends. We were rich!

After we got through thanking Mum and Watson and saying good-bye to everyone, it was time to go home. The next day was . . . the wedding.

(And I still had no idea what to give Mum and Watson.)

13th CHAPTER

Wedding Countdown:
Saturday – Zero Hour

"Ee-iiii!"

It was the Big Day, the day of the wedding.

I woke up with a start and leaped out of bed without really knowing why. Then I remembered. I had to see what the weather was like. The day before had been rainy. If it was still rainy, then (horror of horrors) the wedding would have to be held indoors. The guests would be jammed into Watson's living room like sardines in a can.

I stood at the window and picked up the corner of the shade, but I couldn't bear to pull it back.

If it was raining, Mum would be in one of her moods.

I gathered my courage and lifted the shade.

I was greeted by a clear, blue sky.

"Oh, thank you, thank you, thank you!" I exclaimed. "Now if I could just get an idea for a wedding present."

I ran downstairs thinking, Coffee cups? No. Cheese server? No. Paperweight? No. Pitcher? No . . .

The wedding wasn't until two o'clock in the afternoon, but the morning went by in a flash. There was still a lot to do. Nannie came over to help us out. She gave Mum a hand packing for the honeymoon. Then she and Mum drove to the beauty salon in the Pink Clinker to get their hair done. When they came back, Nannie made us all eat something.

"I'd hate for one of you to faint during the ceremony," she said.

"But I'm too nervous to eat," Mum replied.

"Just a little something," Nannie insisted, and suddenly she sounded very much like the mother, and Mum like the daughter.

After we'd eaten enough to please Nannie, it was time to get dressed. I went to my room, closed the door, and, with a feeling of awe, took my bridesmaid gown out of the cupboard. It had been hanging there in a plastic dry cleaner's bag since the day before.

I was about to put it on when something occurred to me. I ran to my window. "Hey, Mary Anne!" I shouted. I hoped she was in her room. "Mary Anne!"

Mary Anne's head appeared in her window.

"Come over!" I called. "You want to help me get dressed?"

"Sure!"

Mary Anne was in my room in a flash. She helped me remove the dress from the bag. Then zipped me into it.

The dress fitted perfectly. Nannie had done a terrific job.

"Oh, Kristy," whispereed Mary Anne, "you look beautiful!"

"Thanks," I replied. "I feel kind of beautiful."

I put on my white knee-high socks and my new shoes with the heels.

"What if I *trip*?" I cried, the awful thought slamming into my mind like a lorry.

"You won't," Mary Anne assured me.

My bouquet and the flowers for my hair had been delivered to Watson's, so I was as dressed as I could get for the time being. When Mum and Nannie and my brothers were dressed, too (we looked so elegant!), Nannie whisked us over to Watson's.

"See you at the wedding!" I called to Mary Anne from the window of the Pink Clinker.

At the Brewers' house, Mum and Watson

were not allowed to see each other (it was supposed to be bad luck or something), so Mum and Karen and I were taken into a spare bedroom, where Nannie put the finishing touches on us.

Karen was over-excited. She jumped up and down and danced around the room. "Oh, I'm the little flower girl," she sang. "The flower girl, the flower girl. And here are my white magic petals —"

"Karen, sweetie," said Mum patiently, "sit down for a minute. You're going to wear yourself out."

"Mum! Oh, no!" I cried suddenly.

"What is it, Kristy?" Mum asked, alarmed.

"It's a little late for this, but do you have something old, something new, something borrowed, and something blue?"

"Believe it or not, I do," said Mum. "My earrings are antiques, my dress is new, I borrowed Nannie's pearl necklace, and, well, some of my underwear is blue — pale blue."

Karen began to giggle.

"That's a relief," I said.

Nannie left the room for a moment, and Andrew wandered in. His shoes were untied, his shirt was unbuttoned, his hair was a mess, and he was trailing his necktie along the floor.

"Andrew!" exclaimed my mother. "You should be ready by now, honey."

"Everyone's busy," Anderew wailed, "and I need help."

"I'll help you," I said. I put Andrew together and sent him out into the hall, where I caught sight of the Fieldings. "Andrew, you're going to sit with your friends. There are Katherine and Patrick. Stay with them, okay?"

Just as Andrew was running off, Nannie returned. "It's time!" she said excitedly.

Mum and Nannie hugged each other.

I ran to the window and peeped outside. The street in front of Watson's house was lined with cars. "Everybody's here already?" I squeaked.

"They're seated and waiting," replied Nannie.

Yikes!

"Now are you two *sure* you know what to do?" Mum asked Karen and me for the eighty-zillionth time.

"Yes," said Karen.

"Positive," I said.

Nannie led us through Watson's house to the door to the patio. There we were met by Sam and Charlie, looking handsome and solemn and somehow not much like my big brothers.

Sam escorted Nannie down the aisle between the folding chairs, and seated her in the front row. The guests watched, murmuring approvingly. Then he joined Watson, who was standing with David

Michael (the ringbearer) and the minister in front of the guests.

I drew in my breath. I hadn't really had a good look at the garden until then, and I saw that it was beautiful. The minister and my brothers were separated from the guests by garlands of flowers strung between poles. Behind the minister was a sort of arbor, covered with more flowers. It all would have been perfect if not for the sight of Morbidda Destiny's house beyond.

"Okay, Kristy. You're next, honey," said Mum.

There was piano player on the patio, and he struck up the wedding march. I stood still for a moment, collecting myself. Then, holding my bouquet firmly in front of me, I walked slowly up the aisle. I was aware that everyone had turned around to look at me. I tried to smile, especially when I spotted Mary Anne and Claudia, but my mouth trembled as if I were going to cry.

The aisle looked a mile long, but at last I reached the garlands of flowers. I stepped through them and stood next to the minister, on the other side of him from my brothers and Watson. When I was able to focus on the people in front me, I saw Karen walking jauntily up that long aisle in front of my mother, who was escorted by Charlie. Karen was strewing her rose petals and grinning broadly. No stage fright for her.

When Mum walked by Nannie, Nannie burst into tears.

In all honesty, I have to say that the next part of the wedding, the vows and stuff, got kind of boring. I stopped paying attention and looked out at the guests. Mary Anne smiled at me. So did Dawn. Jamie Newton waved and called out, "Hi-hi!" which made several people laugh.

Just as the minister was saying, "You may kiss the bride," I noticed Stacey signalling frantically. She was pointing to me . . . No, not to me, to Karen. I looked down. Karen had turned around and was staring at something behind us. From the look on her face, I thought for sure Dracula was back there.

Then Karen let out an ear-piercing shriek. Luckily, she let it loose just when Mum and Watson were finishing their kiss (a very big smooch, I might add), and people were beginning to rise from their seats with congratulations.

The ceremony was over.

I dared to turn around.

Morbidda Destiny was standing behind me in full black dress, with her snapping eyes and her frazzly, witchy hair.

"The magics!" Karen wailed. "The magics are going to crash!"

Morbidda Destiny looked at Karen, puzzled. Then she turned to me. "I brought the bride and groom something," she said, holding out a box.

"Don't take it!" Karen cried. "It's a wedding spell! It's a —"

A hand was clapped over Karen's mouth. Watson had broken away from the celebrating.

"Why, thank you, Mrs Porter," he said, accepting the box with one hand, while keeping his other hand over Karen's mouth. "That's very nice of you. Won't you join the guests for some refreshm — Ow!"

Karen had tried to bite her father's hand.

"*Daddy* —"

I pulled Karen away. Watson regained his composure, and Mrs Porter did stay at the party for a while. (Karen ran in the house and wouldn't come out until she was gone.)

Later, the caterer wheeled out the wedding cake. The guests gathered around to watch Mum and Watson cut the first slice. They did it together, both pressing down on the cake-cutter. Then they each took a bite of cake, their wrists intertwined. I could see their wedding rings shining in the sunlight.

They're joined, I thought. They're part of each other, and our families have come together to be part of each other, too.

I felt tears spring to my eyes.

And at that moment, I knew what to give Mum and my stepfather.

14th CHAPTER

"Goodbye! Goodbye!"

One after another, our relatives' cars pulled away from Watson's house. The wedding was over, the guests were gone, and now our family was leaving, too.

"See you, Luke! 'Bye, Emma! Behave yourself. Bye-bye, Beth!"

The Meiners were gone.

"Take care of your leg, Ashley! 'Bye, Peter! 'Bye, Grace!"

"May the force be with you!" (That was David Michael saying goodbye to Berk.)

The Millers were gone.

A friend of Watson's pulled up, picked up Karen and Andrew to take them to their mother's, and then *they* were gone.

Last to leave were Mum and Watson. They were going to spend their honeymoon at a little inn in Vermont. My brothers and I would be on our own for a week!

Before Mum got in the car, she ran through a list of last-minute instructions.

"Don't forget to walk Louie before you go to bed. And don't forget to change his water. And lock up the house if you're all going to be out. Charlie, you're in charge. David Michael, remember your vitamins."

"Aw, *Mum.*"

"And Sam —"

"Mum, Mum, we know *every*thing," I said. "Trust us. We won't leave the stove on —"

"Oh, I hadn't even *thought* of that," exclaimed Mum.

"— and we'll run the dishwasher, and we know where the emergency money is."

"And I'll be on call," spoke up Nannie, who was standing behind us. Nannie was going to drop my brothers and me off at our house, and then go home. She looked tired.

"Honey, let's go," said Watson.

"Oh . . . all right." Mum tried to hug all of us at once.

I kissed Watson on the cheek and he told me I'd been a beautiful bridesmaid.

Two minutes later, Mum and Watson were gone, too. Watson hooted the horn all the way down the street.

When Nannie dropped Charlie, Sam, David Michael, and me off, we waved to her as the Pink Clinker hummed down the street. Then we went inside, and all four of us collapsed on the floor in the living room.

Louie joined us, lolling on his back.

Just when I thought every last one of my brothers was asleep, the silence was interrupted by a snort of laughter from Charlie. Then he said in a deep voice, "All right, you guys. You heard Mum. I'm in charge. These are the house rules."

I raised my eyebrows. Leave it to Charlie to let a little responsibility go to his head.

"Dinner every night will be pizza. Everyone must go to bed an hour later than usual. Sam, no eating in the kitchen; food is permitted only in front of TV set *while it's on*. Kristy, you must, I repeat *must*, spend three hours a day talking on the phone. David Michael, go through the *TV Guide* and make sure you don't miss a single cartoon show."

"Do I still have to take my vitamins?" he asked, inspired.

"Yes," replied Charlie. "Don't press your luck."

The four of us were laughing hysterically. It was a good thing, because I'd been just about ready to leak a few tears over the wedding, and Mum's being gone and all.

Instead, when we recovered from Charlie's rules, I went to my room and began working on my idea for the present. Eventually I'd need Claudia's help, but I might as well get my thoughts together before I talked to her. I looked through our encyclopedia for information on family trees. I doodled a bit. I hoped I would have the present ready by the time my mother and stepfather came back.

That night, before David Michael went to bed, he stuck his head in my room and said, "Hey, Kristy, I know what to give Mum and Watson."

"What?" I asked.

"Goldfish," he replied.

And that's exactly what he did give them.

The next day, I talked to Claudia about my idea. I went over to her house so we could look at her art supplies.

"See? It'll show both families," I said, "and how they became one. But I need help with the design. And I need you to draw a bow and show me how to make those little flowers you drew on that art project for Mr Fineman last year."

"Or maybe you should use a real bow," suggested Claudia.

"Oh, that's an idea! And maybe the background could be a really pretty piece of wallpaper or something."

Claudia and I bent busily over our work.

We were interrupted later by the sound of the doorbell. That was followed by the sound of feet — lots of them — running up the stairs. Stacey, Dawn, and Mary Anne appeared in the doorway to Claudia's room.

"Hi, you guys!" said Dawn. "We were looking for you."

"Look what I've got," said Stacey. "Pictures." She held out a fat envelope. "They're from the wedding. Mum and I took them to that one-hour developing place downtown. It was open this morning."

"Ooh!" I shrieked. "Let's see."

Claudia and I abandoned our project. The five of us hopped down on the floor, and my friends peered over my shoulders as I opened the envelope.

"There you are, getting ready to walk up the aisle," said Stacey. "And there you are, walking up the aisle."

"Look at the expression on my face!" I cried.

"You look so nervous!" said Mary Anne.

"No, she looks like she's going to cry!" exclaimed Dawn.

"Both, I think," I said, "Gosh, the dress looks pretty, though, doesn't it?"

"Beautiful."

"Perfect."

"Where is it now?"

"What are you going to do with it?"

We are all talking at once.

"It's in my cupboard in a plastic bag," I told them. "I don't know what I'm going to do with it. I'll probably outgrow it pretty soon."

"Oh, don't!" wailed Mary Anne. "If *you* start growing, then *I'll* be the class shrimp."

"Hey, there's Mum and Watson kissing!"

I exclaimed. "Stacey, I can't believe you took a picture of them doing *that*!"

Stacey grinned slyly. "I thought you'd want the moment captured for ever."

I poked her.

"There's Karen and you and Watson and Morbidda Destiny," said Mary Anne softly. She shuddered.

"It's hard to believe Mor— Mrs Porter is going to be my neighbour soon," I whispered. I quickly stuck the photo on the bottom of the pile. "Here are Mum and Watson cutting the cake," I said, looking at the next picture.

"That's a great photo, Stacey. Hey, you guys, that's what gave me the idea for a wedding present for Mum and Watson."

"What did?" asked Stacey.

"Mum and Watson, when they linked their wrists like that and stuff. Like in the picture. I thought of how their coming together brought our families together to make another different family. And then I thought I could make them a sort of family tree to show the new family. Claudia's helping me. See what we're going to do?"

I showed them what Claudia and I were working on. "Up at the top," I explained, "are Karen and Andrew. Then those lines show that they're Watson's children. In the middle, Mum and Watson are joined by a heart. And the lines under Mum's name show that my brothers and I are her children. And that's the new family."

"That's really something," said Mary Anne.

"Yeah," agreed Dawn. "I think it will mean a lot to your mum."

"I wonder if I can get it framed before the honeymoon is over," I said.

"I bet my mother and I could go with you to the frame store this week, if you wanted help," said Stacey.

"Really? Thanks!"

The members of the Babysitters Club looked at my new family tree. Mum and Watson, Karen and Andrew, Charlie and Sam and David Michael and me. Two families coming together to make a new family. That's what the wedding had been all about.

The Babysitters Club

Need a babysitter? Then call the Babysitters Club. Kristy Thomas and her friends are all experienced sitters. They can tackle any job from rampaging toddlers to a pandemonium of pets. To find out all about them, read on!

1 **Kristy's Great Idea**
2 **Claudia and the Phantom Phone Calls**
3 **The Truth About Stacey**
4 **Mary Anne Saves The Day**
5 **Dawn and the Impossible Three**
6 **Kristy's Big Day**
7 **Claudia and Mean Janine**
8 **Boy-Crazy Stacey**
9 **The Ghost At Dawn's House**
10 **Logan Likes Mary Anne!**
11 **Kristy and the Snobs**
12 **Claudia and the New Girl**
13 **Goodbye Stacey, Goodbye**
14 **Hello, Mallory**
15 **Little Miss Stoneybrook ... and Dawn**
16 **Jessi's Secret Language**
17 **Mary Anne's Bad-Luck Mystery**
18 **Stacey's Mistake**
19 **Claudia and the Bad Joke**
20 **Kristy and the Walking Disaster**
21 **Mallory and the Trouble With Twins**
22 **Jessi Ramsey, Pet-Sitter**
23 **Dawn On The Coast**
24 **Kristy and the Mother's Day Surprise**
25 **Mary Anne and the Search For Tigger**
26 **Claudia and the Sad Goodbye**
27 **Jessi and the Superbrat**
28 **Welcome Back, Stacey!**
29 **Mallory and the Mystery Diary**
30 **Mary Anne and the Great Romance**
31 **Dawn's Wicked Stepsister**
32 **Kristy and the Secret Of Susan**
33 **Claudia and the Great Search**
34 **Mary Anne and Too Many Boys**
35 **Stacey and the Mystery Of Stoneybrook**
36 **Jessi's Babysitter**
37 **Dawn and the Older Boy**
38 **Kristy's Mystery Admirer**
39 **Poor Mallory!**

40 Claudia and the Middle School Mystery
41 Mary Anne Vs. Logan
42 Jessi and the Dance School Phantom
43 Stacey's Emergency
44 Dawn and the Big Sleepover
45 Kristy and the Baby Parade
46 Mary Anne Misses Logan
47 Mallory On Strike
48 Jessi's Wish
49 Claudia and the Genius Of Elm Street
50 Dawn's Big Date
51 Stacey's Ex-Best Friend
52 Mary Anne and Too Many Babies
53 Kristy For President
54 Mallory and the Dream Horse
55 Jessi's Gold Medal
56 Keep Out, Claudia!
57 Dawn Saves The Planet
58 Stacey's Choice
59 Mallory Hates Boys (and Gym)
60 Mary Anne's Makeover
61 Jessi and the Awful Secret
62 Kristy and the Worst Kid Ever
63 Claudia's ~~Freind~~ Friend
64 Dawn's Family Feud
65 Stacey's Big Crush
66 Maid Mary Anne
67 Dawn's Big Move
68 Jessi and the Bad Babysitter
69 Get Well Soon, Mallory!
70 Stacey and the Cheerleaders
71 Claudia and the Perfect Boy
72 Dawn and the We Love Kids Club
73 Mary Anne and Miss Priss
74 Kristy and the Copycat
75 Jessi's Horrible Prank
76 Stacey's Lie
77 Dawn and Whitney, Friends For Ever
78 Claudia and Crazy Peaches
79 Mary Anne Breaks the Rules
80 Mallory Pike, No1 Fan
81 Kristy and Mr Mum
82 Jessi and the Troublemaker
83 Stacey vs the BSC
84 Dawn and the School Spirit War
85 Claudia Kishi, Live on Air
86 Mary Anne and Camp BSC
87 Stacey and the Bad Girls
88 Farewell Dawn